EDUCATION FOR DEMOCRATIC CITIZENSHIP

Education for Democratic Citizenship

Issues of Theory and Practice

Edited by

ANDREW LOCKYER
Glasgow University, UK

BERNARD CRICK
Birkbeck College, London, UK

JOHN ANNETTE
Middlesex University, UK

ASHGATE

Andrew Lockyer, Bernard Crick and John Annette have asserted their right under the Copyright, Designs and Patents Act, 1988, to be identified as the authors of this work.

Published by
Ashgate Publishing Limited
Gower House
Croft Road
Aldershot
Hants GU11 3HR
England

Ashgate Publishing Company
Suite 420
101 Cherry Street
Burlington, VT 05401-4405
USA

Ashgate website: http://www.ashgate.com

British Library Cataloguing in Publication Data
Education for democratic citizenship : issues of theory and
practice
    1. Citizenship - Study and teaching - Great Britain
    2. Civics, British - Study and teaching
    I. Lockyer, Andrew II. Crick, Bernard, 1929 III. Annette,
John
    370.1'15

Library of Congress Cataloging-in-Publication Data
Education for democratic citizenship : issues of theory and practice / edited by Andrew
Lockyer, Bernard Crick, and John Annette.
    p. cm.
 Includes bibliographical references and index.
 ISBN 0-7546-3959-2
    1. Citizenship--Study and teaching--Great Britain. 2. Democracy--Study and
teaching--Great Britain. 3. Education for citizenship and the teaching of democracy in
schools. I. Lockyer, Andrew. II. Crick, Bernard R. III. Annette, John.

 LC1091.E43 2003
 370.11'5--dc22
                                                                    2003058296

ISBN 0 7546 3959 2

April 6, 2004

Printed and bound in Great Britain by Athenaeum Press Ltd., Gateshead, Tyne & Wear.

Contents

Preface

Political philosophy, thriving as never before in the universities, should apply itself more often to clarifying and criticizing the ideas behind policies affecting the public. This book arose from a specialist group meeting on citizenship education organized by John Annette and Andrew Lockyer at the 50th anniversary conference of the Political Studies Association, held at the London School of Economics and at Birkbeck College in 2000. It was a good initiative and a unique occasion. Many political thinkers of the past have argued both that the principles of political philosophy – its concerns with legitimate authority, freedom, justice and human equality – must inform education from the beginning, and that methods of schooling can have a profound influence on political order. In our times, however, political philosophers have rarely thought about schooling, and teachers and educationists have lost touch (though they are far from alone in this) with the tradition of political thought. Nor have British teachers believed that their charges should be prepared for political life.

John Annette and Andrew Lockyer saw the opportunity for bridge-building at that 50th anniversary. The opportunity was the report I had chaired at the invitation of David Blunkett, *Education for the Teaching of Citizenship and Democracy in Schools*. Most of those who presented papers on that possibly seminal occasion appear in this book, but other essays on the theme were adopted or commissioned. Perhaps there is too much in them about 'the Crick Report', but they are certainly not uncritical. For this book is not advocacy, but reasoned analysis and criticism.

Limitations of civic republicanism (or the duty of active citizenship) are suggested. After all, to live in peace under the laws of a liberal state is no mean thing, certainly by comparison. And yet liberal assumptions were also found in the Report which appear to play down positive advocacies of anti-racism and of gender equality. Perhaps the Report's implicit aims became hidden under advocacy of an implicit teaching methodology for a prudent indirect attack – an outflanking, as it were, not a brave frontal attack. But if so, it needed arguing. None of the contributors, however, have pointed to how muted was the Report's discussion of 'teaching democracy', compared with 'teaching citizenship'. I have escaped challenge on that, and it was deliberate. My worries about the rhetorical ambiguities of 'democracy' – long ago clear in my book *In Defence of Politics*, and recently reiterated as a critique of populism in a 'very short book', *Democracy* – are at least as great as the worries of others about the ambiguities of 'citizenship'.

Though partners in the commissioning, John Annette and I for various reasons, good and bad, had to leave the uncertainties of correspondence and the toil of editing to Andrew Lockyer, without whose sweat and sweet entreaties this book would never have seen the light of day. We thank him warmly and deeply.

Bernard Crick

List of Contributors

Andrew Lockyer is Senior Lecturer in the Department of Politics, University of Glasgow.

Bernard Crick is Emeritus Professor of Politics and Fellow of Birkbeck College, London.

John Annette is Professor of Citizenship and Political Studies at Middlesex University, London.

David Archard is Professor of Philosophy and Public Policy, Lancaster University.

Madeleine Arnot is Reader in Sociology of Education and Fellow of Jesus College, Cambridge.

Ian Davies is Senior Lecturer in the Department of Educational Studies, York University.

Elizabeth Frazer is Official Fellow and Tutor in Politics at New College, Oxford.

Graham Haydon is Lecturer in Philosophy of Education at the Institute of Education, University of London.

Will Kymlicka is Professor of Philosophy at Queens University, Kingston, Canada.

Terence McLaughlin is Professor of Philosophy of Education at the Institute of Education, University of London.

Geraint Parry is Emeritus Professor of Politics, Manchester University.

Acknowledgements

While most of the essays in this volume are original, a few make use of previously published material. The editors are grateful to those who have granted permissions.

Will Kymlicka's essay was initially presented as a paper at the 4th International Congress on Philosophy of Education in Madrid, in November 2000, and was published in Spanish in *Educación, Ética y Cuidadanía*, UNED Ediciones, Madrid, 2002.

Elizabeth Frazer's essay is an abridged version of a previously published article, 'Citizenship Education: Anti-political Culture and Political Education in Britain', which appeared in March 2000 in *Political Studies*, Vol. 48(1), pp. 88-103 (published by Blackwell).

Geraint Parry obtained permission from the publishers, the *Oxford Review of Education*, to make use of some passages from his article, 'Constructive and Reconstructive Political Education', which appeared in 1999 in Vol. 25(1-2), pp. 23-39. In the event, his essay in this volume bears little relation to his previous article, but nonetheless we willingly mention the publisher's website: *http/www.tandf.co.uk.*

Some paragraphs of Bernard Crick's essay draw upon 'The Citizenship Order' in *Parliamentary Affairs*, July 2002; 'The Presuppositions of Citizenship Education', in *The Journal of the Philosophy of Education of Great Britain*, Vol. 33(3), 1999; and 'In Defence of the Citizenship Order 1999' and 'Friendly Arguments', in *Essays on Citizenship* (Continuum, 2000).

The editors would also like to express their appreciation for the work which has gone into the preparation of the final text. The principal responsibility for producing the camera-ready copy was borne by Fiona Croesér at Glasgow University. Her editorial expertise has been a great asset to us; she has not only ruthlessly imposed consistency on referencing and indexing, but has gently suggested improvements to the text for the benefit of our readers.

Finally, we must acknowledge the helpfulness of the staff at Ashgate. Special thanks are due to Kirstin Howgate, whose efficiency, tolerance and good humour were a support and encouragement.

Introduction and Review

Andrew Lockyer

In August 2002, as a result of the *Citizenship Order*, the teaching of 'citizenship' was introduced as a compulsory element of the school curriculum in England. In other parts of the United Kingdom it is now either to be recognized as a cross-curricular theme, or integrated into Personal, Social and Health Education and subject to inspection. The immediate impetus and rationale for this came from the Report of an Advisory Group, chaired by Bernard Crick, on *Education for Citizenship and Democracy in Schools*,[1] published in 1998. This was the culmination of the work of a number of agencies and individuals – including academics, teachers and politicians – who have recognized the critical role which education plays in equipping young people to share in democratic life. The Advisory Group's declared aim was

> ... no less than a change in the political culture of this country both nationally and locally: for people to think of themselves as active citizens, willing, able and equipped to have an influence in public life and with the critical capacities to weigh evidence before speaking and acting; to build on and to extend radically to young people the best in existing traditions of community involvement and public service, and to make them individually confident in finding new forms of involvement and action among themselves (Crick Report, 1998, 1.5).

To what extent the aspirations of the Advisory Group can or should be implemented, is open to question on practical and theoretical grounds. This collection of essays brings together the reflections of a number of political, social and educational theorists, who share in common only the belief that citizenship education is a subject which raises important philosophical and practical issues. The collective aim is to examine the presuppositions, principles and implications of the proposals to realize a particular conception of citizenship. However, the issues raised have salience for what an appropriate model of citizenship education beyond Britain might be. They deal with the general question of the state's role in creating or reproducing a citizenry appropriate to the functioning of an economically developed and culturally diverse pluralist liberal democracy.

Whether or not there is a fully cogent concept of citizen education embedded in the Crick Report and stipulated in the English *Citizenship Order* is open to

---

1   The Final Report of the Advisory Group on Citizenship, 22 September 1998, entitled *Education for Citizenship and the Teaching of Democracy in Schools*, is hereafter referred to as the 'Crick Report'. References to the Crick Report give paragraph numbers.

debate. There is significant disagreement reflected here on a number of issues: How radical are the proposals for changes in the school curriculum? Do they reconcile liberal, democratic and republican values? Can they include multiple sub-state national identities and educational traditions? Can religious, ethnic and cultural diversity be accommodated? Is the Order over-prescriptive, or does it miss an opportunity to redress inherited bias and inequalities? The historical juncture at which education for democratic citizenship has finally become a recognized subject for formal education in Britain allows considerable room for extensive debate.

Ideological Origins

Most of the essays in this collection locate the proposals of the Crick Committee in the context of their ideological origins. Many of the tensions and dilemmas found in the Report's proposals arise from the countervailing influence of liberal and civic republican ideas. The prevailing concept of citizenship that emerges is a hybrid or an amalgam of at least these two competing intellectual traditions or bodies of ideas; and there is also a third element in the influence of communitarianism.

The core of classical liberalism is ethically grounded in the protection and promotion of equal individual rights. The primary function of liberal education is to facilitate and maximize individual autonomy within the rules of justice. Democratic choice largely has instrumental value in preventing government from abusing power. Citizenship essentially expresses a series of individual contractual obligations that include the right to engage in public affairs, but which make civic and political life optional. Citizenship is ethically neutral between competing ways of life; it matters only that they are freely chosen and, as far as possible, open to all. Civic republicanism, by contrast, is grounded on an ethic of civic virtue, where human beings are deemed only to have their potential fulfilled as citizens serving the common good, and identifying with the ends and purposes of their 'civic communities' or nation states. Classically, engagement in public affairs is privileged over private, personal or group interests, and democratic citizenship must involve sharing in rule as well as in being ruled.

These two intellectual traditions are not exclusive of other prevailing influences. We should notice that there are both radical and conservative communitarian strains of thought, which either accentuate or diminish the extent to which republican liberal democracy accommodates difference or recognizes ethical pluralism. But most of the antinomies or tensions that arise in the conception of citizenship education discussed in the essays which follow, derive from the compromise to be sought, or the balance to be struck, between liberalism and civic republicanism. To express the same point differently, located within 'republican liberalism' is a debate about what priority to give civic and public duty in relation to the right to pursue private goods and personal autonomy.

It must be said that Bernard Crick views himself as both a liberal democrat and a civic republican, but it is his particular dedication to sustaining and reviving the latter tradition that is his distinctive contribution to British political (and educational) ideas and practice. It is widely recognized that he is in large measure responsible for the concept of citizenship education adopted by the Advisory Group, not simply by his chairing the Committee, but by three decades of teaching, writing and (in the best political sense) 'agitating' to promote politically active citizenship.

Political Background

The fact that Crick's Committee was comprised of members with diverse political backgrounds and allegiances, and that its Report obtained cross-party agreement and a breadth of professional support, suggests either that its proposals were cleverly constructed to mean all things to all bodies of influential opinion, or that they contained significant compromises. There is something of both. The least that can be said is that the content is not anodyne. Its concept of citizenship is broad-based yet robust, and for a committee report, its recommendations are sharply focused. Crick gives a clue in his recent book on *Democracy*, in the 'A Very Short Introduction' series – he wonders 'how many of my group realized that they were signing up to the radical agenda of civic republicanism?' (Crick, 2002).

But the revival of civic republicanism cannot be entirely down to the influence of Labour's Third Way or Sir Bernard's committee management skills. There was significant support for all three elements of the Advisory Group's view of citizenship education – social and moral responsibility, community involvement and political literacy – amongst the élites of all political persuasions, though not for all the elements in equal measure. There is a distinctly Crickian emphasis on the 'active' mode, which was not fully acknowledged to have major implications for introducing democratic practice into schools (leaving aside the empirical question of whether some schools which do recognize this try hard to avoid it).

The explanation of the revival of the citizen ethic was in many quarters a reaction to the dominant social philosophy of the Thatcher years, and the excesses of possessive individualism to which it gave sway. It was Douglas Hurd (one of Mrs Thatcher's ministers) who said in 1989 that 'The idea of Active Citizenship is a necessary complement to that of the enterprise culture'. Hurd went on to say that in Britain 'public service was once the duty of an élite but today it is a responsibility of all' who have benefited from capitalism (quoted in Heaton, 1991, p. 140). This both evokes the element of communitarianism in traditional Tory philosophy – that the better-off should voluntarily 'do something' for the less well-off – and recognizes that, in a more affluent democratic society, the duty now applies to all. With material and social equality comes social responsibility.

Summary of Contents

In the first essay in this volume Bernard pulls together and polishes some previously published articles and addresses the context and the content of the

Report and its implementation. He begins by explaining the proximate historical context, singling out a number of strands: the poor electoral turnout in the 1997 election which swept New Labour to power; the apparent cynicism of the young about politics and politicians; other evidence of youth alienation and crime; the desire for a more inclusive and cohesive society. This same concern is registered in the Crick Report and in *Encouraging Citizenship* (Commission on Citizenship, 1990). There is also an implicit recognition that the primary orientation of state-supported education is now either vocational, or the direct promotion of competitive individualism. The private and independent schools which previously provided an appropriate education for a social, civic and political élite cannot be relied upon to sustain democratic politics.

Crick makes the point that support for the *Citizenship Order* being compulsory came not only from government ministers, but unanimously from his cross-party committee. (He notes the importance of Lord Baker's support in muting any possibility of political opposition.) Several considerations led the government to make the Order compulsory: it was necessary for the constitutional reform which was intended to create a more participative democratic society; it would help to diminish exclusion and cynicism at all levels; and it might 'change our collective mentality from subjects to active citizens' of a democracy. If these are all good reasons why the Order should be universal and statutory, it is regrettable that it can only have full statutory force in part of the UK.

Crick acknowledges here (and elsewhere) that his earlier thinking on political education and political literacy has been extended to recognize the importance of 'community activity' and of the experiential learning that takes place within the groups and associations of civil society. These secondary associations are viewed as essential sites of civic activity to mediate between the individual and the state. The centralist Rousseauian democratic identification of the citizen with the whole political community is modified by the pluralist communitarianism of Tocqueville's 'corporations' and Burke's 'small platoons'. However, it is not wholly clear how much 'democracy', or informal 'politics', is to be expected or found within the organizations, groups and communities of civil society. Nor is it transparent to what extent the emphasis on 'local politics' acknowledges the need to reconceptualize the boundaries of 'political' activity.

It is a feature of the *Citizenship Order* that it offers no precise prescriptions about what ought to be taught. Some regard this as grounds for criticism (see Arnot's essay); it is deemed a fault that the Order does not require teaching to cover specific social issues – it is not, for example, explicitly 'anti-racist' (Osler and Vincent, 2002). It does require, however, that issues are set within a framework of human rights, and that the implications of living in a country 'with diverse national, regional, and ethnic identities' are understood. The justification for the 'light touch' approach offered in the essay is both principled and pragmatic. Governments ought not to make precise proscriptions about the teaching of 'politically or morally sensitive matters', and there should be local discretion as to what schools teach and how they organize the curriculum to give pupils community relevant experience. Not all teachers will be thankful to be left with so much freedom. Some indeed will find it more demanding than following a fully specified curriculum. However, it is Crick's belief that citizenship education is safer in their hands, with an appropriate level of inspection, than in the hands of an elected government (Crick, 2002, p. 114).

The final two sections of the first essay cover ground which may be familiar to some – except that few political theorists read educational journals and few educationists read political philosophy. The first is devoted to setting out the *Presuppositions* upon which the case for the civic republican conception of active citizenship is grounded. The second claims that 'toleration', 'fairness', 'respect for truth' and 'respect for reasoning' can be treated as *Procedural Values* which provide the foundation both for the method of learning and for the conduct of moral and political discourse concerning substantive values. The principles and problems outlined here are taken up in some of the essays which follow.

Reproductive and Remedial

Geraint Parry (in Essay 2) locates the Crick Report in the context of the history of ideas on education and political theory. He identifies two broad approaches among the classical texts on the role that education is intended to play either in 'reproducing' citizens to maintain existing political forms, or in 'remedying' failing political systems by 'reconstructing' citizens to improve social and political structures. The Crick Report's proposals are in the reconstructive idiom. The aim of education is to create a new model of active citizen, fitted for participative democracy, rather than to reproduce a minimally engaged law-abiding subject. Underlying the Report's endorsement of liberal values is a bias in favour of 'strong democracy', which includes local civic participation associated with the ideas of Tocqueville, Dewey and Benjamin Barber. Parry contrasts this participatory 'reconstructive' model of democracy with the 'realist' (or élite) theory, which begins by accepting the division between rulers and ruled, requiring citizens only to judge representatives wisely (following Sartori and Galston).

Parry asks whether a 'maximal' or 'minimal' conception of citizenship education is sustainable. Is the Crick Report's call for activism 'incongruent with the norms of British politics'? Or might the reconstructive conception of citizenship education raise expectations that cannot be satisfied, 'given the present structure of political opportunities'?

The minimalist conception of citizenship might be better able to accommodate multicultural or sub-state nationalism, but could be inadequate to inculcate loyalty to the institutions which enable a plural democracy to survive. A possible compromise between the two approaches is a strategy which teaches the skills and competence associated with the norm of public reasonableness, required by some conceptions of deliberative democracy. These are at one with procedural values endorsed by the Crick Report. Even if the liberal values associated with public reasonableness do not require political activism, they might promote development of the 'politically well-educated citizen and sustain, reinforce and extend the practices of liberal democracy'.

Pluralist Dilemmas

Will Kymlicka (in Essay 3) addresses two dilemmas of citizenship education in pluralist societies where the duties of citizenship are 'quintessentially liberal'. The dilemmas are created by the challenge to liberal democratic states of two kinds of diversity – those created by inclusion of conservative fundamentalist religious groups, and those arising from the problem of privileging the state as a locus of civic identity where there are competing sub-state national groups. Although Kymlicka's essay was written in the first place with a Spanish audience in mind, the problems of citizenship education where there are multiple national identities and competing sites of civic activism are not dissimilar to those of the multinational and multi-ethnic United Kingdom.

The first dilemma is that, even if the duty to privilege political participation and civic identity is played down, passive citizenship requires the religious fundamentalist at least to show the virtue of civility to non-intimates. The teaching of public reasonableness, or the requirement to adopt liberal procedural values, may expose children to different points of view, and thereby constitute a threat to religious fundamentalist ways of life. Kymlicka describes the liberal state's acceptance of faith-based schools, where liberal education is not enforced, as a strategy or 'wager' which historically has been broadly successful, allowing faith groups over time to become reconciled with the liberal polity.

Not all the issues raised for citizenship education by the presence of sub-state national groups which Kymlicka identifies apply in the British case, but the central ambivalence of British national citizenship in combination with competing national identities (and educational systems) does arise. The Crick Report does not directly acknowledge multivalent identities as being a problem. It views 'national identity' as a facet of 'cultural diversity' and looks to

> a common sense of citizenship, including a national identity that is secure enough to find a place for the plurality of nations, cultures, ethnic identities and religions long found in the United kingdom. Citizenship Education creates a common ground between different ethnic and religious identities (Crick Report, 1998, 3.14).

But since the *Citizenship Order* only directly applies to the curriculum in England, and not in those parts of the UK where a sub-state national identity is strong (among some groups at least), there is no guarantee that the approach to citizenship education intended to 'create or restore a common sense of citizenship' will be adopted consistently throughout the UK.

The degree of devolution of political power in the UK which acknowledges territorial, national and cultural difference is – in Kymlicka's terms – a partially successful 'wager'. It remains to be seen whether the citizenship education delivered can both reflect the extent of differences, and endorse to the same degree the multiple sites of civic identity and political activity.

Anti-political Culture

Elizabeth Frazer (in Essay 4) explains the late introduction of citizenship education into Britain as a consequence of an antipathy to teaching about political institutions and culture. Her contention is that, although political education is identified with 'citizenship', the term has a low level of salience for young people. Although citizenship has recurred as a cross-curricular theme, it has tended to be depoliticized by being converted into teaching about personal and social 'values'. Frazer notes it is difficult to generalize, given the differences in the UK's educational systems, but these very differences may be a source of the 'antagonisms and tensions' which are a major factor in making political education contentious.

Frazer finds the teaching of political culture and democracy in the United States, where 'civics' has had an established place in the school curriculum, to be 'in better shape' than in Britain. Other pastures may just look greener. She sees the lack of a written constitution and an agreed historical narrative about state formation as being responsible for some of the difficulty in the British case.

Frazer and Crick share many of the concerns about the anti-political culture in Britain. Frazer's worry is that in Britain politics has come to have entirely negative associations. Whereas liberal 'values' such as equality, liberty, tolerance of difference and concern for human rights and the environment are learned, they are not linked with the institutional structures and political processes that might bring them about. So politics is associated with partisanship and the pursuit of power and stability, where principles are set aside and values compromised. She sees the need to teach 'the basics' about political institutions and political process, whereas Crick is somewhat dismissive of the 'dead-safe, dead boring' approach he associates with civics, or the British equivalent.

Frazer's complaint is that the Advisory Group's conception of political literacy requires no 'formal political education at all', so citizenship education endorses personal responsibility and interpersonal skills and students learn about morality and justice, but in a context which may encourage an antipathy to politics. She concedes that learning about political institutions and process is 'not sufficient', but this does not mean it is unnecessary.

What is unassessed in this analysis is the extent to which participating in school and community involvement shows the relevance of moral issues to politics, and vice versa. For Crick, learning how to use concepts is the key to political literacy (although he does recognize the need for learning about institutions – see Essay 1). Frazer may nonetheless be right to suggest that the need to teach about political systems is understated – if not overlooked.

Moral Responsibility, Civic Virtue, Identity and Inclusion

Graham Haydon's approach (in Essay 5) is to question whether the aims of citizenship education embedded in the Crick Report – social and moral responsibility, community involvement, political literacy, national identity and social inclusion – are fully consistent. Haydon focuses on social and moral responsibility. He suggests that to avoid imposing their own values, teachers are likely to treat it as a facet of political literacy and community involvement. He makes the point that all three elements are not learned in isolation, but require the compliance of others to provide the opportunity for their exercise.

Social inclusion Haydon sees as a collective purpose of citizenship education, and a prerequisite for realizing the elements mentioned above. Some sense of a shared national identity is linked with social inclusion, although Haydon rightly acknowledges that national identity is 'nuanced' and recognized as being 'complex' in the Crick Report. There is no requirement for British citizenship to be the primary identity; rather it must provide common ground for a diversity of plural identities.

Haydon argues that it is preferable for moral and social responsibility to be conceived as compliance with 'rationally shared norms and principles' rather than subscription to a particular ethic of civic virtue. His concern is that the latter requires citizens to acquire certain virtues as attributes of character, which is overly prescriptive, and thus incompatible with the inherent diversity of a multicultural and multi-faith society. People of different faiths and communities will have different ideas about the appropriate virtues to pursue, or how they are to be specified, and these are constitutive of their identities. This is to favour pluralist liberalism over civic republicanism.

Haydon echoes some of Parry's concern that the concept of citizenship embodied in the Crick Report might require too much commitment to common values to be inclusive. He wisely suggests that national identity should not endorse a particular idea of British character. However, his view that commitment to shared values might acceptably be reduced to following norms of conduct suggests that external conformity to principles of reasonableness and being law-abiding are good enough. This liberal concept of what is held in common may be too thin to distinguish the citizen from the resident. But if there is no more sense of shared identity than this, there may be no approved site for public engagement in which diverse citizens will wish to be included.

This points to a recurring theme – that citizenship education must strike a balance between accepting social and cultural diversity, which permits value pluralism, and privileging some values and practices of liberal democracy, which endorses some sense of common identity.

Multicultural Citizenship

Dave Archard's discussion (in Essay 6) picks up the central issue of the tensions inherent in creating an active citizenry, sharing a common civic and national identity, and the persistence of communal and cultural diversity. The starting point is that the Crick Report has to design education for citizenship not simply for a liberal democracy, but for the distinct society which is multicultural Britain.

This tension can be characterized as one between centripetal and centrifugal forces. In civil society there are manifest religious, ethnic and cultural differences pulling subjects apart, while a civic identity with a commitment to a particular set of political institutions is required to pull fellow citizens together. Unlike Haydon, Archard sees the main tensions as not between liberalism and republicanism, but between a liberal citizenship education and the substantive values of particular ethnic communities. He takes British Muslims who are committed to the teaching of Islamic law as an example for exploration in his essay.

He begins with Kymlicka's first dilemma, already discussed. The Crick Report endorses rational or critical autonomy, which requires 'the willingness to be open to changing one's opinions and attitudes in the light of discussion and evidence'. However, fundamentalist Muslims may regard the capacity to 'rationally reflect on, and potentially revise, our conceptions of the good life' as subversive rather than virtuous. Archard's response is to suggest that this radical degree of autonomy might not be required by liberal citizenship. The virtue of autonomy could consist of 'independence of character' and an 'ability to execute one's considered choices', rather than in exposing fundamental beliefs to scrutiny and revision. This might ease the tension of adopting liberal procedural values, but not remove it.

A harder case is presented by minority cultures which do not straightforwardly accept 'gender equality' – not, of course, that this is a preserve of minority cultures. The Crick Report (contra Arnot's interpretation below) enjoins 'a commitment to equal opportunities and gender equality' as essential values and dispositions to be acquired in citizenship education. Archard is sensitive to the view that in Islamic law women and men are equally valued, although traditional Muslim culture generally endorses separate treatment of the genders based on natural differences. If these differentiated gender roles are freely chosen, where there is genuine equality of opportunity, the liberal educator can have no complaint. But the difficulty of choosing to leave a minority religious or cultural community poses problems, not least the loss of identity which it is hard for the national culture or other civil associations to substitute for.

It is not an adequate response to insist that equal citizenship can only be characteristic of the public sphere. Archard points to a huge issue for citizenship education when he makes J.S. Mill's point that what happens in the family is the 'real school' of morality and upbringing. Meaningful citizenship education must not only impinge on the private sphere but arguably, as feminist theory suggests (see Arnot, Essay 7), must also challenge the separation of the public and private spheres. The interrelation of school, home and intermediate groups as sources of life experience and competing identities (and sites of 'politics') gives rise to tensions which the official discourse of democratic citizenship education barely touches upon.

Citizenship Education and Gender

Madeleine Arnot's argument (in Essay 7) is a counterweight, but also a complement, to Archard and Haydon. Whereas the Crick Report is criticized (in this Introduction) from a liberal point of view, for being too prescriptive to accommodate ethical pluralism, Arnot finds it 'strangely silent' on questions of social equality and gender. Despite its claim to signal 'no less than a change in political culture', it makes no attempt to transform the current gender-biased character of contemporary politics.

There are three related lines of argument. Firstly, the *Citizenship Order* fails to include social equality as a goal of citizenship education, and this leaves unchallenged the distinction between the public and private spheres. Secondly, this leads to a failure to question the location of women in the private sphere, and thus address the 'specificity of female citizenship'. The third step is to argue that gender bias leads to privileging the norm of heterosexuality, which has exclusionary consequences for citizens with same-sex relationships.

Arnot finds the association of masculinity with the public arena of politics and the confinement of women to the privacy of family and household – a characteristic feature of classical republicanism – to be left unchallenged by the model of citizenship education now proposed and adopted. Moreover, Arnot reports from her research into student teachers' attitudes to the conceptualization of citizenship in Europe that women were not represented as 'legitimately successful and autonomous in public life', and that the differing political discourse of male and female students tended to reflect traditional gender stereotypes. Given these findings, Arnot sees the need for major support for professional teacher training and curriculum guidance, to avoid citizenship education reproducing conventional male and female citizen identities.

It is clear that in under-specifying the content of citizenship education, the Crick Report also avoids promoting an overtly feminist agenda – whether out of pluralist principle or political discretion we need not guess. As most contributors have noted, there are value presuppositions which derive from the traditions of liberalism and civic republicanism, and these undeniably reflect a masculine conception of citizenship. But there may be more scope for lessening the gender-biased conception embedded in the Crick Report than Arnot acknowledges.

The concept of political literacy does privilege a language of politics which pays dues to what some feminists regard as a masculine conception of rationality, but the emphasis on engagement makes it possible to give equal weight to what Gilligan (1982) and others call an 'ethic of care'. The element of community involvement, a central aspect of active citizenship, has potential for creating new forms of civic engagement that might embrace a distinctively feminized form of political activity (Phillips, 1991; Mansbridge, 1993; Gould, 1993). Of course, if community involvement is no more than traditional voluntary social service, into which schools for preference funnel female pupils, this simply reinforces gender stereotyping.

Gender equality may or may not require the recognition of relevant difference in relation to civic engagement. Arnot is certainly right to insist that this has to be prominently part of the curriculum for teaching teachers, and must be informed by research on gender attitudes.

Political Status of Children

The focus in Essay 8 is on the implications of the Crick Report and *Citizenship Order* for the political standing of children and young people. I suggest that their status as citizens is ambiguous in the Report, and this allows the issue of their political rights to be avoided. I argue that the conception of political literacy embodied in the Report requires active political participation which, given the largely undemocratic character of schools and despite community involvement, they will find difficulty in providing.

The expectation is that the balance between young people's rights and duties, and their dubious status as citizens (without political rights), is likely to become a contentious issue. Thus the programme of citizenship education has radical implications for democracy in schools and beyond.

The final section considers the impact of the implementation of the Crick Report on the case for lowering the voting age. More is at stake than political participation and competency, because treating children paternalistically or granting them full autonomy is linked with the right to vote. I argue that, while there is no reason to confine the attribution of citizenship to those old enough to vote, a strong case can be made for lowering the voting age to 16 in Britain. My conjecture is that this measure might provide the impetus both for rethinking school regimes in relation to young people's rights, and for carrying forward the programme of democratic citizenship education.

Citizenship and Community

John Annette (in Essay 9) sees the idea of community as the key to rethinking the relationship between civil society and the state, and views participation in community politics as the vehicle for democratic renewal and the enhancement of democratic citizenship education. Concern about the 'loss of community', which has animated social theorists and politicians (Putnam to Blunkett), can be addressed by reinvestment in 'social capital' and reactivating 'civic engagement'.[2] This, Annette argues, can only be done within a learning framework provided by the development of an appropriate form of citizenship education.

Of the variety of ways of conceptualizing 'community', Annette's focus is on community as a political ideal. He suggests that civic republicanism offers a substantive account of the importance of community as a location for both the freedom to engage in 'active self-government' and the exercise of civic duty. He refers to the growing literature on crisis in local democracy, but also the response

---

2 Robert Putnam (2000) is the theorist most associated with the movement for civic revival in the US. David Blunkett is the current British Home Secretary, and was the Minister of Education – a former student of Bernard Crick, who was the force behind the citizenship education programme. Despite his centralist politics, his theorizing is heavily communitarian (see his *Politics and Progress: Renewing Democracy and Civil Society*, 2001).

(following J.S. Mill) which sees local government as both 'a site for political activity' and providing a grounding in political education. A growing repertoire of approaches – including referenda, consultative activities and local strategic partnerships – brings deliberative participation into local governance.

In the last section of his essay Annette makes the case for 'service learning' as the key to providing the opportunity for community involvement which the Crick Report endorses as one of its strands. This involves students engaging in, and reflecting upon, voluntary service in the community. For this to be more than simply an exercise in social responsibility, but also to develop the skills and attributes associated with political literacy, the experience must involve reflection and deliberation. It must be linked with the teaching of democratic values.

Annette is concerned that community involvement in the citizenship curriculum could involve a conception of community as simply a place or neighbourhood; and if that is all, it will result in the forms of volunteering that fail to challenge students to think politically. Community involvement based on the pedagogy of 'service learning' as part of citizenship education must address the question of how best to structure their experience to make them become 'political' and 'aware of the political significance of civic engagement in local communities'.

Teaching Controversial Issues

Terry McLaughlin (in Essay 10) offers a philosophical analysis of the difficulties and complexities embedded in the inescapable commitment any form of citizenship education has to 'teach controversial issues'. He acknowledges that the complexities of the particular context in which they are taught comes down to what actually happens in the classroom, but the philosophical perspective can help teachers and education policymakers to identify and tackle tensions related to their work. The focus is on teaching of controversial issues where there is non-trivial, but well-grounded, 'reasonable disagreement' which cannot readily be resolved by appeals to evidence and the exercise of judgement.

The vital and worthwhile role that teaching controversial issues plays in citizenship education is recognized in the Crick Report. It tackles issues which are characteristic of conflict in everyday life, and this is closely linked with the Crickian view of politics as '… the creative conciliation of differing interests, whether the interests are primarily material or moral'. McLaughlin notes that the prescriptions to teachers in the Report are to prepare pupils to deal with controversies 'knowledgeably, sensibly, tolerantly and morally' – in other words, they must learn adherence to liberal procedural values. Teachers are advised on pedagogic strategies to facilitate fair and thorough examination of issues.

However, McLaughlin suggests some 'difficulties and complexities' which go beyond those recognized in the Crick Report. There can be reasonable disagreement about what is controversial – this will depend on the teaching context, the developmental stage of the pupils, whether the school is a 'common' or faith school, and on the sensitivities of parents. The idea of achieving a 'balance' in the treatment of issues is similarly difficult and complex.

The major area of complexity which McLaughlin discusses is the interface between 'the public and non-public domain'. He offers the view (taken from John Tomasi) that the non-public lives of citizens – their non-public virtues and personality traits – are differentially affected by liberal public norms – like those endorsed by the Crick Report. Four citizen types are conjectured who value autonomy in public and personal lives differently. Tomasi's view is that citizenship education should help students explore the *fit* between the public and non-public views that they affirm.

What McLaughlin takes from this is the 'moral texture and complexity' of the relation between non-public values and those of public reasonableness, which must enter into handling of controversial issues. Teachers must have a certain sort of practical wisdom to enable them to achieve balance at the interface between dealing with students' personal and public values. McLaughlin sees this not in terms of a teacher following rules or professional norms, but being 'a certain sort of person'. This raises demanding questions for the nature of teacher education.

Developing Education for Citizenship

Ian Davies (in Essay 11) is writing from the perspective of someone who has observed the failure of previous attempts to teach citizenship education. While he sees challenges and opportunities in the *Citizenship Order* which could lead to 'enormous benefits', he has no illusions about the demands that will be placed upon teachers, and the teachers of teachers.

Citizenship education has had to be wide-ranging to incorporate changing government social policy (and influences from within the European Union), at the same time as being sufficiently flexible and robust to cover matters of legal status, and issues of identity formation and the ability to act effectively. The citizenship agenda has been continuously in danger of overload and loss of coherence – the broad-brush approach, which incorporates the competing ideologies of civic virtue and individualism, risks citizenship education meaning everything and nothing. Davies says this will be the case unless we hold on to central features of citizenship – 'a few substantive concepts related to power, exploration of identity and investigations into the nature of practising citizenship by promoting action'.

Research suggests that at present 'there is no widespread agreement about how to teach citizenship'. Davies offers two models of teaching projects that may stimulate thinking and action on the way forward. The first focuses on learning by identifying procedural concepts which enable students to think and act 'as citizens' rather than learning about citizenship. The second makes use of an international exchange of trainee teachers with support activities, which promotes a comparative national and cultural element in citizenship education. There is also stimulus to reflect upon the forms of identity which go beyond the national state – whether citizenship has a meaningful European and global dimension is a matter for debate – one which can be expected to animate young people, and is aided by a visitor's perspective. These examples are only indicative, but they do substantiate the case for both conceptual and concrete thinking by curriculum planners and teachers.

Summation

A clear message from most of the contributions to this collection is that a huge weight of responsibility for developing democratic citizenship lies with schools and local authorities. Crick tells us this is the cost of keeping partisan political interference at arm's length. At the same time, a liberal democratic state cannot afford to leave citizenship education to chance or private initiative. Learning to be active citizens requires considerable support from outside the classroom and beyond the school. It requires not only inspection and regulation, but also public scrutiny, resources and resourcefulness. Democratic citizenship education must connect with people in all modes of life.

The partial success or relative failure of the proposals in the Crick Report (they cannot totally succeed, and they must not completely fail) will have much to do with how well the issues debated in this book are understood and tackled. These are issues of 'politics' and 'education' in the widest sense. They demand some critical re-evaluation of the way these activities have been conceptualized and engaged with in the past. They are not simply matters for professional politicians and educators, nor only for students of politics and education. They concern the character and depth of our democracy. The issues of citizenship education, theoretical and practical, are matters for all citizens to reflect upon critically and actively explore.

References

Blunkett, D. (2001), *Politics and Progress: Renewing Democracy and Civil Society*, Demos and Politicos, London.
Commission on Citizenship (1990), *Encouraging Citizenship*, Her Majesty's Stationery Office, London.
Crick, B.R. (2002), *Democracy: A Very Short Introduction*, Oxford University Press, Oxford.
Gilligan, C. (1982), *In a Different Voice*, Harvard University Press, London.
Gould, C. (1993), 'Feminism and Democratic Community Revisited', in J. Chapman and I. Shapiro (eds), *Democratic Community: Nomos XXXV*, New York University Press, New York and London.
Heaton, D. (1991), 'Citizenship: A Remarkable Case of Sudden Interest', in *Parliamentary Affairs*, Vol. 44(2), pp. 140-56.
Mansbridge, J. (1993), 'Feminism and Democratic Community', in J. Chapman and I. Shapiro (eds), *Democratic Community: Nomos XXXV*, New York University Press, New York and London.
Osler, A. and Starkey, H. (1996), *Teacher Education and Human Rights*, Davis Fulton, London.
Osler, A. and Vincent, K. (2002), *Citizenship and the Challenge of Global Education*, Trentham Books, Stoke-on-Trent.
Phillips, A. (1991), *Engendering Democracy*, Polity Press, Cambridge.
Putnam, R. (2000), *Bowling Alone in America*, Simon and Schuster, New York.

1

The English Citizenship Order 1999: Context, Content and Presuppositions

Bernard Crick

Considering how much political philosophy – and in modern times how many political philosophers – have been embedded in education, it is curious how little attention university political philosophers have paid to what is taught in schools. For it is here that all the practical implications of differing concepts of freedom and authority and their varying relationships first come together. We note in passing, of course, the importance that Aristotle, Rousseau, and John Stuart Mill (even Hobbes, though coming to a perverse conclusion) attached to education, as the right schooling of the young, as the precondition for a just state – notice, but usually pass on. Perhaps one should also add the name of John Dewey, who saw a radically more democratic schooling as the essential precondition for (in his sense) a genuinely democratic society. But despite a magisterial effort at revival (Ryan, 1995), few thinkers in the United Kingdom outside schools of education see him as part of the canon of political thought.

The existence of citizenship as a subject in schools has, in the main, been driven by political events rather than political thought. The teaching of citizenship arose in high schools in the United States and paralleled the rise of Political Science in the colleges, as a response to mass immigration in the last decades of the nineteenth century. In Mexico it followed the revolution, just as in the postwar Federal Republic of Germany (indeed, in most of continental Europe) and in Japan, it was seen as an essential part of postwar reconstruction. In France it was introduced into schools after the defeat of 1870 as part of a patriotic revival, but soon degenerated into learning the constitution by heart (as could be the all-too-common nervous line of least resistance elsewhere) when faced with deeply and bitterly divided views on the true nature of *La Patrie* (Heater, 1990; Oliver and Heater, 1994).

However, whatever the history and context surrounding such potentially major changes, the actual form they take must everywhere contain some philosophical, or at least theoretical, presuppositions. One thinks of J.M. Keynes' remark that the economist who boasts of being purely practical is usually parroting the views of an academic scribbler of yesterday. And one might also think of Collingwood or Oakeshott. But before coming to presuppositions, some context is needed to explain why citizenship was introduced so late to English schools.

The Context

Dr Johnson once said, while considering in didactic mode 'the nature of fancy', the 'purpose of life' and 'why were we born?' that the real question was 'why were we not born before?' Why, indeed, did it take so long for England to make citizenship a statutory subject in a National Curriculum? Only since 1986 has England had a statutory National Curriculum, and only in 2002 was citizenship added to the six compulsory subjects. It was legislated for in 1999, but schools were given two-and-a-half years to prepare – in fact longer, because in 1997 the new Labour Government announced its intention to introduce citizenship, but left its definition largely to an independent committee (the Advisory Group, which I chaired). The Advisory Group's report came out quickly the following year as *Education for Citizenship and the Teaching of Democracy in Schools* (Crick Report, 1998).[1]

Britain was the last country in Europe to add citizenship to the curriculum. Previously we had thought that we did not need it. Were we not the 'Mother of Parliaments'? Had we not won *the* war – well, with a little help from the Americans and the Soviet Union, of course? And had not our private, independent schools produced a famous ethos of public service and leadership, albeit in empire, army, church and the higher civil service? But by 1997 it was clear that most of the products of the independent schools were going into business, not public service, and that in the common schools where about 90 per cent of our children were educated (the local authority schools, commonly called 'state schools'), there was no consistent or effective preparation for participation in community, local and national affairs, or for leadership in more democratic contexts. And it was not unnoticed, even amid the euphoria of the leaders of New Labour at their sweeping electoral victory, that victory was won on the lowest turnout ever – and that of all age groups, turnout was lowest among the 18- to 24-year-olds, only about 44 per cent of whom claim to have voted (Park, 1999). Moreover, a lot of the non-voting was widely reported to be deliberate and pointed – 'What's the use?', 'What's the difference?', 'They are all in it for what they can get', 'A plague on both your houses'. Politicians, pundits, programme-makers and parents became worried about the behaviour of youth, about increased petty crime, drug-taking and alcohol abuse, as well as cynicism about politics and politicians. Quite apart from these worries, some public-spirited voluntary bodies had long campaigned for schools, as part of preparation for adult life, to equip young people with the skills as well as the knowledge they needed to be effective in a democracy – indeed, to give them positive experiences of participation and responsibility.

---

1 The Final Report of the Advisory Group on Citizenship, 22 September 1998, entitled *Education for Citizenship and the Teaching of Democracy in Schools*, is hereafter referred to as the 'Crick Report'. References to the Crick Report give paragraph numbers.

The terms of reference given to the Advisory Group are interesting:

> To provide advice on effective education for citizenship in schools – to include the nature and practices of participation in democracy; the duties, responsibilities and rights of individuals as citizens; and the values to individuals and society of community activity (Crick Report, 1998, p. 4).

Someone had been doing a little thinking. There was a lot in that tight space to unpack. The official language was by no means bland. 'Effective education for citizenship' presumed political action and social engineering – and why not? 'Participation' went beyond individualism. 'Rights and duties' had a fine civic, republican ring to it, somewhat modifying Quentin Skinner's recent pessimism on that score (Skinner, 1998), even if 'responsibility' might only be as yet undefined moral rhetoric. 'Community activity' broadened the older concept of political education into citizenship education.

Back in the 1970s there had been a voluntary movement for schools, campaigning for what we then called education for political literacy. Some may suspect a mere politic play with words in moving from 'political education' to 'citizenship education': opinion surveys showed that parents favoured the idea of citizenship education, but political education would perhaps always have worried them. But there is classic political philosophy behind this shift. Did not De Tocqueville, in *Democracy in America*, argue that the very foundations of liberty depend on 'corporations' or self-governing groups intermediary between the state and the individual (Oldfield, 1990)? Edmund Burke extolled 'the small platoon' as a pillar of the state, and also the revival of an old term of the Scottish eighteenth-century enlightenment, 'civil society' (a rare example of a learned term becoming widely familiar), referring to all those groups intermediary between the individual and the state – numerous and vibrant in Western Europe, sadly lacking, diminished or destroyed in old countries formerly under Communist rule. Aristotle had argued in *The Politics* that if a tyrant was to be secure he must destroy all intermediary groups, because however apolitical they were, it was participation in such social groups which created *mutual trust* between individuals. Mutual trust was an essential precondition for the *polis* or citizen state, without which opposition to tyranny and misgovernment in general was futile.

The political context was that of a reforming government, anxious to convince its new voters (and the hitherto Conservative voters whose deliberate abstention was an important factor) that New Labour was more democratic than it was socialist – if people still thought that it perpetuated the democratic socialist tradition. But why then was there no Conservative attack on the Crick Report and the subsequent curriculum order? Cries of 'indoctrination' had been expected, however balanced the report in tone and conclusions. It was very balanced, but there was also considerable public support (less at first among overburdened and over-managed teachers) for the idea, even if partly based on a misunderstanding: that citizenship meant *good* citizenship – that is, good behaviour – and not also *active* citizenship – that is, acting together to change things or to resist change.

Tocqueville is again helpful. There are great social changes and there are contingencies, whether benign or malign. In his *Souvenirs*, he says that when great changes take place politicians believe that it is because they have pulled the right strings, whereas men of letters believe that they can identify general causes underlying and unfolding social forces, laws of society and of history. He says that they are both wrong, or perhaps half right. These underlying forces come to nothing if particular men do not seize the opportunity and act, but men of action can effect nothing if the time is not ripe (Tocqueville, 1948). The time was ripe: the old hierarchical orders of British society were breaking down. Both in a Thatcherite and a slightly different Blairite mode, the common man was replacing the gentleman as the preferred social image. The particular enthusiasm of the then Secretary of State for Education, David Blunkett, was crucial – perhaps taking the view that if he could no longer hope to be creating socialism, he could at least help fashion a more radically democratic society (Blunkett and Crick, 1988; Blunkett, 2001). And there was also the former Secretary of State for Education, Kenneth Baker, the architect of the National Curriculum itself, quite new to England – in force only since 1986. He had let it be known that he had favoured making citizenship a compulsory subject in 'his' National Curriculum, but that 'she' had quite simply said 'no'. Her reasons have to be imagined, since she did not waste time in argument. In joining the Advisory Group, Lord Baker was not merely immensely supportive and useful in preventing the proposed curriculum being attacked by his former colleagues as Blairite or indoctrinatory; he was also crucial to the group's decision to advise that citizenship must be compulsory, not just advisory. He had seen to it, at the time of the National Curriculum, that some excellent cross-curricular advisory papers were produced, including one on citizenship. But he told the group that they had all been ignored and had had very little influence at all. With such a full, crowded National Curriculum, any major new initiative must either be statutory or else it would be a faint prayer (Crick, 2002).

So the Advisory Group were unanimous in wanting citizenship made statutory in secondary schools. The history of take-up for the voluntary cross-curricular guidance papers had, indeed, been derisory. Also, the very idea of democratic citizenship must surely be a universal one. So it had to be a universal entitlement. Admittedly, one can take a horse to water and it may not drink. But unless water is provided it cannot drink at all. The civic 'drink' must be a universal entitlement, clearly there for all. The government accepted that. But in the way governments work, especially Tony Blair's, it cannot be ascribed just to the enthusiasm of one departmental minister and a few allies. If any ministers had doubts that citizenship should be compulsory, three broad considerations prevailed:

1. Citizenship education in schools and FE colleges was seen as a necessary condition for the success of constitutional reform, if part of its object is gradually to create a more participative, self-sustaining and genuinely democratic society.
2. Citizenship education in schools and further education colleges is a necessary condition for a more inclusive society, or for helping to diminish exclusion

from schools, cynicism, welfare-dependency, apathy, petty criminality and vandalism, and the kind of could-not-care-lessitude towards voting and public issues unhappily prevalent among young people.

3. After all, Britain is a democracy, however imperfect, and its legal citizens should know how it works, and how it could be improved if we could change our collective mentality from being subjects of the Crown to being both good and active citizens. This is all part of a liberal education, part of liberalism in the broadest sense.

The Content

The Report that led to the Order made a bold declaration:

> We aim at no less than a change in the political culture of this country both nationally and locally: for people to think of themselves as active citizens, willing, able and equipped to have an influence in public life and with the critical capacities to weigh evidence before speaking and acting; to build on and to extend radically to young people the best in existing traditions of community involvement and public service, and to make them individually confident in finding new forms of involvement and action among themselves (Crick Report, 1998, 1.5).

But it came down to earth, stating three 'practical ideals' later developed into what Blunkett called a 'light touch' curriculum:

> Firstly, children learning from the very beginning self-confidence and social and moral responsible behaviour both in and beyond the classroom, both towards those in authority and towards each other. ... Secondly, learning about and becoming helpfully involved in the life and concerns of their communities, including learning through community involvement and service to the community. ... Thirdly, pupils learning about and how to make themselves effective in public life through knowledge, skills and values – what can be called 'political literacy', seeking for a term that is wider than political knowledge alone (Crick Report, 1998, 2.11).

The *Citizenship Order* itself was 'light touch' in that it was, although a statutory Order, remarkably shorter and less detailed than the other National Curriculum subjects (Department for Education and Employment, 1999). The virtue of the Order was that its generality left schools and teachers with a great freedom and discretion, more so than in the other subjects. Some were dismayed, having unhappily grown used to precise directives, while others were delighted to be given some freedom and professional discretion for once. In any case, plenty of advisory materials and lesson plans began to appear, but not from the government itself (e.g. Alexander, 2001; Association for Citizenship Teaching, 2001; Citizenship Foundation, 2002; Community Service Volunteers, 2000; Potter, 2002; Qualifications and Curriculum Authority, 2002). This occurred, I think, for two reasons. Firstly, it would not be appropriate for the government to give precise prescriptions on some politically or morally sensitive matters – the detail should be at arm's length from the state (it will be for school inspectors, local authority advisers and school governors to watch for gross bias or bad teaching). Secondly, in the very nature of citizenship (somewhat concerned with enhancing freedom, after all) there must be local discretion. It would have been paradoxical for a subject designed to encourage thought and action, action based on thought, to be too prescriptive. For instance, the Order prescribes *inter alia* that:

Pupils should be taught to:

(a) research a topical political, spiritual, moral, social or cultural issue, problem or event by analysing information from different sources …
(b) express, justify and defend orally and in writing a personal opinion about such issues, problems and events
(c) contribute to group and exploratory class discussions, and take part in formal debates (DfEE, 1999, p. 15).

But that is all – there is no prescription about *which* problems, issues and events. The advice *usually* given is that, using the words of the Report, a teacher's choice of problems should consider what the pupils think are real problems and that, whenever possible, pupils should choose. (Of course, this way some of the objectively most important problems of the real world may be ignored; but the aim was not knowledge as such. It was to develop skills of analysis, advocacy, empathy and information discovery which can then be applied when knowledge of the ever-changing problems of the real world is needed.)

There have been objections that, for instance, 'anti-racism' was not explicit in the *Citizenship Order* (Osler and Starkey, 1996). But what was set down was only a way in, to be adapted to different schools with different mixes in different circumstances. Lack of prescriptive detail was deliberate – neither evasive nor a bizarre oversight, but rather a suggested way of putting problems of race relations into a broader context of diversities and tolerances familiar to all:

Pupils should be taught about:

(a) the legal and human rights and responsibilities underpinning society …
(b) the origins and implications of the diverse national, regional, religious and ethnic identities in the United Kingdom and the need for mutual respect and understanding …

Non-governmental bodies – some charities, some educational publishers – offer detailed materials for teachers and pupils on parts of the Order that specifically or implicitly mention civil and human rights, political doctrines, race relations, sustainable development, global citizenship, constitutional reform, civil liberties, consumer rights and financial literacy. The Order allows for considerable flexibility. What is not ruled in is not ruled out; therefore, so long as everything in the Order is covered to a basic level of understanding, some topics can be stressed more than others, and used as major gateways into the whole curriculum.

In the main the Order followed the Report, even if the Order is terse and prescriptive (the actual curriculum is only just over two pages), whereas the Report offers justifications and explanations of its recommendations. Teachers are urged to read them together, especially in relation to the teaching and discussion (there is great stress on discussion) of 'events, issues and problems'. The Report says *'controversial'*, and the Order less controversially says *'contemporary* issues and problems'. But in two respects the Order went radically further than the Report. The Report strongly recommended pupil participation, both in school and in the local community, as good practice, but not to be part of a statutory order – 'value-added', if you like. The Advisory Group thought they were being politically prudent and that the classroom curriculum was enough for a beginning, without overloading teachers. But the Secretary of State sent word to the working party of civil servants, teachers and advisers who were drafting the actual Order that participation could be mandatory, if they thought fit. (We did.) The final Order said that 'Pupils should be taught to negotiate, decide and take part responsibly in school- and community-based activities'.

Without the experiential, participative side of citizenship learning, some schools could turn the brave new subject into safe and dead, dead-safe, old rote learning about institutions – old civics. So easily examinable. There is an awful lot which could be learnt about local government law. A recent book on education for participation begins by quoting a Yoruba proverb: 'The child carried on the back does not know the length of the road'. The editors wisely comment:

> The process of assisting children to become active citizens requires the teacher to keep a delicate balance between providing security and offering challenge. Children must be motivated by being allowed to discuss issues that are real to them (Holden with Clough, 1998).

The motivation to learn about institutions comes when there is a problem to be solved; then it becomes relevant to know what the powers of various institutions are.

'To take part responsibly' can sound 'a dying fall'. Perhaps, but the Report carefully glossed 'responsibly' to bring out how strong its practical implications can be, and to rescue it from high-minded moral vagueness:

> So our understanding of citizenship education in a parliamentary democracy finds three heads on one body: *social and moral responsibility, community involvement* and *political literacy.* 'Responsibility' is an essential political as well as a moral virtue, for it implies (a) care for others; (b) premeditation and calculation about what effect actions are likely to have on others; and (c) understanding and care for the consequences (Crick Report, 1998, 2.11, 2.12).

Presuppositions

The Report, in one explicit quotation, showed that its emphasis on active citizenship was part of a particular tradition of political thought which might not have been apparent to the general reader (nor possibly to some members of the Advisory Group itself). David Hargreaves wrote:

> Civic education is about the civic virtues and decent behaviour that adults wish to see in young people. But it is also more than this. Since Aristotle it has been accepted as an inherently political concept that raises questions about the sort of society we live in, how it has come to take its present form, the strengths and weaknesses of current political structures, and how improvements might be made … Active citizens are as political as they are moral; moral sensibility derives in part from political understanding; political apathy spawns moral apathy (Hargreaves, 1994, pp. 37-8).

Hargreaves takes us back to the very beginning of discourse about citizenship and education. Aristotle reasoned that to be a good man one must also be a good citizen, even if he admitted that it was possible to be a good citizen without being a good man. But in 1820 Benjamin Constant drew a mordant distinction in his once-celebrated essay, 'The Liberty of the Ancients Compared with that of the Moderns':

> The aim of the ancients was the sharing of social power among the citizens of the same fatherland: this is what they called liberty. The aim of the moderns is the enjoyment of security in private pleasures; and they call liberty the guarantees accorded by institutions to these pleasures.

In our yet more modern or post-modern era, these liberties are now guaranteed by the United States of America enforcing on the rest of the world a free-market economy (except when it touches some of their own domestic interests)

Mark Philp has recently written in an essay on 'Citizenship and Integrity' that it is not difficult to see the attraction of citizenship in the classical mode: 'the vision of a virtuous, active citizenry, engaged in deliberation on the proper ends of their association and taking turns at ruling and being ruled – especially when coupled with the assumption that civic virtue provides the natural completion of the broader moral virtues.'

Something of this ancient ideal is a presupposition of democratic states when they command or influence the content and manner of educational systems. However, Philp goes on to remind us that this noble view 'has little moral significance for most people'. Not merely can many people live a purely self-centred life, almost entirely dominated by acquisition, sport, shopping and sex, well protected by a liberal state, but the private life at its best – better than all that – can be claimed to be more virtuous than public life as pictured by Aristotle and, in our times, by Hannah Arendt in one way, or by John Dewey in another. Philp embarrasses the citizenship thesis by quoting the great *politique*, Montaigne, to this narrowing effect:

> Storming a breach, conducting an embassy, ruling a nation are glittering deeds. Rebuking, laughing, buying, selling, loving, hating and living together gently and justly with your household – and with yourself not getting slack nor betraying yourself, is

something more remarkable, more rare and more difficult. Whatever people say, such secluded lives sustain in that way duties which are at least as hard and as tense as those of other lives (Philp, 1999, pp. 20-21).

So the case for active adult citizenship should not be overstated. It cannot be made universal by persuasion, nor compulsory by law. If made compulsory, it is either trivial (where voting is made compulsory, anything can be scrawled on the reluctant ballot paper), or it is ideological and intense – as in one-party states and in ultra-nationalist regimes.

However, a state that does not have a tradition of active citizenship deep in its culture, or cannot create in its educational system a proclivity to active citizenship, is a state that is running certain risks. The extreme risk is lack of support in times of war or in times of economic crisis. The more usual risk is lawlessness within society; perhaps not general, but at least when some minority groups feel alienated from public concerns, disaffected, or driven to or open to a high degree of antisocial behaviour. Philp concedes that despite his 'sceptical caveats, the arguments advanced … show that modern democratic states will be politically stable only if most of their citizens see compliance with their civic responsibilities as a requirement of personal integrity' (Philp, 1999, p. 21).

A common-sense case for education for citizenship might be that since politics, rather like sex, cannot be avoided – indeed civilized life depends on it, on them – then it had better be faced. Since it cannot be avoided, care and time should be given to it, always striving to act with integrity. And since it is an interesting subject, it should be taught in an interesting manner. Civilized life and organized society depend upon the existence of governments, and what governments should do and can do with their power and authority depends, in turn, on both the political structure and the beliefs of inhabitants and groups within society. Taking a Greek or a Jacobin view of the matter may now appear to be going too far – that a person is only at his or her best when acting politically (Arendt, 1958; Crick, 1962). But it remains true that a person is still regarded as less of a human being when he or she has no public spirit, has no concern for, and takes no part in, all the jostlings of self-interest, group interests and ideals that constitute a political society. Only a few would maintain that the good life for all or most consists in the avoidance of public concerns. But nearly all would recognize that our whole culture or style of life is less rich – that is, less various and shapely – and less strong – that is, less adaptable to change and circumstances – if people of any age group or either sex believe they should not, or cannot, influence authority. Feelings of helplessness and powerlessness to have any effect create a widespread could-not-care-lessitude, if not a potentially corrosive cynicism.

These may sound like abstract generalities, but the implications for education are embarrassingly concrete. Any worthwhile education must include some explanation and, if necessary, justification of the naturalness of politics: that people both do and should want different things and, indeed, have differing values and aspirations which are only realizable or attainable by means of, or by leave of, the public power. So pupils must both study and learn to control, to some degree at least, the means by which they reconcile or manage conflicts of interests and ideals, even in school. Michael Oakeshott's radical scepticism (politics is simply keeping a ship afloat on a voyage with no predetermined destination, and therefore it cannot be learned from a book, but only from experience) is at least half right; but it is also half wrong. The conservative and the progressive should come together (Rousseau, of all people, is their go-between) in recognizing that just as a strong experiential element is needed in an education for politics, so is some knowledge of institutions and history (or in terms of Oakeshott's metaphor, both navigation and manuals on how to make running repairs at sea). It is a somewhat arbitrary arrest of experience to make the distinction between schooling and adult experience too sharp, and therefore to privilege fitness to govern to those reared in a class experienced in governing.

The point of departure is, however, all-important. When we ask for directions, there are occasions when we should receive the famous reply of the English rustic asked the way to Biddecome: 'I would not start from here if I were you'. In practice we have to start from where we are – perhaps as inhabitants of a state that conceives politics as neither subversive nor divisive, nor yet as the implementation of a single and authoritative set of ideological or patriotic truths which are to be extolled, but not questioned. But in education in a reasonably free society (and education in its full sense can only exist in reasonably free societies), we are reasonably free, despite practical limitations of various kinds, to start where we choose. So we should start with the nature of politics itself and the realities of political life. If we start from some other point, from conventional and innocent-sounding points of departure such as 'the rule of law', 'good citizenship', 'real justice' or even 'human rights', we risk reinforcing preconceptions too often unappraised. To choose any such single overriding concept is always to beg the question, to think that a political education should lead to a single Platonic answer. A political education is, on the contrary, a way of learning to mediate both morally and practically the differing values and interests which Aristotle found even in the free *polis*, let alone what we are confronted with in the diversity of large modern states.

To mediate we must understand. We understand through concepts. We explore possible meanings, actual meanings and the context of the usage of concepts. There is no choice about beginning with concepts or not: the real choice in education is between beginning with the concepts of a theoretical discipline and simplifying them, or beginning by exploring the actual use of concepts among those we are teaching. (I favour the anthropological or conversational method rather than the didactic.) But people 'do not first make generalizations and then embody them in concepts,' wrote Peter Winch, 'it is only by virtue of their possession of concepts that they are able to make generalisations at all' (Winch, 1958, p. 89). Ernest Gellner, however, was to reprove Winch for what he saw as his Wittgensteinian arrogance in assuming that to understand the concepts of a society is to understand the institutions of that society. For, said Gellner:

> Concepts and beliefs are themselves, in a sense, institutions among others; for they provide a fairly permanent frame, as do other institutions, independent of any one individual, within which individual conduct takes place. In another sense, they are

correlates of *all* the institutions of a society: and to understand the *working* of the concepts of a society is to understand its institutions (Gellner, 1973, p. 128).

If it is, indeed, by the *working* of concepts that one understands a society, then we must start by explicating meanings of such concepts as 'power' and 'authority', *inter alia* – not to show their true meaning, but to explain the role these terms play in, for instance, different political doctrines, and in the power-structures of different social groups (another concept). Concepts are not true or false, they are simply public and useful. Philosophers need to simplify for their pupils and public the basic concepts by which we understand political and social life, and need not simply explore perpetual qualifications and complications among themselves.

Procedural Values

We go wrong at the beginning of complicated enterprises. Any learned fool can elaborate ideas in a PhD or treatise. It needs a certain brave simplicity to begin at the beginning. In the Hansard Society report *Political Education and Political Literacy* (Crick and Porter, 1978), some of us were bold enough to stipulate 12 basic concepts for teachers of citizenship, which we suggested could constitute a vocabulary adequate for a basic understanding of the political world – give or take synonyms and negations, of course. It would be provocative to repeat that intellectual escapade (though some teachers found it helpful). Suffice it to say that some such way in is needed once one comes to think of education as, indeed, *inducare* – a lead-in, an induction, and therefore a progression. Part of the point of this book is that some who think deeply about concepts at the highest level never think of progression from the elementary, the basic, the simple. But one idea from the Hansard thinking is worth reviving – the suggestion that, as well as substantive political and moral values to be debated, there are fairly obvious *procedural values* which must be respected in education, if there is to be any hope of agreement about substantive values in any particular situation or argument. Some of these concepts can also be defined in a substantive way, but they are thought of here as procedures to be followed if there is to be any rational hope of agreement. They are all very familiar: freedom, toleration, fairness, respect for truth, respect for reasoning.

Freedom is the active making of choices of public significance, or potentially of public significance, in a self-willed and uncoerced manner. This is not merely a basic concept and a value, it is a procedural value, for without freedom there can be no way forward to either knowledge of, or voluntary participation in, politics. True, some regimes deny freedom and thus knowledge of politics is limited, but even the secret writings of the samizdat or the philosopher in his study are some sign of freedom, however minimal, and perhaps of potential importance. To conceive of a political education for citizenship that did not seek to nurture freedom would be paradoxical.

Toleration is the degree to which we accept things we disapprove of. It is often confused with permissiveness. The need for toleration would not arise if there were not disapproval. Perhaps 'respect for others' can be seen as a procedural value as well as a moral virtue, but then the case is no better – total respect is either lack of moral discrimination or love (and love, in any absolute sense, is plainly an unrealistic and unnecessary precondition for civil society). Toleration is a two-dimensional concept: it signals disapproval, but also restraint, forbearance and hopefully respect – the hope is for mutual respect. Thus, to be tolerant is to express or imply a disapproval, but in a fair way, and without forcing it on another. But absence of force does not at all imply absence of any attempt to persuade, or refusal to signal some degree of disapproval. What is fair and just by way of persuasion is relative and depends on the circumstances. (We should be more tender in discussion with a pupil in a classroom than with another adult in a meeting.) Those who say they do not want to be tolerated but to be accepted and respected, or that toleration is condescension, may somewhat be missing the point that to tolerate is to recognize that some differences which the other values are real. To be tolerant of someone who holds strongly to a different ideology or religion needs considerable understanding and empathy. It is better to be mutual, but social contact or legal necessity cannot always wait for that. Empathy is a skill to be developed in education, indeed in all of life, quite as much as self-confidence and the propensity to participate. Indeed, it strengthens both. Toleration is neither simply a disposition towards others nor a knowledge of others, but is both together. Even in political life, empathy has great tactical value. The dogmatic activist all too often fails to understand his opponents, commonly lumping them all together as reactionaries or dangerous Lefties or whatever, and therefore adopts inappropriate tactics. 'Know thy enemy as thyself', said Koestler to Orwell.

'*Fairness*' may seem vague compared with 'justice', but it is the concept of common usage. The most ambitious modern attempt to state a philosophical theory of justice, John Rawls' *A Theory of Justice*, resolves the overly legalistic, traditional discussion of justice into the more general considerations of what is thought to be fair and what is fair. Earlier, though certainly influenced by Rawls, W.G. Runciman's work on equality, *Relative Deprivation and Social Justice*, showed empirically that working people judged other people's wages not in absolute monetary terms, but by whether the differences were 'fair' or not (some were thought to be fair, some not). Runciman concluded, like Rawls, that whereas *equality* cannot be defined precisely nor sensibly adopted as an unqualified social ideal, yet 'less unjustifiable inequalities' (or less unfairness) can. So it is reasonable to demand that all inequalities should justify themselves. (It is right and fair, says Runciman, to respect all men equally, but unfair to praise them equally.) Certainly fairness, however vague, is to be preferred to the misleading precision of 'rule of law', which many would make a prerequisite both for political-democratic order and for citizenship education. 'What rules of law?' can legitimately be asked. Anyone who has ever refereed under-11 football will know that there is little knowledge of the actual rules, but an intense contextual sense of fairness.

Respect for truth raises the immediate issue that, even in a parliamentary democracy, the practice of politics and citizenship education do not always see eye to eye. A politically literate person will ask awkward questions early. Political literacy must involve knowing that truths have to be faced, however embarrassing or difficult. The child is surely shocked by parents quarrelling openly, with hysterical selfishness. If Joe and Joanne have to be made aware of why this can happen in the world, this does not imply habituating them to it. Formidable arguments were once made, based upon 'reasons of state', that there are some things only knowable by natural rulers, and that there is some knowledge which must always be kept from the people if order is to be preserved – the *arcana imperii* or the mysteries of power. This might seem utterly discredited. But some modern concepts of ideology were sophisticated versions of this old *politique* argument: that for the welfare of the state – or the party – lies may be told. Truth is what is useful. The 'ideologically correct' is what will be tomorrow if all goes well. But as modern writers like Orwell and Koestler have argued, there is a simple sense in which a lie is still a lie, and a half-truth is a half-lie, whether told for country or party; and that regimes which depend upon systematic lies are neither worthy of support, nor likely to be stable without systematic coercive oppression.

Put positively, a necessary condition of good government is that the truth can be discovered and publicly told about how decisions of government are made. There are obvious practical limitations: security, anticipation of economic decisions, confidentiality and libel. In times of emergency, there are occasions when limitations on truth-telling and public expression are justifiable. But the literate person must presume a right to know, and that everything should be told unless there are compelling and generally acceptable known reasons to the contrary. In hard times lying or not telling the truth can be regarded as a test of party loyalty or even patriotism, but never of a political education. Particular governments may be damaged, but it is a test of free regimes that no amount of truth-telling can endanger them.

Respect for reasoning would seem almost otiose as a precondition for citizenship education, if it were not so uncommon in the rhetoric and sound bites of politicians. But some have argued (and this is still a powerful cultural tendency and educational doctrine) that if an opinion is *sincerely* held, it should not be questioned; nor should one press for reasons or justifications in respect of actions held to be *authentic* expressions of personality. Others regard reasons as unnecessary if actions can be certified as authentic or typical emanations of some group interest – 'working class solidarity', 'respectable opinion' or 'my community believes'. Respect for reasoning comes from analogy and from examples in the polity, the home and the school. We are only discussing the latter, but the context is always there. The teacher must give reasons why things are done in certain ways, particularly when meeting a new class or when changes are made. It is beside the point to object that young children may often not understand reasons given to them. The real point is that the habit of giving reasons, and expecting them to be given, is basic both to intellectual method (as distinct from memorizing) and to political democracy (as distinct from passive obedience, or simply slagging off the other side).

The demand to give reasons does not destroy legitimate authority either in the classroom or in political life – on the contrary, the refusal to give reasons and to encourage reasoning creates cynicism, indifference or even contempt for the political. To consider only the mass media, there are now so many tendencies inimical to reasoning in modern society, it should be clear that citizenship needs citizenship education, and that its presuppositions are those of the long tradition, threatened but still alive, of civic republicanism.

References

Advisory Group on Citizenship ('Crick Report') (1998), *Education for Citizenship and the Teaching of Democracy in Schools*, Final Report of the Advisory Group on Citizenship, 22 September 1998, Qualifications and Curriculum Authority, London.

Alexander, T. (2001), *Citizenship Schools: A Practical Guide*, Campaign for Learning, London.

Arendt, H. (1958), *The Human Condition*, University of Chicago Press, Chicago, Ill.

Association for Citizenship Teaching (2001), 'Apathy: Can Citizenship Help Turn the Tide?', *Teaching Citizenship*, Vol. 1, Summer, Birmingham, *www.teachingcitizenship.org.uk.*

Blunkett, D. (2001), *Politics and Progress: Renewing Democracy and Civil Society*, Politico's Publishing, London.

Blunkett, D. and Crick, B. (1988), *The Labour Party's Aims and Values: An Unofficial Statement*, Spokesman Pamphlet No. 87, Nottingham.

Citizenship Foundation (2002), *Young Citizen's Passport*, 5th ed., Hodder and Stoughton, London.

Community Service Volunteers (CSV) (2000), *Active Citizenship: A Toolkit*, Hodder and Stoughton, London.

Crick, B. (1962), *In Defence of Politics*, Penguin, Harmondsworth.

Crick, B. (2000a), *In Defence of Politics*, 5th ed., Continuum, London.

Crick, B. (2000b), *Essays on Citizenship*, Continuum, London.

Crick, B. (2002), 'The Citizenship Order', in *Parliamentary Affairs, A Journal of Comparative Politics*, Oxford University Press, Oxford.

Crick, B. and Porter, A. (1978), *Political Education and Political Literacy: The Report and Papers of and Evidence Submitted to the Working Party of the Hansard Society's 'Programme for Political Education'*, Longman, London.

Department for Education and Employment/Qualifications and Curriculum Authority (1999), *Citizenship. The National Curriculum for England*, DfEE/QCA, London.

De Tocqueville, A. (1948), *The Recollections of Alexis de Tocqueville*, ed. J.P. Mayer, translated by A. Teixeira de Mattos, The Harvill Press, London.

Gellner, E. (1973), *Cause and Meaning in the Social Sciences*, Routledge, London.

Hargreaves, D. (1994), *The Mosaic of Learning: Schools and Teachers for the Next Century*, Demos, London.

Heater, D. (1990), *Citizenship: The Civic Ideal in World History, Politics and Education*, Longman, London.

Holden, C.E. with Clough, N. (1998), *Children as Citizens: Education for Participation*, Jessica Kingston, Exeter.

Oldfield, A. (1990), *Citizenship and Community: Civic Republicanism and the Modern World*, Routledge, London.

Oliver, D. and Heater, D. (1994), *The Foundations of Citizenship*, Harvester Wheatsheaf, Hemel Hempstead.

Osler, A. and Starkey, H. (1996), *Teacher Education and Human Rights*, Fulton Publishers, London.

Park, A. (1999), 'Young People and Political Apathy', in *British Social Attitudes 16th Report*, National Centre for Social Research, London.

Philp, M. (1999), 'Citizenship and Integrity', in A. Montefiore and D. Vines (eds), *Integrity in the Public and Private Domains*, Routledge, London.

Potter, J. (2002), *Active Citizenship in Schools*, CSV with Kogan Page, London.

Qualifications and Curriculum Authority (2002), *Schemes of Work for Citizenship Key Stage 4*, QCA, London.

Runciman, W.G. (1966), *Relative Deprivation and Social Justice*, Routledge, London.

Ryan, A. (1995), *John Dewey and the High Tide of American Liberalism*, W.W. Norton, New York.

Skinner, Q. (1998), *Liberty Before Liberalism*, Cambridge University Press, Cambridge.

Winch, P. (1958), *The Idea of a Social Science*, Routledge, London.

2

Citizenship Education: Reproductive and Remedial

Geraint Parry

The regularity with which political thinkers throughout history have written on education is striking but should not be surprising. Whilst political theory is concerned with the roles in government of adults (sometimes rulers, sometimes subjects, sometimes citizens), many theorists turn to education to prepare the next generation to succeed to those parts. Education might be aimed at rulers (Machiavelli), their child heirs (Erasmus) or their court (Castiglione). Alternatively, those to be educated might be the subjects of absolute rulers (Hobbes) or of a mixed government (Locke). The re-emergence of republicanism and representative government called for an education of 'citizens', many of whom might have received little education of any sort (Rousseau, James Mill, John Stuart Mill).

The context, content and discourse of political education alter over time. There is, nevertheless, a detectable element of continuity. Human beings always face the question of how far they should, or are able to, mould their young to support or to change the ways of the parental generation. A number of responses to this problem can be discerned. One distinction that may be drawn is between 'reproductive' and 'remedial' education. The idea of education as reproductive is common and has been elaborated by Bourdieu (Bourdieu and Passeron, 1990; Bourdieu, 1996). Even where, it is claimed, the school system appears autonomous, it fulfils 'simultaneously its social function of reproducing the class relations, by ensuring the hereditary transmission of cultural capital, and its ideological function of concealing that social function ...' (Bourdieu and Passeron, 1990, p. 199). Despite Bourdieu, however, much educational theory has been remedial in character. It calls on the new generation to redress the failures of the old. Past and present political systems and rulers are perceived as corrupt and schools as, indeed, reproducers of corruption. The remedy is to isolate the young from this environment and make new persons – an aspiration shared by many radicals since the French Revolution, inspired in no small measure by Rousseau (Parry, 2001).

The distinction between reproductive and remedial has some affinity with a contrast between 'constructive' and 'reconstructive' education (Parry, 1999). This makes use of a difference Dennis Thompson drew between two concepts of citizenship (Thompson, 1970, pp. 43-52). The ideal of constructive citizenship is attained through reforms, whilst reconstructive citizenship requires a qualitative change in economy, politics and society. Similarly, a constructive citizen education seeks to redirect the existing priorities and interests of pupils towards the goals that promote society's needs. A reconstructive education looks to effect a transformation of the belief systems of its subjects and produce 'new persons'. There is not a neat identification between the two suggested sets of categorization. A constructive education may have some remedial objectives, but the remedies tend to involve reforms that will serve to reproduce the essentials of existing practices. Reconstructive education has a firmer association with radical remedial measures and political novelty. More than occasionally, it is true, it may seek to reproduce an ideal that is long past – Rousseau in certain of his moods presents one instance. But this too is tantamount to a reconstruction of pupil, society and polity.

Recent developments in citizenship education in Britain may be offered as illustrations of these broad distinctions between reproductive and remedial, constructive and reconstructive education. For Britain even to address the teaching of citizenship in a self-conscious manner smacks of novelty. State-sponsored citizen education has been variously neglected, regarded as superfluous or seen as politically dangerous and illiberal. For such a change in attitudes to occur there must be something in the state that appears to require a remedy. The Crick Report[1] must be the starting point.

Transformation and Activism

The Introduction to the Report contains a bold statement that catches the vision behind the enterprise:

> We aim at no less than a change in the political culture of this country, both nationally and locally: for people to think of themselves as active citizens, willing, able and equipped to have an influence in public life ... (Crick Report, 1998, 1.5).

This paragraph of the Report ends by citing with approval a speech by the Lord Chancellor in which he declared that 'unless we become a nation of engaged citizens, our democracy is not secure'. This language is clearly in the reconstructive idiom. Indeed, the Report alludes to a political tradition 'stemming from the Greek city states and the Roman Republic', in which citizenship has implied active involvement in public affairs, participation in debate and direct or indirect influence on laws and decisions. The Report proceeds to distinguish this tradition from a more minimal notion of the citizen, associated with the rise of the nation state, that was scarcely differentiated from the status of 'subject'. Britain is cited as a country in which the inheritance of the Crown has meant that the

---

1   The Final Report of the Advisory Group on Citizenship, 22 September 1998, entitled *Education for Citizenship and the Teaching of Democracy in Schools*, is hereafter referred to as the 'Crick Report'. References to the Crick Report give paragraph numbers.

concepts of British citizen and British subject have appeared identical to most people (Crick Report, 1998, 2.1-2.2).

The Report goes on to endorse the revival of the term 'good citizens' at the expense of 'good subjects' who might largely fulfil their obligations by upholding the rule of law. Active citizens require a range of skills to enable them to distinguish between law and justice (Crick Report, 1998, 2.4). The Report repeatedly emphasizes the development of a critical capacity in the citizen. The cultivation of such a faculty is to be accompanied by an education in tolerance, sympathy, respect for others, openness to alternative opinions and civility. Since it is 'active citizenship' that is to be instilled in the young, there is a proportionate stress on action and on doing. As befits a Report that cites John Stuart Mill and Alexis de Tocqueville, there are frequent recommendations that a sense of responsibility and of respect for others is best learned through the exercise of responsibility, and through engagement with others. This can start in primary school, explicitly rejecting any suggestion that this is a pre-citizenship or pre-political stage of life (Crick Report, 1998, 2.11). Citizen virtues are to be encouraged, from early on, by school councils, involvement with local voluntary organizations or in charitable fund-raising. The Report is far from neglecting the importance of formal acquisition of information (Crick Report, 1998, 6), but the value of 'experiential learning' is insisted upon throughout. 'Learning through action' (Crick Report, 1998, 6.3.2) is, literally, stressed as a means of developing the virtues, and of providing the pupils with the qualities they will need as adult citizens. The purpose of citizen education is declared to be that of increasing 'the knowledge, skills and values relevant to the nature and practices of participative democracy' (Crick Report, 1998, 6.6).

The need for a critical disposition seems to underlie the acquisition of the other virtues. The Report suggests that the prerequisite for being a responsible citizen, which includes building upon existing traditions, is the critical capacity 'to weigh evidence before speaking and acting' (Crick Report, 1998, 1.5). This may seem entirely innocuous. Who would wish for educational practices that did not aim to produce the critical mind? Nevertheless, this stress upon critique can also be said to be part and parcel of a specific conception of democratic politics and its attendant dispositions that pervades the Report, and is not one to which all democrats or advocates of citizen education would necessarily adhere.

The Report openly displays a strong partiality toward a reconstructive notion of citizenship. Suggestions of political 'bias' in citizen education are scarcely surprising, given the 'reproductive' potential of schooling. The issue is addressed by the Report (Crick Report, 1998, in section 10) and Crick himself has acknowledged that any citizen education worthy of the name must handle controversial and divisive issues. He has consistently and robustly relied upon the professionalism of teachers to manage any problem (Crick, 2000, pp. 35-57). Generally, however, what commentators have in mind when fearing bias are matters of partisan or religious dispute. The 'bias' of the Report lies in its deeper partiality to participatory democracy.

The citations to political thinkers in the Report are to some of the great names in the participatory tradition – Aristotle, John Stuart Mill, De Tocqueville. Only

Rousseau, Dewey and Arendt are missing and the last-named has always featured as an influence on Crick's own thought. The language of the Report alludes frequently to that of these classic authors. Central to Aristotle's conception of a polity was that citizens should learn to rule and be ruled in turn. In contrast with Plato's reliance on rule by a guardian élite, Aristotle argued that fully developed human beings needed to be able to make political judgements for themselves but also, and crucially, in co-operation with their fellow citizens. The judgement of each should be contributed to the judgement of all through an exchange of views in debate. Implicit in this was a commitment to civic education to enhance the capacity for public discourse. With his almost instinctive sympathy for ancient liberty, Rousseau picked up this central concern with personal engagement in civic responsibilities. He needed, however, to reconcile the modern concept of the autonomous individual with a sense of the community, with which it was often in tension. The individual needed to 'think his own thoughts'. But the citizen had to be seen as a fraction of the whole. Rousseau sought to bridge this gap in a series of highly influential works on personal and citizen education. His degree of success in resolving the difficulty is debatable (Parry, 2001). What each attempt had in common was, by means of education, a reconstruction of the values of the individual – making a new person or, at the political level, the transformation of a subject into a true citizen. Citizenship in particular required that one learned to think and speak on public affairs with only the public, and not one's personal or group interest, in mind. A specifically public or citizen discourse had to be learned. But, in a circularity of cause and effect pervading Rousseau's political analyses, such a discourse could only be acquired in the context of a reconstructed political order that expanded the citizen's opportunities for political participation.

John Stuart Mill saw the problem of citizenship in a remarkably similar way to Rousseau. Starting from a much more robustly individualist, libertarian position, he nevertheless sought also to evoke the ideal of Greek citizenship and its commitment to a public good. At the personal level, it was essential that any education instilled in the pupil a capacity for independent judgement. The critical capacity should be at its core and Mill was celebrated, perhaps notorious, for his insistence on fearless criticism of tradition and popular prejudice. But this intellectual distancing of the individual from others had, in Mill's view, to be balanced in a person of character by a willingness to take on social and political responsibilities. This was something that had to be learned. Just as Mill himself had found that he had needed 'to begin the formation of my character anew' (J.S. Mill, 1958, p.118), such a re-educative process would be required more generally in an active citizenry. In formulating this re-education Mill, as Garforth put it, changed 'the focus from the teacher and the teaching to the pupil and his learning', whilst in politics he switched it 'from government to governed' (Garforth, 1980, pp. 179-80).

The purpose of education, Mill argued, was not to teach, but to fit the mind for learning. Politics was not a science to be professed, but a topic about which students should be taught to think:

What we require to be taught on that subject, is to be our own teachers. It is a subject on which we have no masters to follow; each must explore for himself, and exercise an independent judgment (J.S. Mill, 1984, p. 244).

The prime way to teach oneself politics was by doing. Here the great example was ancient Athens, where every citizen had to act upon a stage and where it was the experience of actual power that was the teacher. A correlative of this, however, was that modern politics would have to be reconstituted, however gradually, to provide some semblance of the opportunity structure that had existed in Athens. Mill repeatedly described politics as a school, but it followed that to be an effective school, the institutions of government had to provide facilities for learning. Hence Mill's advocacy of local government, voluntary associations and forms of industrial democracy as fora in which one could learn to understand the viewpoints of others, the burdens of choice and the moral and political responsibilities of true citizenship.

This 'discovery learning' was to become associated particularly with John Dewey's 'progressive education'. Experiential learning was at the core of Dewey's epistemology, educational thinking and democratic politics. Experience is a transaction between the individual and the world by which a person acts upon the world, is affected by the consequences of that action, and learns and changes as a result (Dewey, 1966, pp. 139-51). Traditional formal education, based upon mastery of distinct disciplines, fails to exploit this transactional experience and leads to stultification. By contrast, education by means of problem-solving, which might be through individual or collective projects, prompts students to test and reconstruct their experiences in a way that 'adds to the meaning of experience, and which increases ability to direct the course of subsequent experience' (Dewey, 1966, p. 76). Politics becomes a similar continuing process of 'reconstruction of experience'. Institutions, practices, rules and rights are never fixed but are constantly subject to testing and deliberation by a community of citizens.

For some, Dewey's anti-foundationalism is liberating (Rorty, 1989, pp. 68-9). Others fear the loss of guarantees offered by the relative fixity of constitutions and conventions on civil and human rights (see discussions by Flew, 1977; Bantock, 1984; Ryan, 1995, pp. 345-65). Similar considerations might influence responses to the work of Benjamin Barber who, like Mill and Dewey, combines radical political and educational reconstruction. Barber confronts the problems of political apathy that trouble the Crick Report. His explanation for the apolitical nature of modern electorates is that the political system itself offers little incentive to become political. Representative democracy keeps the people at a distance. For most citizens, political action consists, at best, in voting every few years (Verba, Nie and Kim, 1978; Parry, Moyser and Day, 1992). Barber's response is to declare that people are 'apathetic because they are powerless, not powerless because they are apathetic' (Barber, 1984, p. 272). In these circumstances there is no urge to gain a citizen education.

The solution, as with Mill and Dewey, is to reconstruct democracy and citizenship education side by side. Barber proposes a 'strong democracy' – a 'self-governing community of citizens who are united less by homogeneous interests than by civic education ...' (Barber, 1984, p. 117). Such individuals can achieve a common purpose, become a people, through the civic attitudes that are formed by the experience of participatory institutions. Citizens have to learn to analyse and to talk politically. They can only do this through new modes of political action – neighbourhood assemblies, town meetings, interactive forms of referendum, workplace democracy, even types of national service.

This is, of course, adult citizen education rather than the preparatory stage with which the Crick Report deals, but the instances of action recommended by Barber and by the Report have a clear family resemblance. Moreover, Barber sees school and university education in much the same light. Like Dewey, he regards teaching via the disciplines and their established canon with suspicion. This canon, he alleges, resists reformulation and reinvention. Knowledge must be openly recognized as 'socially constructed ... conditioned and thus conditional'. It will be persuasive only to the extent that it can be seen to be openly and democratically arrived at: 'The only truth the modern school can have is produced by democracy: consensus arising out of an undominated discourse to which all have equal access' (Barber 1994, p. 214). However, if all are to share in such an undominated discourse, there needs to be a congruence between the school and its environment. Barber shares with Dewey, one of his heroes, the dilemma that experiential education, with its transactions with the world, can result in cognitive dissonance when impoverished surroundings clash with the aims of the school (Barber, 1994, pp. 215-16). This is a version of the circularity that perplexed Rousseau and led him, and some other educationists, to wish to isolate the child from its corrupting environment in order to enable it to transcend that environment. Rousseau's tutor in Emile had been untouched by society, and his counterpart is the school as an enclosed academic world free, so far as is possible, from the distracting pressures of everyday life. This solution is not available to the communitarian Dewey or Barber, or to the Crick Report. Their hope is reform from inside. The school should involve itself with the community by incorporating in the curriculum opportunities to learn the citizen virtues by participating in voluntary service (Barber, 1994, pp. 230-61; Crick Report, 1998, 5.3).

The ultimate hope of participatory theorists is, in the words of Rousseau warmly endorsed by Barber, that such a democracy will produce 'a remarkable change in man' by developing faculties and broadening understanding and sympathies. Concomitant with this effect on reconstructed persons is its impact on society through a shared commitment to public discourse. These would seem to be the ambitions, expressed in less utopian rhetoric than a Rousseau or a Barber, of the Crick Report, when it calls for 'a change in the political culture' of the country, or suggests that without reformed citizen education the 'hoped-for benefits both of constitutional reform and of the changing nature of the welfare state' would be diminished, or that the goal is 'to create a nation of able, informed and empowered citizens' (Crick Report, 1998, 11.1).

'Realism' and Reproduction

The participatory vision is not, however, the only account of democracy that is currently on offer. An alternative conception of democracy, or of how the goals of democracy can be most fully realized, plays down the need for, and sometimes even the desirability of, active citizenship (for the essentials of the dispute see Weale, 1999, pp. 84-105). For these theorists the evocation of ancient, classical or republican models of politics is misplaced, since it ignores the changed 'reality' of modern democracy. A 'realist democrat' starts from the fundamental fact that, since the end of the eighteenth century, representative government has been the only actual claimant to the title of 'democracy'. James Mill termed it 'the grand discovery of modern times' (J. Mill, 1992, p. 21). Central to the idea of representative government is, as Schumpeter later expressed it, a 'division of labour' between the politician and the public (Schumpeter, 1943, p. 295). Moreover, this distance was not regarded as merely an unfortunate consequence of adapting democracy to large nation-states instead of the city-states of the ancient world. The elected representative was to be a person with the knowledge and skill to sift the demands of the populace and legislate for the longer-term interest of the nation. A different social and educational standing from the voter was often seen as particularly appropriate when many electors were persons of little property and learning.

From the outset of representative government there was a widespread, albeit not universal, view that an active citizenry was not an essential requirement when, for the most part, political involvement was confined to the periodic selection of members of the legislature. It is true that radicals, including here James Mill, sought to restrict the discretion of representatives by frequent elections, which would have had the side-effect of increasing the regularity of electoral participation. Nevertheless, apart from elections to the US House of Representatives, this was seldom adopted. Generally, therefore, if electoral politics is at the core of modern democracy, it does not demand a high level of citizen activity, and to expect it might be deemed unrealistic. As Manin has put it:

> What is today referred to as a crisis of political representation appears in a different light if we remember that representative government was conceived in explicit opposition to government by the people, and that its central institutions remain unchanged (Manin, 1997, p. 232).

If an active citizenry is not to be assumed, what do realist democrats see as the role of citizen education? James Mill, as well as writing the classic early British defence of representative government, also composed a treatise on education fully congruent with his position on political motivation. In politics, as in life generally, individuals were moved by a concern to promote or protect their own happiness. The task of politics and of education was to redirect the natural pursuit of private advantage so that it coincided with the national interest. This did not involve any reconstruction of humanity in the manner of Rousseau. In contrast to his son John Stuart, James Mill placed more emphasis on the teacher, whose skill lay in the employment of rewards and sanctions so that pupils would be taught regularly to associate their own pleasure with those activities that promoted public benefits (J. Mill, 1931, pp. 54-6). Rulers were prone to abuse power and act in a manner contrary to the greatest happiness. Electors had to learn to protect their own and the general interests by adopting a suspicious attitude to government. The mechanism was the electoral sanction of defeat for governments that set private over public interest, and the reward of re-election for those promoting the greatest happiness. Such a political system could function without the acquisition of a strong sense of civic virtue on the part of either rulers or ruled.

Subsequent realist democrats have a similarly thin conception of citizen education. Most notorious and provocative was Schumpeter, for whom the people not only have a limited role in modern democracy, but rightly so. He claimed that once average persons enter the political arena, they lack the kind of knowledge and judgement they normally possess in their private lives (Schumpeter, 1943, p. 262). They understand what is involved in choosing a pair of shoes or in making a business decision. However, their fundamental and inescapable remoteness from political events and the factors surrounding them renders ordinary persons unable to act in a sensible and informed fashion. The task of electors is to choose between competing political élites and, once they are elected, allow them to get on with the business of governing without any 'back-seat driving'. Even their electoral choice is heavily influenced by the rival political leaderships who, in effect, determine the agenda and employ all the techniques of the modern advertiser to shape the will of the voters. No answer can be found by seeking to revive the classical conception of democracy and the active citizen, and the attendant civic education. The reality of competitive élite politics precludes such utopian gestures.

By far the most subtle presentation of the realist position is that of Giovanni Sartori. Here, too, the ideal of ancient participative democracy is rejected not only as outmoded, but as incompatible with modern liberalism and individualism. The participatory vision carries with it, according to Sartori, a legacy of collectivism (Sartori, 1987, pp. 278-97). Like Schumpeter, he holds that modern democracy is not to be defined in terms of the rule of the people, but of the selection by the people of those who are to rule. Unlike Schumpeter, he does not believe that electoral choices in a free society are so readily manipulated by the élites. Most people, Sartori believes, are capable of gaining sufficient political knowledge to make a choice between the packages of policies on offer from the rival parties. Beyond this, however, there is little incentive on a purely cost-benefit analysis for most people to gain more detailed political understanding and develop a rationally ordered set of policy preferences. The vote is a blunt instrument for or against a party programme and cannot, in normal electoral circumstances, discriminate between different parts of a manifesto or rank them (Sartori, 1987, pp. 106-10).[2]

Sartori, therefore, regards any call for a transformation of the voter into an active citizen with the aid of civic education as unrealistic and betraying a misunderstanding of representative democracy. The modern citizen is not an active

---

2 For a clear introduction to voting and preferences see Weale, 1999, pp.124-47.

citizen so much as a controller and, even at that level, requires only modest political knowledge such as can exist in a free society with a relatively autonomous public opinion. The true need for political education, Sartori argues, is at élite level, equipping the political class to make judgements on behalf of the electors in the face of the accumulation of 'expert' scientific and technical information that they need to assess to reach policy decisions in a world of complexity.

Despite the total indifference to citizen education displayed by Schumpeter and the relative neglect shown by Sartori, it remains the case for other realist democrats that even the modest political role assigned to the average person requires some preparation. Democratic self-control is a discipline to be learned. It is the counterpart of learning how to be an active citizen in the rival conception. Each within its system of thought is a virtue. William Galston has proposed the kind of education for representative democracy that has 'congruence with the basic features of the society it is intended to sustain' (Galston, 1991, p. 246). He identifies these basic features as the election of representatives and the limited sphere of competence of the liberal state. In the tradition of Madison he argues that an advantage of representative politics is the distance between the political class and the people. This is coupled with the intervals between appeals to the electorate, which mean that the system allows the legislature to distinguish between 'momentary public whim and the settled will – that is, the considered judgement – of the community'. The corresponding civic education will concentrate on 'the virtues and competences needed to select representatives wisely ... and to evaluate their performance in office soberly' (Galston, 1991, p. 247). These capacities may be related to, but can be distinguished from, those needed for direct participation. They include the ability to assess the talents and characters of office-holders and candidates, respect for others, readiness to moderate demands and acceptance of the rule of law. They do not include any sense of a duty of active participation or any grander notion of civic virtue (Galston, 1991, p. 253). It is the aspirants to political office who should be expected to display enhanced political capacities and virtues.

To demand more of citizens in a representative democracy and to reinforce this demand by civic education is, Galston argues, to go beyond the remit of a liberal polity. The call for an active, critical citizenry is 'to endorse a politics of transformation based on a general conception of the political good external to the concrete polity in question' (Galston, 1991, p. 246). A liberal representative state is fully justified in advancing a civic education confined to inculcating what is necessary to sustain itself. Indeed, it is permitted to propagate a positive version of itself and its history.[3] However, the liberal state may not shape education positively to 'foster in children skeptical reflection on ways of life inherited from parents or local communities' (Galston, 1991, p. 253). This would be to enshrine in law a specific world view not shared by all citizens and not required for the maintenance of the framework of the state.

---

3   On the potential dangers of such civic myths, see Callan, 1997, pp. 100-31; Barry, 2001, pp. 230-32.

This restriction on the role of citizen education is shared by what, since the work of John Rawls, has come to be termed 'political liberalism'. Rawls argues that, in a modern society in which citizens hold a variety of 'reasonable' comprehensive moral positions, often in conflict with one another on significant issues, it would be improper for the state to employ its resources to advance any one such doctrine over another (Rawls, 1993). The state should seek to be neutral. It is not, nevertheless, required to be neutral about its own neutrality. Children may be educated to acquire the political virtues so as to become 'fully co-operating members of society' (Rawls, 1993, p. 199). These virtues apply specifically to the political realm and are supportive of a system of rules and behaviour that Rawls believes are consistent with all major reasonable comprehensive doctrines and can, therefore, be supported by an overlapping consensus in a liberal polity.

The content of such a civic education would include an understanding of civil rights and the promotion of political toleration. Children would need to learn that political justice requires that each acknowledge the equal political rights of others, and that no group may seek to use the state to enforce its own moral doctrines on others. Future citizens also need to learn a specific form of discourse appropriate to the conduct of liberal democracy. This 'public reason' is a mode of argumentation that confines itself to the terms of political justice (Rawls, 1993, pp. 212-54). Any case for a modification of the procedures of liberal democracy must be couched, as Rousseau argued, in the language of public principles and not of private interests or belief systems. As a consequence, the range of civic education is, at first glance at least, restricted and is deliberately not transformative or reconstructive. A more participatory-minded civic education appears to be ruled out because of its alleged close association with a specific comprehensive moral doctrine, in particular one grounded on the cultivation of the reflective, critical, autonomous individual as its goal – a position derivable from Rousseau, Kant or certain passages in the earlier Rawls of *A Theory of Justice* (Rawls, 1971, pp. 453-76).

Remedial Education – Minimal and Maximal

There are, therefore, powerfully argued sceptical alternatives to an education for active citizenship. They are constructivist and reproductive in tone, arguing for schooling that would broadly support the existing arrangements of liberal representative government, albeit perhaps with gradual reforms. A distinction, along such lines, between a 'minimal' and a 'maximal' form of citizen education appears to be discernible in educational practices across the world (Kerr, 2000; Hahn, 1999). Where a country might appear, on a notional continuum from minimal to maximal, depends on many factors. These include the specificity of the curriculum, the degree of national testing, the emphasis on teaching or learning, whether citizenship is a distinct subject or is incorporated within other school subjects, and how far a state adopts a 'values explicit' or a 'values neutral' stance (Kerr, 2000). Where a state might be placed on the continuum will also be affected by judgements by researchers, teachers or educational authorities as to what counts as 'political' in education. At one extreme it may be confined to an understanding of the workings of government. At the other one might wish to include training in social behaviour and community discipline, such as the pupils' rota of cleaning or meal service in a Japanese school, designed to promote a sense of cohesion and identity (Cummings, 1980, pp. 109-19; McCargo, 2000, pp. 129-33). The comparative study of citizen education suggested that there had been a shift in many countries away from a 'narrow, knowledge based approach' to one 'encompassing knowledge and understanding, active experiences and the development of student values, dispositions, skills and aptitudes' (Kerr, 2000, p. 23). This shift was, however, slow, partly as a consequence of school cultures in which teaching, the transmission of factual information and testing were the norms and, in the case of politics, one can surmise, perhaps also due to fears of allegations of bias or government pressure.

In the face of this widespread alternative understanding and practice of citizen education, is the call by the Crick Report for an education in activism incongruent with the norms of British politics? Might its reconstructive conception of civic life arouse expectations of political involvement that cannot be satisfied, given the present structure of political opportunities?

One defensive move would be to argue, with Crick, that the National Curriculum for citizenship education in UK schools is 'a light touch order' (Crick, 2000, p. 118). It indicates goals and some broad topics which are to be covered in a curriculum. It does not stipulate the events or problems that might be used by teachers as illustrations. Nor are there, as in some countries, officially prescribed textbooks. This points to an arm's-length liberal solution proposed more generally for education by John Stuart Mill in Chapter Five of *On Liberty*. The state might set public examinations in a subject, whilst permitting schools to prepare the pupils by whatever teaching methods and with whatever materials they considered appropriate. Each school would offer its distinctive approach to a common set of questions – 'competing experiments', as Mill termed them (J.S. Mill, 1989, pp. 104-8). From a strict libertarian standpoint the difficulty remains that the examinations could be a means of introducing state control by the back door. Mill sought to obviate this problem by restricting public testing largely to factual knowledge – a solution that would go against the broader goals of the Crick Report. Nevertheless, this model of public examinations might deserve more attention from those who recognize a need for educational yardsticks, but disapprove of the prescriptivism of national curricula – and not merely in citizenship education.

The Rawlsian argument that liberal neutrality implies that civic education must not endorse any comprehensive moral doctrine, but should confine its remit to what is required to sustain political justice, might be countered by defenders of the Crick Report at two levels. First, one could contend that the Report meets both requirements. The Report defends its position in political terms, as might be expected from the author of *In Defence of Politics*. It justifies its stance in consequentialist terms by the effect of citizen education on the nature of political life. It does not get too far into deeper water by arguing that its belief in active citizenship is justifiable by appeal to notions of moral autonomy or another such comprehensive moral position.

It may, however, teeter on the edge of doing so, which leads to the second line of defence, which is also a line of attack. This is to argue that strict liberal neutrality is an unsustainable position in education. In *Political Liberalism*, Rawls suggests that civic education should teach not only that others have equal civil rights, but that this permits them to express, but not seek to enforce by law, their own moral positions. Civil tolerance demands that people must understand alternative views sufficiently to appreciate their reasonableness. One effect might be that religious schools be legally required, as part of their civic role, to teach comparative religious education in such a way that their pupils are able to assess the strengths, weaknesses and reasonableness of the alternatives and, perhaps, as a consequence, of their own religion. The aim of educating the reasonable, tolerant citizen of a neutral state may result in a self-consciously critical individual whose world view is indistinguishable from a comprehensive moral liberal. Indeed, it is in the context of education that Rawls acknowledges that the effect, if not the intention, of political liberalism might be to encourage the spread of moral liberalism. These 'unavoidable consequences of reasonable requirements for children's education may have to be accepted, often with regret' (Rawls, 1993, p. 200). As Callan has put it, the 'upshot of all this is that Rawlsian political liberalism is really a kind of closet comprehensive liberalism' (Callan, 1997, p. 40). Rawls' critics, even those within the liberal camp, claim in different ways and to different degrees that liberalism is a more substantive doctrine, and that this has to be reinforced by an education with more explicit political and cultural content (Frazer, 2000; Levinson, 1999). It is the contention of the Crick Report that liberal politics needs active citizenship for its sustenance. Moreover, it alleges that liberal democratic politics in Britain is suffering from a crisis of confidence and infers that citizenship studies should be viewed as a form of remedial education.

The urgent need for citizen education is to help redress the apparent decline in the already low levels of political participation. The Report cites evidence that even voting, the only political activity in which a large majority of the population regularly engages, has declined, particularly amongst the young. Signs of a greater interest in voluntary organizations and single-issue politics, such as environmentalism, might offer the promise of resuscitation. Yet this preference for involvement in the articulation of interests accompanied with disdain for the process of aggregation, which is the balancing and compromising business of parties and governments, can itself be regarded as a potentially dangerous misunderstanding of the essentials of democratic politics.

Beyond the decline in electoral politics one can detect an increasing uncertainty as to the fundamentals of British politics (Holliday, Gamble and Parry, 1999). What are termed 'fundamentals' at any period are usually constructions of statecraft by élites. They are maps of power and markers for both the political class and subjects or citizens. It is arguable that we are now living through a period of deconstruction of fundamentals in almost every sphere of life. In British politics the monarchy, the House of Lords, the sovereignty of parliament, the voting system and the lines of executive accountability have all undergone substantial change in the last few decades. As recently as 1970, a classic textbook could portray Britain as possessing a 'homogenized' culture, as no longer facing a nationalities, religious or constitutional problem and, to a large extent, as enjoying a substantive consensus (Finer, 1970, pp. 132-40). Thirty years later Britain was being routinely redescribed as multicultural, multinational and as constitutionally in democratic deficit (Parekh, 2002; Holliday, 1999; Beetham and Weir, 1999).

In such a plural and deconstructed world citizens can lose their bearings. One response of constitutional theory and civic education is to seek a minimal citizenship to which all might consent. It might involve a defensive form of politics, institutionalizing distrust of government and placing heavy reliance on strengthened constitutional checks and balances to limit the reach of the state (Parry, 1976). Such a response does not have to eschew all notions of positive citizenship but can, with the help of education, seek to build a consensus around the core features of liberal procedures, as Rawls and Galston have proposed. Engagement in these procedures would not carry with it any associations with comprehensive moral doctrines, ethnicity or religion, or any legacies of such other identities (Parekh, 2002). Such a minimalist conception of citizenship may, however, have difficulties in inspiring ideas of loyalty to a particular polity – to Britain as distinct, say, from any other liberal nation within the European Union (see Simmons, 1979 on the 'particularity requirement in political obligation'). Even if this is not a drawback, there must be a question whether an education for such a thin conception of citizenship can engender enough commitment and enthusiasm to remedy the curious combination of political demands with alienation that is alleged to be threatening the liberal democratic state. But for the defenders of such a minimalist notion of citizenship, it is precisely political self-restraint that must be learned if pluralist democracy is to survive.

The alternative strategy is the rediscovery of the active citizen. The hope is that people can learn to create a distinctive trusting society through talking and doing. This approach has one thing in common with the more defensive, minimalist responses. It also seeks to establish a discourse that is directed to the public good. However, rather more than the minimalist conception that distrusts politics and would set limits to the political realm, it hopes to achieve a strong civic bond through expanded political action – trust engendering trust. In Barber's ideal of strong democracy:

> Individuals become involved in government by participating in the common institutions of self-government and become involved with one another by virtue of their common engagement in politics. They are united by the ties of common activity and common consciousness – ties that are willed rather than given by blood or heritage or prior consensus on beliefs ... (Barber, 1984, p. 223).

These two contrasting responses to democratic governance and to the problems of fulfilling its promises have existed since the emergence of modern forms of democracy. For the realist, participatory democracy is, at best, a long haul and its outcome a long shot. At its worst it overemphasizes the populist at the expense of the liberal elements within liberal democracy. It does so by placing the construction and reconstruction of rights or other constitutional constraints in the hands of the collective. The participationists, by contrast, fear that the distrust of the political realm and the distance that realists put between the citizens and the political class can be self-confirming and result in apathy or cynicism. Of course this is taking the contrast to its extreme. A strong democrat, such as Barber, acknowledges (if perhaps too briefly) that there must be some constraint on the political will (Barber, 1984, pp. 307-11). Crick, whilst nailing his colours to the activist mast, has criticized those who appear to admire participation for the sake of participation (Crick, 2000, pp. 30-32). Conversely no realist, even James Madison, has relied solely upon constitutional mechanisms to maintain liberal procedures. Realists recognize that people have to perceive the need for sufficient active political involvement to protect the public realm – however restricted that realm may be. There is, nevertheless, a significant difference of view either about the nature of democracy or, at least, about what is necessary to fully attain the core ideals of democracy.

There may be ways of narrowing the gap between these approaches. It is possible, for example, that greater transparency in government might help to assuage political cynicism, which is the dangerous extension of what can often be healthy political distrust. But transparency would have to be accompanied by an education in political understanding for politicians, media and the public alike. Arguments within governments or oppositions might need to be recognized as debates between intelligible options, rather than as personal or sectional conflicts to be leaked or suppressed. Reasonable compromise might need to be seen, as Burke saw it, as a political virtue, not a vice, if interests are to be aggregated and not articulated as non-negotiable demands.[4]

It may follow from this that civic education should not be fixated on the idea of active citizenship, but attempt something less demanding, yet not inconsistent with that aspiration. This would be to teach the stronger form of public reason advocated by certain theorists of deliberative democracy, such as Joshua Cohen (Cohen, 1997). Cohen argues that a deliberative view of democracy, in which all participants are equally required to offer reasons for their arguments that are politically acceptable to others, implies an inclusive political community. Whilst such an approach is highly congruent with a participatory view of democracy, such as Cohen's own, it does not demand it. There is no pressure on individuals to reconstruct or transform themselves. It does require that where people do step out of the private into the public sphere, they couch their arguments in terms of what others can be brought to recognize as reasonable claims for collective endorsement.

This was also the essence of Rousseau's requirement that each true citizen has to possess a general will – an appreciation of how to present a case in public terms. At its most elevated it may, as participationists from Rousseau to Barber or Cohen have hoped, generate civic virtue and community. This can be learned by practising public deliberation. But at a very basic level many people already have an inkling of what is involved in the adoption of public reason, even when it is employed merely as a political strategy. Teachers may call for higher pay, but to count as a persuasive public reason, they learn to rephrase it in terms of a common

---

4   See the still relevant analysis of 'pluralistic stagnation' by Beer, 1982.

benefit – better education that will allegedly be produced through the recruitment or retention of teaching staff – about which all can deliberate, instead of a sectional desire over which there can be little profitable debate. Local protesters may not wish a development in their own backyard, but need to find public reasons to appear convincing. The lack of sincerity may be disappointing but is not necessarily disturbing or relevant. The essential is that all are required to find publicly acceptable formulations of their demands. Such formulations can be supported by evidence and reasoned argument that can be challenged in debate.

Deliberative citizenship education would, therefore, aim to produce one of the conditions required for reasonable political decision-making. It aims to teach the modes of argumentation appropriate to liberal democracy. This would incorporate much that the Crick Report enjoins, but also that would be acceptable to realist democrats. There would still be disagreements between participationists and some political liberals about the remit of politics. But there might be more agreement about the capacities that citizens could be expected to acquire. Pupils would learn how to reason, criticize, marshal evidence and debate. They would also learn to listen to others and respect their equal rights to advance claims that are similarly phrased in the terms of public discourse. To meet the 'particularity' requirement, they would still need to learn how these skills are normally exercised in their own country (in Britain, say, rather than in another liberal state that follows other styles of governance) – something necessarily involving some historical understanding of how this came about. It also follows that, if all citizens are to be taught this knowledge, it will seem less discriminatory to ask incomers to learn some abridgement of it. Here particular care still needs to be taken by educational authorities that this public language is not so narrowly defined as to exclude certain categories of the population, on the grounds that they do not display adequate levels of communicative competence. Plural democracies have to be ready to consider a number of modes of political expression. Nevertheless a citizen education in a democracy can be expected, with suitable safeguards, to aim at a common level of competence in the language of politics. The realist will insist that in this there should be no inbuilt expectation that the students become activists, only that when they do so they know how to go about political activity guided by a norm of political reasonableness. The hope and expectation of participatory democrats is that competence breeds competence and that confident, politically well-educated citizen activism is more likely to sustain, reinforce and extend practices of liberal democracy.

References

Advisory Group on Citizenship ('Crick Report') (1998), *Education for Citizenship and the Teaching of Democracy in Schools*, Final Report of the Advisory Group on Citizenship, 22 September 1998, Qualifications and Curriculum Authority, London.

Bantock, G.H. (1984), *Studies in the History of Educational Theory, Vol. II, The Minds and the Masses, 1760-1780*, Allen and Unwin, London.

Barber, B. (1984), *Strong Democracy: Participatory Politics for a New Age*, University of California Press, Berkeley.

Barber, B. (1994), *An Aristocracy of Everyone: The Politics of Education and the Future of America*, Oxford University Press, Oxford.

Barry, B. (2001), *Culture and Equality*, Polity Press, Cambridge.

Beer, S. (1982), *Britain Against Itself: the Political Consequences of Collectivism*, Faber and Faber, London.

Beetham, D. and Weir, S. (1999), *Political Power and Democratic Control in Britain*, Routledge, London.

Bourdieu, P. (1996), *The State Nobility*, translated by L.C. Clough, Polity Press, Cambridge.

Bourdieu, P. and Passeron, J-C. (1990), *Reproduction in Education, Society and Culture*, 2nd edition, translated by R. Nice, Sage, London.

Callan, E. (1997), *Creating Citizens: Political Education and Liberal Democracy*, Oxford University Press, Oxford.

Cohen, J. (1997), 'Procedure and Substance in Deliberative Democracy', in J. Bohman and W. Rehg (eds), *Deliberative Democracy: Essays in Reason and Politics*, The MIT Press, Cambridge, Mass.

Crick, B. (2000), *Essays on Citizenship*, Continuum, London.

Cummings, W.K. (1980), *Education and Equality in Japan*, Princeton University Press, Princeton, N.J.

Dewey, J. (1966), *Democracy and Education*, Free Press, New York.

Finer, S.E. (1970), *Comparative Government*, Allen Lane, The Penguin Press, London.

Flew, A. (1977), 'Democracy and Education', in R.S. Peters (ed.), *John Dewey Reconsidered*, Routledge and Kegan Paul, London.

Frazer, E. (2000), 'Citizen Education: Anti-political Culture and Political Education in Britain', *Political Studies*, Vol. 48(1), pp. 88-103.

Galston, W (1991), *Liberal Purposes: Goods, Virtues, and Diversity in the Liberal State*, Cambridge University Press, Cambridge.

Garforth, F.W. (1980), *Educative Democracy: John Stuart Mill on Education in Society*, Oxford University Press, Oxford.

Hahn, C. (1999), 'Citizenship Education: An Empirical Study of Policy, Practices and Outcomes', *Oxford Review of Education*, Vol. 25(1 & 2), pp. 231-50.

Holliday, I. (1999), 'Territorial Politics', in I. Holliday et al., *Fundamentals in British Politics*, Macmillan, Basingstoke, pp. 119-41.

Holliday, I., Gamble, A. and Parry, G. (eds) (1999), *Fundamentals in British Politics*, Macmillan, Basingstoke.

Kerr, D. (2000), 'Citizen Education: An International Comparison', Paper presented to the Annual Conference of the Political Studies Association of the UK, London.

Levinson, M. (1999), *The Demands of Liberal Education*, Oxford University Press, Oxford.

Manin, B. (1997), *The Principles of Representative Government*, Cambridge University Press, Cambridge.

McCargo, D. (2000), *Contemporary Japan*, Macmillan, Basingstoke.

Mill, J. (1931), 'Education', in F.A. Cavenagh (ed.), *James and John Stuart Mill on Education*, Cambridge University Press, Cambridge.

Mill, J. (1992), 'Government', in T. Ball (ed.), *James Mill: Political Writings*, Cambridge University Press, Cambridge.

Mill, J.S. (1958), *Autobiography*, The World Classics, Oxford University Press, London.

Mill, J.S. (1984), 'Inaugural Address Delivered to the University of St. Andrews, 1867', *Collected Works of John Stuart Mill*, Vol. XXI, Toronto University Press, Toronto.

Mill, J.S. (1989), *On Liberty and Other Writings*, Cambridge University Press, Cambridge.

Parekh, B. (2002), 'Being British', *Government and Opposition*, Vol. 37(3), pp. 301-15.

Parry, G. (1976), 'Trust, Distrust and Consensus', *British Journal of Political Science*, Vol. 6, pp. 129-42.

Parry, G. (1999), 'Constructive and Reconstructive Political Education', *Oxford Review of Education*, Vol. 25(1 & 2), pp. 23-8.

Parry, G. (2001), '*Emile*: Learning to be Men, Women and Citizens', in P. Riley (ed.), *The Cambridge Companion to Rousseau*, Cambridge University Press, Cambridge, pp. 247-71.

Parry, G., Moyser, G. and Day, N. (1992), *Political Participation and Democracy in Britain*, Cambridge University Press, Cambridge.

Rawls, J. (1971), *A Theory of Justice*, Harvard University Press, Cambridge, Mass.

Rawls, J. (1993), *Political Liberalism*, Columbia University Press, New York.

Rorty, R. (1989), *Contingency, Irony, and Solidarity*, Cambridge University Press, Cambridge.

Ryan, A. (1995), *John Dewey and the High Tide of American Liberalism*, Norton, New York.

Sartori, G. (1987), *The Theory of Democracy Revisited*, Chatham House Publishers, Chatham, N.J.

Schumpeter, J. (1943), *Capitalism, Socialism and Democracy*, Allen and Unwin, London.

Simmons, A.J. (1979), *Moral Principles and Political Obligations*, Princeton University Press, Princeton, N.J.

Thompson, D. (1970), *The Democratic Citizen*, Cambridge University Press, Cambridge.

Verba, S., Nie, N. and Kim, J-O. (1978), *Participation and Political Equality*, Cambridge University Press, Cambridge.

Weale, A. (1999), *Democracy*, Macmillan, Basingstoke.

3

Two Dilemmas of Citizenship Education in Pluralist Societies

Will Kymlicka

Introduction

Whenever societies seek to educate children for citizenship, they always have a particular model or conception of citizenship in mind, implicitly or explicitly. These models of citizenship vary over time, and from place to place. But throughout the Western democracies for the last century, two characteristics have been central to our models of citizenship.

The first concerns the values of citizenship, which have typically been defined in *liberal* terms. If citizenship can be understood in part as a package of rights and responsibilities, then this package has been defined by reference to liberal values. At the heart of our citizenship rights are individual liberties. These include the freedom of association, speech and conscience, and more generally the freedom of choice about how to lead our lives. Similarly, our duties as citizens are quintessentially liberal duties e.g. the duty to be tolerant, to accept the secular nature of political power and hence the separation of church and state, and to exercise our individual autonomous judgement and critical reasoning when engaging in voting or public reasoning.

The second key characteristic concerns the scale or boundaries of citizenship, which has invariably been defined in *national* terms. If citizenship can be understood as membership in a political community, then the traditional model of citizenship emphasizes membership in national political communities. The nation-state has been seen as the privileged locus for political participation, self-government and solidarity. If democracy is the rule 'of the people', then it is the nation that defines 'the people' who are to rule themselves. We exercise self-determination by electing national legislatures, and our citizenship rights are protected by national constitutions.

This picture of citizenship as based on liberal values institutionalized in national political communities has been very powerful in the recent history of Western democracies. And it remains influential. Western democracies have had great success in promoting and inculcating this model of citizenship. The levels of popular commitment to both liberal values and national institutions are surprisingly high in most countries. (It is surprising when we remember that there were very few political communities that were either liberal or national 200 years ago.) And schools have surely played an important role in the successful propagation of this liberal/national model of citizenship. Despite the limited resources and low priority given to citizenship education in many countries, and despite the lack of an agreed or effective pedagogy for teaching it, it is inconceivable that this level of support for liberal values and national institutions could have arisen without the use of the schools as arenas for civic education.

However, this traditional model of citizenship is increasingly challenged by the facts of diversity in our society. We live in an era of increasing diversity and, more importantly, an era when more and more groups – even long-standing ones – feel entitled to demand public recognition and support for their differences. This trend is often labelled as a 'politics of difference' or a 'politics of recognition' (Kymlicka and Norman, 2000).

Two Challenges

In this paper, I want to discuss two separate challenges that diversity raises to our traditional models of citizenship. First, we have some groups which challenge the underlying liberal values, and who view liberal norms of secularism, tolerance, individual autonomy and public reason as a threat to their way of life. Such groups are typically conservative or fundamentalist religious groups. In Europe, this threat is often associated with Muslim immigrants. In North America, by contrast, the issue has typically arisen in the context of well-established Christian and Jewish groups, such as the Amish in Wisconsin, the Hasidic Jews in New York, or evangelical Protestants in the southern United States.

A second challenge is raised by groups whose members accept the underlying liberal values of the traditional model, but who dispute the privileging of the nation-state as the appropriate scale of political community, and indeed who view this as a threat to their own distinct sense of political community. This challenge has been raised most forcefully by certain substate national groups that have mobilized along nationalist lines to demand self-government. Examples include the Basques and Catalans in Spain, Scots in Britain, Québécois in Canada, Flemish in Belgium, and indigenous peoples in the Americas, New Zealand and Australia.

Surveys show that the members of these national groups often share the same liberal values of secularism and individual liberty (Kymlicka, 2001, chs 10-15). However, they insist that they form their own distinct political communities, with the right to govern themselves through their own legislatures. (This may take the form of outright secession, or some form of federal autonomy within the larger state.) They also insist that citizenship education should promote participation in, and attachment to, their own political community.

Others challenge the national scope of citizenship from the opposite direction, arguing that citizenship should be focused on certain supranational forums, like the European Union. According to this view, citizenship education should focus on training children to participate in, and identify with, supranational political communities. Both the substate nationalists and the transnationalists argue that the historical privileging of the nation-state is arbitrary, and that other political communities at other levels are the appropriate locus for the exercise of liberal citizenship.

So we confront challenges to the *liberal content* of citizenship from conservative religious groups, and challenges to the *national scale* of citizenship from substate minorities. Both of these raise many important issues. Political philosophers have tended to focus on the first challenge, at least in the American literature (e.g. Macedo, 2000; Levinson, 1999; Feinberg, 1998; Spinner-Halev, 2000; Burtt, 1996; Galston, 1995; Reich, 2002). However, the second challenge is equally important, and both must be addressed in any systematic theory of citizenship education.

I will not try to resolve either of these two challenges in this paper. However, I do want to examine them in more detail, and consider how Western democracies have dealt with them. I will start with the challenge to liberal values.

The Challenge to Liberal Citizenship

Conservative religious groups often object to the liberal conception of citizenship education, and indeed to liberal models of education more generally. In particular, they reject two key components of a liberal conception of citizenship: public reasonableness and civility. In order to explain their objections to these values, I need first to explain why they are important to liberals.

Certain virtues are needed in virtually any political order, whether it is liberal and democratic or not. These include general virtues, such as courage and law-abidingness, as well as economic virtues, such as the capacity to delay self-gratification or to learn a productive skill or trade (Galston, 1991, pp. 221-4). Religious groups rarely object to these general virtues, and indeed are often seen as exemplars of these virtues. But there are other virtues that are distinctive to a liberal democracy, relating to the basic principles of a liberal regime, and to the political role citizens play within it. It is these distinctively liberal-democratic virtues, such as public reasonableness and civility, to which some conservative religious groups object.

By public reasonableness, I mean the ability and willingness to engage in public discourse about matters of public policy, and to question authority. These are perhaps the most distinctive aspects of citizenship in a liberal democracy, since they are precisely what distinguishes 'citizens' within a democracy from the 'subjects' of an authoritarian regime.

The need to question authority arises in part from the fact that citizens in a liberal democracy elect representatives who govern in their name. Hence an important responsibility of citizens is to monitor those officials and judge their conduct. The need to engage in public discourse arises from the fact that the decisions of government in a democracy should be made publicly, through free and open discussion. But the virtue of public discourse is not just the willingness to participate in politics, or to make one's views known. Rather, as Galston notes, it 'includes the willingness to listen seriously to a range of views which, given the diversity of liberal societies, will include ideas the listener is bound to find strange and even obnoxious. The virtue of political discourse also includes the willingness to set forth one's own views intelligibly and candidly as the basis for a politics of persuasion rather than manipulation or coercion' (Galston, 1991, p. 227).

This is the virtue of 'public reasonableness'. Liberal citizens must give reasons for their political demands, not just state preferences or make threats. Moreover, these reasons must be 'public' reasons, in the sense that they are capable of persuading people of different faiths and nationalities. Hence it is not enough to invoke Scripture or tradition. Liberal citizens must justify their political demands in terms that fellow citizens can understand and accept as consistent with their status as free and equal citizens. It requires a conscientious effort to distinguish those beliefs that are matters of private faith from those that are capable of public defence, and to see how issues look from the point of view of those with differing religious commitments and cultural backgrounds. As I discuss below, this is a stringent requirement that many religious groups find difficult to accept.

The virtue of public reasonableness is less relevant for citizens who do not wish to participate in political affairs, and there will always be a portion of the population who have little desire to be politically active. Some people will find their greatest joys in other areas of life, including the family, the arts, or religion. A liberal democracy must respect such diverse conceptions of the good life, and should not compel people to adopt a conception of the good life that privileges political participation as the source of meaning or satisfaction. For these more or less apolitical people, the virtue of public reasonableness may be less important.

But even for these passive citizens, the requirements of liberal citizenship are by no means trivial. The obligations of passive citizenship are often described in purely negative terms, i.e. the obligation not to break the law, and not to harm others or restrict their rights and liberties. Passive citizenship, in short, is often seen as simply requiring non-interference with others. However, this ignores one of the most basic requirements of liberal citizenship – namely, the virtue of civility or decency. This is a virtue that even the most passive citizen must learn, since it applies not only to political activity, but also – indeed, primarily – to our actions in everyday life, on the street, in neighbourhood shops, and in the diverse forums of civil society.

Civility refers to the way we treat non-intimates with whom we come into face-to-face contact. To understand civility, it is helpful to compare it with the related requirement of non-discrimination. The legal prohibition on discrimination initially only applied to government actions. Government laws and policies that discriminated against people on the basis of race or gender have gradually been struck out in Western democracies, since they violate the basic liberal commitment to equality of opportunity. But it has become clear that whether individuals have genuinely equal opportunity depends not only on government actions, but also on the actions of institutions within civil society – corporations, schools, stores, landlords etc. If prejudiced shop-owners or real estate agents discriminate against people, they deny them equal citizenship, even if the state itself does not discriminate. Hence legal requirements of non-discrimination have increasingly been applied to 'private' firms and associations.

This extension of non-discrimination from government to civil society is not just a shift in the scale of liberal norms, it also involves a radical extension of the obligations of liberal citizenship. For the obligation to treat people as equal citizens now applies to the most common everyday decisions of individuals. It is no longer permissible for businesses to refuse to hire black employees, or to serve black customers, or to segregate them. But not just that. The norms of non-discrimination entail that it is impermissible for businesses to ignore their black customers or treat them rudely, although it is not always possible to legally enforce this. Businesses must, in effect, make blacks feel welcome, just as they do for whites. Blacks must, in short, be treated with *civility*. The same applies to the way citizens treat each other in schools or recreational associations, and even in private clubs.

This sort of civility is the logical extension of non-discrimination, since it is needed to ensure that all citizens have the same opportunity to participate within civil society. But it now extends into the very hearts and minds of citizens. Liberal citizens must learn to interact in everyday settings on an equal basis with people for whom they might harbour prejudice (Spinner, 1994, ch. 4; White, 1992).

So we have two basic requirements of a liberal-democratic conception of citizenship: (a) for those who participate actively in politics, there is the requirement of public reason; (b) for all citizens, even for those who do not participate politically, there is the requirement of civility. Conservative religious groups often feel threatened by these two aspects of liberal citizenship, since both indirectly promote autonomy, i.e. they encourage children to interact with the members of other groups, to understand the reasonableness of other ways of life, and to distance themselves from their own cultural traditions.

Consider civility. I emphasized earlier that norms of civility and non-discrimination protect ethnic and religious groups from prejudice and discrimination. This means that groups wishing to maintain their group identity and cultural practices will face fewer legal barriers or social stigmas. But civility also increases the interaction between the members of different groups, and hence the likelihood that individuals will learn and adopt new ways of life. Historically, cultural boundaries have often been maintained by the visible expression of prejudice towards outsiders; people stayed within their group because they were not welcome elsewhere. The spread of civility in social institutions (including schools) means that these boundaries tend to break down. Children from one group are more likely to co-operate with and befriend children of other groups, and so learn about other ways of life and possibly adopt new identities.

Simply by teaching and practising civility, schools promote this sort of mingling and fraternizing between the members of different groups, and hence make the breakdown of cultural barriers more likely. In some cases, adopting other ways of life may be done in an unreflective way, simply by imitating one's peers, and hence does not count as the exercise of autonomy. But schools also promote a more reflective process, by teaching the virtue of public reasonableness. Because reasonable people disagree about the merits of different religions and conceptions of the good life, children must learn to distinguish reasons based on private faith from reasons that can be publicly accepted in a diverse society. To develop this capacity, children must not only learn how to distance themselves from beliefs that are taken for granted in their private life, but they must also learn to put themselves in other people's shoes, in order to see what sorts of reasons might be acceptable to people from other backgrounds. The virtue of public reasonableness does not require that children come to admire or cherish other ways of life. But it does require that children be exposed to competing ways of life, and be encouraged to view them as the expressions of coherent conceptions of value that have been sincerely affirmed by other reasonable people. Learning to view other ways of life in this way does not inevitably lead to the questioning of one's own way of life, but it surely makes it more likely, since it requires a sort of broad-mindedness that is difficult to combine with an unreflective deference to traditional practices or authorities.

For all these reasons, education for liberal citizenship will almost unavoidably, albeit indirectly, promote autonomy. Through citizenship education children become aware of alternative ways of life, and are given the intellectual skills needed to understand and appreciate them. As Gutmann puts it, citizenship education involves 'equipping children with the intellectual skills necessary to evaluate ways of life different from that of their parents', because 'many if not all of the capacities necessary for choice among good lives are also necessary for choice among good societies' (Gutmann, 1987, pp. 30, 40).

As a result, those conservative religious groups that rely heavily on an uncritical acceptance of tradition and authority, while not strictly ruled out, are bound to be discouraged by the critical and tolerant attitudes that civic education encourages (Macedo, 1990, pp. 53-4). So they feel threatened by attempts to educate their children for liberal citizenship. They often respond either by seeking to establish separate religious schools or by seeking exemption from certain aspects of the curriculum where these liberal virtues are learned and practised (e.g. exemptions from sex education, or from integrated physical education classes) (McLaughlin, 1992; Halstead, 1991).

Conservative religious groups may not explicitly challenge the principle that citizenship education should be part of the curriculum, and may indeed accept it as part of the curriculum in separate religious schools. *De facto*, however, they resist teaching these liberal virtues by eliminating the situations where it is necessary to exercise these virtues, i.e. by eliminating situations where students are required to interact and debate in a civil and reasonable way with people from different cultural or religious backgrounds. In homogeneous separate schools, the occasion to exercise these virtues simply does not arise.

How have Western democracies responded to these demands from conservative religious groups? Most countries have generally accepted some of these demands. They have allowed such groups to avoid participating in educational contexts that require the learning and exercising of civility and public reasonableness, either through the establishing of separate schools or through exemptions within common schools. States often impose a requirement that religious schools teach citizenship education, and may assert the right to monitor these schools to ensure compliance, but in fact most states do not actively monitor whether these liberal virtues are indeed being taught in religious schools.

As a result, there is a gulf between the principles and practice of citizenship education in many Western democracies. In principle, even conservative religious groups endorse the values of public reasonableness and civility as norms for citizenship education, yet they subvert it in practice. The liberal state seeks to maintain the fragile consensus on these values by a mixture of threats and bribes directed at conservative religious groups, and claims to enforce these values through a mandatory common curriculum. But in practice the state does not look too closely at whether religious schools are actually living up to these principles. The conservative religious groups pretend to believe in these values, and the state pretends to enforce them.

This may be a risky strategy for states to adopt, since it gives illiberal groups a space within the education system to avoid learning liberal citizenship. But it reflects what we can call a 'liberal wager', or what Rosenblum calls the 'liberal expectancy' (Rosenblum, 1998). The hope and expectation is that liberal democracy has a 'gravitational pull' that draws illiberal groups into its orbit. Even if religious groups manage to establish separate schools, they will still be subject to pervasive influence from liberalizing forces in the media, law, economy and political process. The members of these groups, it is assumed, will over time see the attractions of liberal democracy, and accept its underlying values and requirements.

This indeed is what we have seen historically with non-liberal religious groups. For example, most Catholics and Jews who emigrated to North America in the nineteenth century had been taught by their religious leaders to fear liberalism, which was seen at the time as a Protestant doctrine. Yet over time the mainstream of both the Catholic and Jewish communities in North America have fully internalized liberal values, and most commentators in the United States, Canada and Australia expect the same to take place with more recent Muslim and Hindu immigrants. Indeed, prior to September 11th, the question of whether Muslims can or will accept liberal values was largely a non-issue in North America or Australia. It was simply taken for granted that they would do so, although people recognize that (as with Catholics and Jews in the nineteenth century) this process takes time, and only fully occurs on an intergenerational basis.

The strategy may still seem risky, but many people argue that it is much safer to accommodate conservative religious groups and trust the long-term gravitational pull of liberal society, than to aggressively seek to impose liberal norms right away, and in effect declare war on these groups (Spinner-Halev, 2000; Macedo, 2000). This liberal wager requires that the larger society be willing to accept the inclusion and participation of religious minorities, and welcome them as they liberalize. The liberal wager will fail if members of the larger society seek to exclude religious minorities, and discriminate against them. If members of religious minorities feel that they will never be accepted in the larger society, even if they accept liberal values, then liberalism will have no gravitational pull.

This may partly explain the differential response to Muslims in the New World immigrant countries like the United States, Canada and Australia, compared to the Old World countries of Western Europe. Immigrant countries expect and trust new immigrant groups to liberalize, and so show a certain openness to them. This openness then encourages immigrants to try to integrate into the liberal mainstream. Some European countries, by contrast, do not expect Muslims to liberalize, and so fear their participation in the larger society, and seek to exclude them. These acts of exclusion eliminate any incentive for Muslims to integrate. In other words, hopes and fears about the willingness of Muslims to liberalize are partly self-fulfilling.

In any event, the approach that a state takes to conservative religious groups will depend, at least in part, on its confidence in this liberal wager. If a state hopes and expects that religious groups will liberalize over time, it is more likely to offer partial accommodations or exemptions for these groups from the requirements of education for liberal citizenship. This is the wager that has paid off in the past for conservative Christian and Jewish groups, and that some countries expect to work for Muslims as well.

The Challenge to the Nation-state

The second challenge to the traditional model of citizenship involves the scope of citizenship. Let's assume that most people accept the legitimacy of liberal values (as indeed the overwhelming majority of citizens do in most Western democracies). We must still confront the question of what the appropriate scale or boundaries of the political community are within which citizens should exercise these liberal virtues and rights.

The traditional model asserts that the nation-state is the primary locus of citizenship participation and popular sovereignty. Within the Western democracies, however, there are many minority groups that view themselves as distinct 'nations' or 'peoples' with a right to exercise self-government. These are typically groups whose homeland was involuntarily incorporated into a larger state, and who may have historically exercised some form of self-government that was limited or abolished when they were forced into a larger state. As I noted earlier, examples include the Catalans and Basques, Québécois, Flemish, Scots, and indigenous peoples in the Americas, Australasia and Scandinavia.

Such groups typically object to the privileging of existing nation-states as the locus of democratic citizenship, even if their individual rights are fully respected within these states. For one thing, this often involves linguistic assimilation. In order to participate in the state's elections, legislature or courts, they are required to speak the majority's language. Moreover, they often form a permanent minority within these state institutions, and are continually faced with the threat of being outvoted on decisions crucial to their interests. In short, according to the traditional model of citizenship, national minorities are expected to participate in state institutions they do not identify with, operating in a foreign language, and in which they are a permanent minority.

Since participation in state institutions often involves linguistic assimilation and/or political marginalization, national minorities are understandably sceptical of any form of citizenship education that takes these state institutions as given, and as the primary forum of political action and political loyalty. This sort of citizenship education is often seen as simply a tool of cultural assimilation and political oppression. For example, in the Canadian context, both aboriginals and the Québécois have historically seen citizenship education as culturally destructive, although both now have substantial control over citizenship education in their own schools (Osborne, 1996; Bear Nicholas, 1996; Lévesque, 2003).

National minorities demand instead to be recognized as peoples with rights of self-government, including the power to make political decisions in their own institutions, operating in their own language and culture. They also insist that citizenship education should focus on training their members for participation in these more local institutions. (Thus citizenship education in Catalonia should prepare students to participate in Catalonia's autonomous institutions, operating in the Catalan language, as much as preparing them to participate in Spain's central state institutions, operating in Castilian.)

How have Western democracies responded to this challenge? As with the challenge from conservative religious groups, the predominant response has been partial acceptance of these demands. In fact, national minorities in most Western democracies have acquired extensive powers of self-government through some form of territorial autonomy, including substantial control over education, all the way from primary through to post-secondary education. This is true of the large national minorities in the West like the Québécois, Puerto Ricans, Catalans and Walloons, all of whom are over 2.5 million in number. But it is equally true of smaller national minorities like the Swedes in Finland (285,000), German-speakers in South Tyrol (303,000) or the Italian-speakers in Switzerland (500,000). All of these groups have territorial autonomy, official language rights and schooling (and university education) in their own language.

This may seem like a risky strategy for states to adopt, since it gives control over education to groups that dispute the sense of common nationhood underlying the state's claim to legitimacy. It allows these substate minorities to use the education system to promote their own distinct sense of nationhood, and to promote a substate loyalty and allegiance that may conflict with loyalty to the larger state. How can we be sure that these groups, once accorded self-government within the larger state, will not start demanding complete independence? Once we've legitimized their national aspirations, what is to prevent these groups from pushing their nationalism towards secession?

As with conservative religious groups, the state's willingness to accept the claims of national minorities can be seen as a kind of wager. In fact, it reflects a double wager. First, states are gambling that satisfying modest nationalist aspirations for self-government will prevent mass support for the more radical option of secession. States are predicting that if members of national minorities feel that their identities are respected, and their aspirations for self-government are accepted as legitimate, this will actually reduce the potential for secession, as compared to a situation where national minorities feel culturally oppressed and politically marginalized.

Second, states are gambling that these national minorities will exercise their self-government in ways that are consistent with basic liberal values of human rights, secularism and tolerance, and will not attempt to establish islands of illiberal tyranny within the larger framework of a liberal-democratic state.

So far at least, this double wager seems to have been successful. No democratic state that has accorded self-government to its national minorities has yet broken apart. To be sure, there are secessionist political parties in many Western democracies, but they have not been able to gain a democratic mandate for secession. By contrast, many countries around the world that have suppressed minority nationalist aspirations for self-government have had to deal with violent, and sometimes successful, secessionist movements (Gurr, 1993, 2000; Kymlicka and Opalski, 2001).

Moreover, these self-governing arrangements have all operated within the constraints of basic human rights and of liberal constitutionalism. Self-governing national minorities in the West are no more (or less) likely to infringe the rights of women, migrants, gays, political dissidents or religious minorities than the central state (Keating, 1996; Keating and McGarry, 2001; Kymlicka, 2001, chs 12-15).

Some optimistic people would argue that the existence of minority nationalisms should not be a source of conflict at all. After all, it is natural for people to have multiple loyalties and identities, operating at various levels from the local to the regional, national and global. People can identify with, say, Barcelona, Catalonia, Spain, Europe and the world. All of these identifications can have significance for people, and it would be absurd to insist that they must choose only one of them. There is no reason why these different identities should be seen as zero-sum, or as inherently competing with each other, as if being Catalan precluded individuals from also feeling Spanish or European. People can be proud of all these identities. So rather than assume that one identity must take precedence, why not assume that it is inevitable, and indeed desirable, for people to have multiple identities operating at different levels, all of which complement each other? And if so, why can citizenship education not prepare students for citizenship at all of these levels? The problems we confront as citizens today must be addressed at different levels. Some can only be dealt with at local levels. Others require collective action at the level of the nation, Europe or the world. So why should we not educate children to be able to act as citizens at all these levels?

In this optimistic view, the phenomenon of minority nationalism is just one example of the more general fact that we live in a world of multiple and multi-layered identities. This fact may challenge the traditional assumption that the nation-state is the only or most important locus of citizenship. But this is not a problem or a threat – rather, it should be seen as enriching and supplementing our traditional practice of citizenship, by adding new forums for the exercise of citizenship. It supplements, rather than replaces, the traditional emphasis on the nation-state.

There is much truth in this optimistic view about people's ability to reconcile multiple and multi-layered identities, and to act as citizens in various levels of political community. However, I believe that the phenomenon of minority nationalism poses certain unique difficulties that make it difficult to reconcile with the traditional model, and that remain to be resolved in many Western countries. Let me briefly mention three of them.

First, there is a political dispute about which level of political community should exercise *jurisdiction* over education, including citizenship education. Who should decide on the curriculum, textbooks and pedagogical activities? Should this rest with self-governing regions, or central states, or with the European Union? Whoever has this decision-making authority will wield considerable influence over the political socialization of the next generation, and can use this power to emphasize the primacy or centrality of their own political community (Osborne, 1996; Lévesque, 2000). If the Catalan government has this jurisdiction, it will teach children first and foremost about Catalonia, even if also acknowledging the relevance of Spain and Europe. If the Spanish government exercises this jurisdiction, it will teach children first and foremost about Spain, even if also acknowledging the relevance of autonomous regions and the European Union. And so too if it is the European Union that exercises this jurisdiction. Since each political community wants its existence to be central in the minds of young citizens, rather than peripheral or secondary, it will seek to maintain or acquire jurisdiction over citizenship education.

Note that this dispute over jurisdiction will exist even if people at all levels agree on the same basic liberal values, and also agree on the general principle that citizenship should be seen as a multi-layered concept. Each level of political community will still want to ensure that priority is given to teaching about *its* history, symbols, institutions and accomplishments. And this requires some degree of control over education. So each level will jealously guard its jurisdiction over citizenship education, and indeed seek to expand its jurisdiction at the expense of the other levels.

Second, there is a pedagogical question about whether it is truly possible to educate people to be effective citizens at all of these levels of political community. One crucial limitation here concerns the linguistic competences required for effective citizenship. Given that it is important for citizens to be able to communicate with each other, and with the government, what language or languages should they able to speak and understand? This question is surprisingly neglected in the literature on citizenship and citizenship education. There is much talk about the importance of dialogue and communication, but less talk about the language in which this communication should take place.

The need for citizens to understand each other has often been given as a justification for policies of linguistic homogenization, and for the suppression of minority languages e.g. the suppression of Basque or Breton in France. It is linguistic minorities who have typically been asked to pay the price of promoting citizenship – minorities are compelled to learn and use the dominant language in public life, while little pressure is put on the linguistic majority to learn the minority's language. To be a good citizen of France, one must speak French – this is the explicit position of the French government. Similarly, the United States insists that to be a good American citizen, one must speak English – indeed, immigrants cannot legally acquire citizenship unless they can speak English (although this requirement is waived for elderly immigrants).

The long-term result of these linguistic homogenization policies has often been the gradual disappearance of minority languages. This is, I believe, a real injustice, and many linguistic minorities in Western democracies have fought for the right to speak their language in public forums, even if this reduces the efficiency of communication amongst citizens. At the level of each nation-state, a certain linguistic *modus vivendi* has developed, often after years of painful struggle, and this has been crucial to developing an acceptable model of citizenship within these countries. Linguistic minorities refused to accept a model of the core competences of citizenship which made the speaking of their language a liability, rather than a competence, of citizenship.

These questions have been settled, more or less, at the level of each state, at least within Western democracies (they remain far more controversial in Central and Eastern Europe). But now we are faced with the emergence of a pan-European citizenship, and so we need to think about the linguistic competences which are appropriate at this new level of citizenship. To be a good citizen of Europe, what language or languages should one be able to speak and understand, and how are we to balance the need for shared understanding with justice to linguistic minorities?

This is a difficult issue, because the linguistic competences required to be a good citizen of Europe may stand in tension with the linguistic competences required to be a good citizen of one's nation-state. For example, there is evidence that (French-speaking) Walloon children in Belgium now prefer to learn English, rather than Flemish, as their second language. This may make them better citizens of Europe, given the de facto predominance of English in pan-European settings, but it may undermine the linguistic *modus vivendi* that has held Belgium together. If Walloon children do not learn Flemish, and Flemish children do not learn French, this does not bode well for the long-term stability of Belgium. The Walloons and Flemish may be able to speak to each other in English, but they will have no access to each other's language, culture and media, and so will become almost complete strangers to each other.

We see the same dynamic in Switzerland, where French-speakers are apparently more interested in learning English than German as their second language. If in 25 years' time children in Geneva speak French and English but not German, this does not enhance the prospect of future stability of Switzerland.

These are just a few examples of the difficulty of developing a satisfactory account of the linguistic competences needed for multi-layered citizenship.[1] The linguistic skills needed to be a good citizen within one's neighbourhood or city may be different from those needed to be a good citizen at the regional or national level, which may be different again from those needed to be a good citizen of Europe. (For example, should a Moroccan immigrant to Barcelona learn to speak Moroccan, Catalan, Castilian or English?) And how do we ensure that it is not always linguistic minorities who pay the price for promoting communication amongst citizens?

One could argue that children should learn three or more languages. Indeed, this is the official position of the European Union. But many people will resist having to master multiple languages. And even if they learn the rudiments of three or more languages, it is doubtful that they will feel comfortable participating in politics in their third language.

Because many people resist having to master multiple languages, each level of political community will put pressure on other levels to accommodate its preferred language. Thus Catalonia will promote the use of the Catalan language in both Spain and the European Union, so that Catalonians need not master other languages in order to participate at these other levels. Similarly, Spain will promote the use of Castilian in both Catalonia and the European Union, so that Spaniards do not have to master another language to participate at these other levels. And the European Union will discourage any policies in either Spain or Catalonia that would require members of other EU states to learn either Castilian or Catalan in order to participate at these levels. For example, the EU is putting pressure on Catalan universities to teach some courses in languages other than Catalan, so that students from other EU countries can enrol in them.

People typically desire to use their preferred language at all levels and in all forums of political participation, and thereby minimize the need to master any other

---

1   For a more in-depth discussion of this problem, see Kymlicka, 2003.

language. This desire is natural and understandable, but it cannot universally be satisfied. Some decisions will need to be taken about which languages will have priority in which contexts, and these decisions will invariably advantage some people and disadvantage others. As with disputes over jurisdiction, these conflicts over language policy will remain a source of conflict even amongst people who agree on basic liberal values, and who accept the basic principle of multi-layered citizenship. While all sides may agree on the basic values, they will nonetheless jealously guard their linguistic rights and privileges, and seek to extend them at all levels.

Finally, there is a philosophical question about the definition of 'the people'. The principle of popular sovereignty states that a political community belongs to 'the people', rather than to élites or royalty, and should be governed by the people. The people are seen as having an inherent right to govern themselves – a right which is not delegated to them by any superior authority, but which arises simply from the fact that they are indeed 'the people'. This principle is fundamental to democracy, and is the basis for the claim to legitimacy by democratic states.

But who are 'the people' with an inherent right to govern themselves? The traditional model states that the citizens of each nation-state form 'the people' who exercise inherent sovereignty. This does not preclude the possibility that power can be exercised at other levels, above and below the level of the nation-state, such as cities and regions, or the European Union. But according to the traditional model, any exercise of power by these subnational and supranational institutions is *delegated* not inherent. According to the traditional model, neither cities/regions nor the European Union have any inherent right to exercise political power. They acquired this power only if, and insofar as, nation-states granted them this power, and in principle nation-states can always revoke this delegation and reassert their original sovereignty. (Recall Thatcher's decision to dissolve the Greater London Council, and increase central state control over the metropolis.)

Thus even when states establish self-governing arrangements for national minorities, they typically insist that these arrangements do not rest on any principle that the minority forms a nation or people with inherent rights of self-government. States continue to insist that there is only one nation or people in the state, composed of all citizens, and it is the people in this sense who are the only legitimate claimant to popular sovereignty. The people may decide to decentralize power in various ways, and this may benefit minorities, but this does not mean that minorities form separate 'peoples' with rights of self-government. These arrangements are seen as delegations of the popular sovereignty that is possessed by 'the people' of the state as a whole, not as assertions of the separate peoplehood or nationhood of a minority.

This is precisely what national minorities reject. They argue that they do form separate nations or peoples with inherent rights to govern themselves. They argue that their powers of self-government are theirs by right, not simply by delegation from a central state, and that the central state cannot rightfully deprive them of this self-government. Indeed, if anything, national minorities often argue that it is the central state whose powers are delegated, rather than inherent. They argue that the right of the central state to rule over their territory depends on their consent, and that they have the right to revoke this consent if and when the central state fails to respect their inherent right to self-government.

So we have two different views of the relationship between central states and self-governing national minorities. According to the traditional view, all the citizens of the larger state form a single people, and they exercise their popular sovereignty by delegating powers to certain regions. Thus the people of Spain have an inherent right to govern all of Spain, and they choose to exercise this inherent sovereignty by delegating certain powers on a regional basis. Any power that the Catalan government possesses, therefore, is delegated, not inherent. For minority nationalists, however, the national minority forms a separate people, and they exercise their popular sovereignty by consenting to stay within a larger state, so long as this larger state respects their inherent rights of self-government. So the people of Catalonia have an inherent right to govern themselves, and they choose to exercise this inherent sovereignty by belonging to Spain. Any authority that the Spanish government exercises over Catalonia should therefore be seen as delegated, and conditional upon the ongoing consent of the Catalan people.

Notice that this disagreement can arise even when both sides agree on the merits of establishing federal autonomy for national minorities. This is a dispute not about the merits of allowing national minorities to exercise certain powers, but about the underlying conception of nationhood and of political community. In effect, it is a dispute between those who view the state as a nation-state that has chosen to decentralize and those who view the state as a federation of distinct peoples or nations who have chosen to live together in a multination state.

The problem here is that citizenship education cannot be neutral between these two views. The idea of popular sovereignty is fundamental to citizenship education, and there is no way for educators to avoid the question of who the people are. This is why minority nationalists want to ensure that citizenship education teaches and legitimizes their claim to nationhood. This indeed is one reason why national minorities are so insistent on having jurisdiction over education. If the central state were responsible for education, they might teach students about the merits of federal autonomy for national minorities, but they are unlikely to teach students that these national minorities form distinct peoples with inherent rights to self-government. Conversely, the central state will want to insist that citizenship education not undermine its claim that the citizens of the state form a single nation or people, and so will seek to ensure that its conception of nationhood is taught and legitimized in schools.

There are at least three reasons – relating to conflicts over jurisdiction, language, and definitions of popular sovereignty – why minority nationalism will continue to pose important challenges to our models of citizenship education, even if all sides agree on the same liberal-democratic values. While identities can indeed be multiple and multi-layered, it is harder to multiply jurisdictions, linguistic competences, and popular sovereignties. For these reasons, the claims of minority nationalisms will continue to pose a major challenge to our models of citizenship education.

It would be overly optimistic to expect that the claims of minority nationalisms can be seamlessly integrated into a single harmonious conception of multiple and multi-layered citizenship. However, while conflicts over citizenship will be enduring and endemic in countries with minority nationalisms, they have not so far proven to be destructive or destabilizing. As I noted earlier, Western states have wagered that these conflicts will be less violent and less destabilizing if minorities feel that their basic identities and aspirations for self-government are respected. And, to date, this wager seems to have paid off in most cases.[2]

Conclusion

In this paper, I have discussed two challenges to the traditional model of citizenship underlying citizenship education in the West: a challenge to its liberal values from conservative religious groups, and a challenge to its national scope from substate national minorities. In response to these two challenges, Western states have modified their conception of citizenship education, allowing religious groups a partial exemption from the most demanding forms of liberal citizenship education, and according national minorities the power to administer their own education systems. Western states are gambling that it is safer to accommodate these two types of groups than to try to suppress them.

In my view, these two wagers have so far worked reasonably well. The accommodations made for these forms of religious and national diversity have enabled Western societies to avoid what might otherwise have been dangerous conflicts. However, it is too early to tell whether these will be enduring settlements. Will liberalism continue to exercise a gravitational pull on conservative religious groups? Will national minorities continue to remain satisfied with internal self-government rather than outright secession? If not, we are likely to see even more radical critiques of existing models of citizenship education in the future.

Acknowledgement

This essay was initially presented as a paper at the 4th International Congress on Philosophy of Education, in Madrid, November 2000, and has been published in Spanish in *Educación, Ética y Cuidadanía,* UNED Ediciones, Madrid, 2002, pp. 111-30.

---

2   One exception to this rule is the Basque Country, where significant forms of regional autonomy have not quelled separatist terrorism. Minority nationalism is also the source of violence in Corsica and Northern Ireland, but in these cases the minorities have not received the sort of recognition and self-government accorded most national minorities in the West. One can still hope that the wager of self-government will eventually pay off in these two cases as well.

References

Bear Nicholas, A. (1996), 'Citizenship Education and Aboriginal People: The Humanitarian Art of Cultural Genocide', *Canadian and International Education*, Vol. 25(2), pp. 59-107.

Burtt, S. (1996), 'In Defense of Yoder: Parental Authority and the Public Schools', in I. Shapiro and R. Hardin (eds), *NOMOS 38: Political Order*, New York University Press, New York, pp. 412-37.

Callen, E. (1997), *Creating Citizens*, Oxford University Press, Oxford.

Feinberg, W. (1998), *Common Schools, Uncommon Identities*, Yale University Press, New Haven, Conn.

Galston, W. (1991), *Liberal Purposes: Goods, Virtues, and Duties in the Liberal State*, Cambridge University Press, Cambridge.

Galston, W. (1995), 'Two Concepts of Liberalism', *Ethics*, Vol. 105, pp. 557-79.

Gurr, T. (1993), *Minorities at Risk: A Global View of Ethnopolitical Conflict*, Institute of Peace Press, Washington, D.C.

Gurr, T. (2000), 'Ethnic Warfare on the Wane', *Foreign Affairs*, Vol. 79(3), pp. 52-64.

Gutmann, A. (1987), *Democratic Education*, Princeton University Press, Princeton, N.J.

Halstead, J.M. (1990), 'Muslim Schools and the Ideal of Autonomy', *Ethics in Education* 9(4), pp. 4-6.

Halstead, M. (1991), 'Radical Feminism, Islam and the Single-Sex School Debate', *Gender and Education*, Vol. 3(1), pp. 263-78.

Keating, M. (1996), *Nations Against the State: The New Politics of Nationalism in Quebec, Catalonia and Scotland*, Macmillan, London.

Keating, M. and McGarry, J. (2001), *Minority Nationalism and the Changing International Order*, Oxford University Press, Oxford.

Kymlicka, W. (2001), *Politics in the Vernacular: Nationalism, Multiculturalism and Citizenship*, Oxford University Press, Oxford.

Kymlicka, W. (2003), 'Multicultural States and Intercultural Citizens', *Theory and Research in Education*, Vol. 1(2), forthcoming.

Kymlicka, W. and Norman, W. (2000), *Citizenship in Diverse Societies*, Oxford University Press, Oxford.

Kymlicka, W. and Opalski, M. (2001), *Can Liberal Pluralism Be Exported? Western Political Theory and Ethnic Relations in Eastern Europe*, Oxford University Press, Oxford.

Lévesque, S. (2003), 'Rethinking Citizenship Education in Canada', in R. Blake and A. Nurse (eds), *The Politics of Nationality: Essays on Canadian Nationalism, Citizenship, National Identity*, Harcourt-Brace, Toronto.

Levinson, M. (1999), *The Demands of Liberal Education*, Oxford University Press, Oxford.

Macedo, S. (1990), *Liberal Virtues: Citizenship, Virtue and Community*, Oxford University Press, Oxford.

Macedo, S. (2000), *Diversity and Distrust: Civic Education in a Multicultural Democracy*, Harvard University Press, Cambridge, Mass.

McLaughlin, T.H. (1992), 'The Ethics of Separate Schools', in M. Leicester and M. Taylor (eds), *Ethics, Ethnicity and Education*, Kogan Page, London, pp. 114-36.

Osborne, K. (1996), 'Education is the Best National Insurance: Citizenship Education in Canadian Schools, Past and Present', *Canadian and International Education*, Vol. 25(2), pp. 31-58.

Reich, R. (2002), *Bridging Liberalism and Multiculturalism in American Education*, University of Chicago Press, Chicago.

Rosenblum, N. (1998), *Membership and Morals: The Personal Uses of Pluralism in America*, Princeton University Press, Princeton, N.J.

Spinner, J. (1994), *The Boundaries of Citizenship: Race, Ethnicity and Nationality in the Liberal State*, Johns Hopkins University Press, Baltimore.

Spinner-Halev, J. (2000), *Surviving Diversity: Religion and Democratic Citizenship*, Johns Hopkins University Press, Baltimore.

White, P. (1992), 'Decency and Education for Citizenship', *Journal of Moral Education*, Vol. 21(3), pp. 207-16.

4

Citizenship Education: Anti-political Culture and Political Education in Britain

Elizabeth Frazer

Introduction

In this essay I discuss reasons why there is, and has been, no well-established tradition of 'education for citizenship', 'education for democracy' or 'political education' in UK schools' curricula. The most important set of reasons, I argue, lie in the lack of any wide assent to, consensus on or even well-articulated dominant account of the nature of politics, civic life or the constitution.

Several constituents of this dissensus are salient. One is the weakness of the discourse or ideal of citizenship in UK political culture and institutions. A second is the fact that, with the discrediting of a (crudely speaking) 'Whig' view of British history, no very robust conception of political processes has been substituted for it in history teaching in schools. Third, even though politics is construed only vaguely, nevertheless its negative connotations are extremely powerful. This factor is connected, I believe, with the fact that in the course of recent discussions about 'citizenship education' and 'education for democracy', commentators from markedly different political and pedagogical positions have argued that the important thing is not education in politics, but education in values.

Nick Tate (then Chief Executive of the England and Wales Schools Curriculum and Assessment Authority, now Chief Executive of the Qualifications and Curriculum Authority which has replaced it) has been personally identified with the promotion of 'values education' and 'moral and spiritual education' in schools. In a speech on the subject of 'education for citizenship' he linked the 'promotion of moral reasoning' and consideration of 'core values and virtues' to basic knowledge of history, geography and economy, but steadfastly avoided mentioning either 'politics' or 'citizenship' (Citizenship Foundation, 1997, pp. 17-20).

Richard Pring, Professor of Education at the University of Oxford, takes a different argumentative route to the same conclusion. Pring argues against any 'instrumentalist' approach to education at all. 'Education for citizenship', like education 'for parenthood' or 'for work' or 'against drugs', misses the educational point, which is to foster students' capacities for knowledge, for reason and for independence. 'Education for citizenship' is particularly suspect when it is legislated for by a government with unprecedented levels of centralized control over curriculum, teaching methods, assessment and the governance of schools. Instead, education should itself be democratic in its structures and pedagogy. 'Democratic education' in the humanities would enable people to acquire the ability to reason about 'issues of supreme political importance: sexual relations, social justice, the use of violence, the respect (or disrespect) for authority, racism and so on. ... There is no need for a subject set apart' (Pring, 1999, p. 81).

It is my contention in this essay that the emphasis on 'values', in the UK context, is an explicitly depoliticizing move in the debate about political education.

Citizenship Education in Recent British Government Policy

In the last two decades of the twentieth century there was a steady stream of projects aiming to have education for citizenship and democracy taken seriously in schools and other educational institutions – for instance, youth clubs (e.g. British Youth Council, 1986; Citizenship Foundation, 1997; Commission on Citizenship, 1990; Fogelman (ed.), 1991; John, 1991; Lansdown, 1995; Lynch, 1992; Review Group on the Youth Service in England, 1982; Smith, 1989; Smith, Southworth and Wilson, 1985; Williamson, 1997). Promoters of this educational effort must have been pleased when 'citizenship' was named as a 'cross-curricular theme' in the National Curriculum and curriculum guidance was drawn up (National Curriculum Council, 1990). However, citizenship went the way of all attempts to institutionalize political education in previous decades and, indeed, the way of all cross-curricular themes, although one commentator has remarked that it does seem to have been the one which was ignored most often! (Davies, 1999). A survey of how, if at all, 'citizenship education' was being delivered in schools (conducted in 1989 as the curriculum guidance was being drawn up) elicited reports of volunteer projects and general studies sessions – courses that are notably light on political content (Fogelman, 1991; Fogelman, 1997). In the last decade there have been debates about 'values education', concern about the aims and objectives of 'personal and social education', the promotion (and denigration) of sex education, legal education and environmental awareness, and official enthusiasm for 'moral and spiritual education' in schools (Schools Curriculum and Assessment Authority, 1995; Schools Curriculum and Assessment Authority, 1996).

After all this determined evasion of 'politics', the Labour government's White Paper, published two months after it came into office, seems to strike a distinctive note (Secretary of State for Education and Employment, 1997). It expresses a determination that schools should 'help to ensure that young people feel that they have a stake in our society and the community in which they live by teaching them the nature of democracy and the duties, responsibilities and rights of citizens'. (Secretary of State for Education and Employment, 1997, 6.42, p. 63) It identifies citizenship education as 'part of schools' wider provision for personal and social education, which helps more broadly to give pupils a strong sense of personal responsibility and of their duties towards others' (6.42, p. 63). But it explicitly emphasizes that 'citizenship' is not exhausted by 'values' or 'moral and spiritual' or 'personal and social' education. 'Citizenship' is a specific issue which, it is implied, has been left 'undeveloped' (6.25, p. 62). The White Paper committed the Department for Education and Employment to setting up 'an advisory group to discuss citizenship and the teaching of democracy in our schools'.

The Advisory Group on Citizenship was set up:

> To provide advice on effective education for citizenship in schools – to include the nature and practices of participation in democracy; the duties, responsibilities and rights of individuals as citizens; and the value to individuals and society of community activity (Crick Report,[1] 1998, p. 4).

Its terms of reference mention

> the teaching of civics, participative democracy and citizenship, and may be taken to include some understanding of democratic practices and institutions, including parties, pressure groups and voluntary bodies, and the relationship of formal political activity with civic society in the context of the UK, Europe and the wider world (Crick Report, 1998, p. 4).

These terms of reference, with their mention of 'civics' and 'civic society', of 'practices' and 'institutions' and 'formal political activity', already bear something of the stamp of the Chairman of the Advisory Group on Citizenship. In the 1970s Bernard Crick was a leading figure in that decade's most prominent campaign for serious political education in schools – the Programme for Political Education, supported by the Hansard Society, and with considerable overlap of personnel with the Politics Association – organized around the motif of 'political literacy' (Crick and Porter, 1978). The idea of the specificity of political relations and political processes, their non-assimilability into the generality of morals and values, or social relations, is the key point of much of Crick's work (e.g. Crick, 1993). It seems significant that the then Labour Secretary of State for Education and Employment, David Blunkett, had been Crick's student.

It is not possible to generalize from data and analysis from schools in England and Wales to those in Northern Ireland or Scotland. The questions and problems regarding 'political education' or 'education for citizenship' in the sectarian and divided society of Northern Ireland are distinct, focused as they are on the political and social outcomes of the churches' and state's delivery of education to Catholic and Protestant children, and on the prospects for the 'common school' (Dunn, 1993). The Scottish curriculum differs somewhat from that of England and Wales, with Scottish Highers based on examination in a wider range of subjects than their counterpart, the English and Welsh Advanced Level qualifications. However, neither 'civics' nor anything like it has been a standard fixture of the Scottish curriculum (although some relevant material may be covered in 'Modern Studies'). Anyway, judging by relevant publications in this period, 'citizenship' and so on was not a preoccupation, or even a concern, of educators in Scotland. A report on

---

1   The Final Report of the Advisory Group on Citizenship, 22 September 1998, entitled *Education for Citizenship and the Teaching of Democracy in Schools*, is hereafter referred to as the 'Crick Report'.

Promoting Social Competence in schools focuses on 'emotions, behaviour and social skills', 'contact with the local community' and the importance of access to 'role models for the full range of roles to be found in the world of work ... professional people, graduates, skilled workers, carers, entrepreneurs, disabled people ...' (Scottish Office, 1998, tables 3.1 and 5.1). The importance of social competence for citizenship is not mentioned, and this list of salient roles and role models is striking for the absence of roles drawn from public life, such as representatives, campaigners or volunteers. A report on Scotland from Her Majesty's Inspectors of Schools makes a number of comments about 'religious and moral education', 'health education' and 'enterprise education' (H.M. Inspectors of Schools, 1999, 2.1). In the section on 'school ethos', opportunities to 'take responsibility', for example by participation in pupils' councils, are mentioned, but none of the terms 'politics', 'democracy' or 'citizenship' are used, although 'charity' and 'partnership with parents and the local community' are (H.M. Inspectors of Schools, 1999, 2.5). By contrast, the White Paper on Scottish education bears the stamp of the Labour government with the striking addition of 'citizenship' to educational objectives:

> [we are committed to] ensuring that we have a world class schools system in Scotland where young people will
> Be confident, motivated and well rounded
> Be literate and numerate – to a level at or above their peers in the rest of the world
> Fully understand and be able to play their part as citizens of a democratic society
> Seize opportunities open to them regardless of their background, culture or race
> Be able to work flexibly and to embrace change on a continuing basis
> (Secretary of State for Scotland, 1999, p. 14).[2]

Citizenship Education in the UK

Differences between the constituent countries of the UK mean that it is difficult to generalize about educational policy. Indeed, the political salience of those very differences, and the antagonisms and tensions they generate, is one major factor which explains the difficulties of establishing political education in schools in Britain generally, and England in particular. The explanation certainly cannot be that there has been no interest in, or no perceived need for, political education, education for citizenship, or education for democracy, civics or constitutional studies in the UK. I remarked earlier that in the last few decades there has been a constant stream of projects to promote such education. But the same applies to every decade since a widened franchise prompted anxieties about the capacity of uneducated or poorly educated people to vote responsibly (Harris, 1993, p. 191; Goldman, 1999, pp. 89-101). The anxiety tends to come in waves – prompted by constitutional changes such as the extensions of suffrage (for instance, the Hansard

---

2   I discuss a more recent Scottish document – a discussion and consultation paper by the Review Group on Education for Citizenship – later in this essay.

Society project of 1970 was prompted by worry about the lowering of the age of majority to 18 years in the Representation of the People Act, 1969) (Stradling, 1977); by threats such as totalitarianism in the 1930s; and by social changes conditioned by the end of wars (see Brindle and Arnot, 1999; also Batho, 1990).

It is interesting and notable that 'citizenship' is the term that promoters of political education have invariably used to underline and to propel into the debate ideals and values such as responsibility, political equality, participation, duty and public service. It is a curious choice of term, because equally notable is that it either lacks salience for significant sections of the intended audience, or invokes an antipathetic response. In comparative research in England and the USA, Conover, Crewe and Searing found that English respondents did not themselves use the concept 'citizenship' in connection with their own political identities. For some there was clear discomfort with its connotations of 'foreignness' (Citizenship Foundation, 1997, p. 4; Conover et al., 1991). That in Britain 'we are not citizens but subjects' became a commonplace critical point in debate about British political culture and constitution in the 1980s and 1990s. The implications of this and other relevant factors in the British political system, political history and current political culture can be traced by looking at research which allows comparison between Britain and the USA in particular, and Britain and some European countries.

In the USA 'civics' is a ubiquitous item in schools' curricula. Although not all states mandate 'civics', 'government' or 'citizenship', those which do not, tend to mandate 'social studies'. In states where there is no state mandate, some school districts do have such a mandate. Thus Hahn and her colleagues calculate that by the age of 15 or 16 most students will have had 'deliberate instruction' in government. Furthermore, most 14- to 15-year-olds will have been taught about democracy, political institutions and rights and responsibilities in a course in US history. The significance of 'civics' in US schooling is clear from the fact that it is evaluated in the National Assessment of Educational Progress.

Hahn reports that 'There is a broad consensus in the country that it is the responsibility of schools to teach about democracy and to prepare students to be effective democratic citizens' (Hahn, 1999, p. 588). Students in the US focus groups were able to talk about 'democracy', and reported that they had learned about branches and levels of government (a few used the terms 'executive', 'legislature', 'local, state and national levels' and the like, while others mentioned 'people who make laws' and 'courts'). Most reported learning about the US Constitution and the Bill of Rights, some about 'checks and balances', and the history behind the Constitution such as the Magna Carta, the Declaration of Independence and the Articles of Confederation. They mentioned rights, jury duty, voting and military service. They also cited a predictable enough list of notable individuals, including presidents (e.g. Washington, Jefferson, Roosevelt, Kennedy), and Martin Luther King Jr., Rosa Parks, Harriet Tubman and others. Data from these focus groups, and those with teachers, suggest that although there is variation in the statutory provision from one state and district to another, there is little variation between classrooms. History and civics teachers reported teaching about democracy when they teach about the Mayflower Compact, Magna Carta, the colonial period, the Articles of Confederation, the Civil War, the Constitution,

Bill of Rights, landmark Supreme Court cases and the denial of rights to women, black people and native Americans.

But Hahn comments that most content in 'teaching democracy' is presented as uncontested, and that the teaching of democracy is done in a very conventional pedagogical fashion, with little emphasis on critical thinking or controversy. In Hahn's sample the teachers themselves seemed to be conscious of 'superficiality' and worse. They commented on the need for these subjects to be treated critically, and some commented on issues such as the difficulty of 'teaching democracy' in schools where the values of docility and quietness were uppermost.

One factor explaining hostility to launching a similar civics curriculum in the UK is scepticism about the effectiveness of the kind of 'deliberate instruction' in government and related topics which is imparted in US schools, and a sense that the resulting 'knowledge' is superficial. It is clearly true that, although education as such has a powerful effect on a range of political outcomes including 'political knowledge' or 'expertise', as well as political attitudes and levels of political engagement, the difference explicit political education makes has been rather unclear. A number of studies failed to find any clear difference in knowledge, attitudes or engagement when students who had, and those who had not, studied politics at A Level or sat through civics classes were compared (Furnham and Gunter, 1983; Langton and Jennings, 1968; Lister, 1973; Mercer, 1972; Stradling, 1977). However, more recent analysis of the 1988 NAEP data by Niemi and Junn suggest these findings may have been influenced by research design and questionnaire design. Niemi and Junn show that discussing current events in class and studying 'government' or 'civics' (and a decent range of topics under these headings) do have independent effects on school students' ability to correctly answer questions about the US polity (Niemi and Junn, 1998, pp. 120-3, 142-3, 144-5).

In any case, I would argue, it does not follow from the lack of a direct and strikingly measurable effect on knowledge that formal political education is insignificant. For one thing, teaching mathematics in schools often has rather disappointing results, but nobody infers from that that we should not bother to teach mathematics. For another, I take it that to have heard and ignored, or to have listened and forgotten, or to have tried but not understood, is not epistemically the equivalent of never having been told at all. With this in mind, the important thing is that, whereas US schoolchildren are told important things about the system of government under which they live, UK children for the most part have been told nothing at all.

However, critics might argue, despite the established place of civics in the school curriculum, US political culture and democracy are not in noticeably better shape than our own. Superficiality of knowledge outcomes is likely to be connected to superficiality in the material taught. The depiction of US history as progressively enlightened, just and democratic is culpably romantic. The discourses of rights, equality and freedom are naïve and uncritical. Basic work needs critical content, and must be supplemented by participation in decision-making, the experience of political debate and conflict and the critical study of political power.

The striking point is that, whereas in the USA there can be, and is, an argument about how to take a more critical and practical approach to the basic study of constitution, political institutions, political processes and political history, in the British case there is no such 'basic study' to take a critical and practical approach to. The consensus on the key events and texts that form the narrative of US history as taught to schoolchildren in all the states has no counterpart in Britain or England. Although it is conceivable that a group of politics and history teachers would come up with a fairly definite list of key events – including perhaps the Magna Carta, the Commonwealth, the Restoration, 1689, the Reform Bills – two things are notable. One is that such a list is in no wise a constituent of a widely promulgated or articulated political culture. Another is that any such list will be highly controversial – or, rather, that the meaning of the various events will be vigorously, and systematically, contested. The role of capital and the nature of class rule, imperialism and the colonial oppression of Welsh, Scots and Irish people, the dominance of Protestantism over Catholicism – these are all features of British history that tend to underline division and oppression rather than convergence and agreement.

Now this fact of the controversial nature of the events that can be seen as ingredients of the long and messy process of British 'state formation' should not in itself be a bar to their place in the school curriculum. After all, US teachers must deal with slavery, segregation, the fate of native American people, and contests between rich and poor, employers and labour. A number of teachers mentioned to Hahn the process of discussing with pupils 'when democracy doesn't work', the negative experience of being Black in a racist society, and the different meanings of 'citizenship' to migrant and non-migrant children. These episodes are subject to competing theories and value interpretations, just as much as are the execution of Charles I, the long delays before granting women the vote, or recent patterns of migration to Britain.

But another striking aspect of the US situation when viewed from a British perspective is that the constitution – both the fact of its codification and its pre-eminent symbolic status in US political and indeed social life – makes US teachers' task of teaching the structures and functions of government, the nature of rights and duties, and the battles for representation and participation, more straightforward than it would be in the UK. The uncodified nature of the British Constitution does not entail that it is obscure. However, it is notable that study of the British Constitution is advanced, and optional, work only for university students in law, history and politics (Mount, 1992; Johnson, 1977). Similarly, when it comes to teaching political values, US teachers have a number of obvious documents to use: the Mayflower Compact, the Declaration of Independence, Martin Luther King's 'I have a dream …'. UK teachers would find it more or less impossible to put such a package together. (They would have to have recourse to international documents such as the UN Declaration of Human Rights.)

This obscurity of constitutional principles, and the unarticulated nature of political ideals, are reflected in the difficulties research respondents have with the language and idea of citizenship. A survey of British trainee teachers before, during and after their Postgraduate Certificate of Education courses at two large teacher education institutions in England suggests that, as Conover, Crewe and Searing's respondents mentioned earlier, this group has difficulties with the language of citizenship (Wilkins, 1999). The idea of a 'good citizen' prompted negative images such as 'disgusted of Tunbridge Wells', 'stiff upper lip and bowler hat', 'neighbourhood watch and writing letters to the parish council' – that is, stereotypes of a particular kind of English middle-class identity. Questions about 'traditional values' prompted expression of fear that such values are imposed rather than being consensual or truly universal, as well as derisive references to 'British bulldogs' and 'roast beef', and sceptical references to 'class deference' and 'acceptance of hierarchy'. When, at the end of their courses, these respondents were asked about 'teaching citizenship', they were even more uncertain and sceptical than they had been at the beginning of the study, both because of continuing vagueness about what citizenship is, and because of recognition of the pressures on timetables and the pre-eminence of effort directed to basic skills in literacy and numeracy, and to 'packaging and assessment'. Perhaps most notable is that the younger students surveyed expressed cynical and negative attitudes to 'politics' itself – as 'not affecting me', as 'a joke'. Older students (26 years and over) were often involved in campaigns and action, but expressed a sense of disempowerment by conventional politics – that is, party and Parliament.

It is obviously difficult to come to grips with what these respondents (university degree-holders) are really saying. Are they saying that it does not matter which party is in government in a political system – that policies affecting the fates of ordinary people are always the same? Are they assuming that, however the competition for the power to govern goes, the degree of physical and social security they enjoy will not diminish – that things could not be worse? Are they saying that it is satisfactory to leave politics to a special class of people? If so, how do they think politicians should be recruited and checked? Speculatively, it could be any of the above, or indeed none, that is being 'said'.

Anti-political Culture

The research and analysis considered so far, then, suggests a number of factors about British culture and politics that are obstacles to any easy reform of the curriculum.

First, from one political and social perspective 'citizenship' is a foreign concept which already goes some way to undermining the traditional constitutional relationships between ruler and ruled. Second, from a different political perspective citizenship is identified with a particular class identity, and with a deferential attitude to values such as hierarchy and respectability which should be contested. Third, there is no widely assented-to historical narrative or corpus of texts, which would mean that the teaching of history and the teaching of 'politics' or 'civics' or 'citizenship', were such a curriculum slot to be institutionalized, would reinforce one another. A fourth, and key, issue is that the meaning of 'politics' itself is construed both vaguely and negatively, even by people with a high level of education.

In fact, we can see deep-seated antipathies to politics both within structured political discourse and within political theory. Take, for example, the common identification of 'political' with 'partisan'. The Education Act, 1996 enjoined education authorities, governing bodies and head teachers to forbid '(a) the pursuit of partisan political activities by registered pupils at maintained schools who are junior pupils and (b) the promotion of partisan political views in the teaching of any subject in the school' (406). The point is that, if educators find it difficult to specify a meaning of political that is distinct from partisan, this proscription is likely to sweep political content out together with partisan content. Hahn reported to one teacher in an English school that her sixth-formers had said they wished to know more about politics. The teacher was 'surprised' and 'admitted that the school does not do much with that in the sixth-form course "because it is difficult. If you have someone from one party then you have to have someone from the other parties too"' (Hahn, 1998, p. 68).

This proscription was first enshrined in the 1986 No. 2 Education Act, and was clearly prompted by suspicion that bias and even propaganda were present in subject teaching in some schools. Suspicion at that time came from the right wing of the political spectrum. It was fixed, of course, on socialism, Marxism and pacifism, as doctrines that can be insidiously and subversively promulgated among vulnerable populations (the young being thought of as particularly vulnerable). But it is important that a comparable level of suspicion about political education also comes from the left wing. Subjects like 'citizenship', 'democracy', 'constitution' and 'civics' are interpreted as biased vehicles for a quietist ideology, as is 'politics'. For many left-wing thinkers and activists, not just Marxists, economic relations are 'real', and really significant in determining people's life chances. Democratic representation and parliamentary politics have not made, and perhaps cannot make, significant differences to people's economic fates. At worst, democratic government has been seen as a charade which distracts individuals and groups from a genuine understanding of the nature of economic power and their place in the structure (Freeden, 1996, pp. 438-42; Phillips, 1993, p. 77). At best, 'politics' for socialists has been working-class, party politics which, as we have seen, can have no place in schools. To the extent that the left-right axis has dominated debates in policymaking and in society (and it certainly has, for the larger part of the industrial period), then the kind of 'political education' in schools discussed here has had determined and powerful opponents from both left and right.

Of course, this left-right axis, with conservatives and the interests of capital on one side and liberals, socialists and the interests of labour on the other, has not been universally admired or participated in. Particularly since the 1960s, a number of interests and articulated positions have emerged which say, more or less, 'a plague on both your houses'. Feminists in particular, environmentalists, some pacifist groups, those committed to solidarity with the developing world and anti-racists have all found – in both the ideas and theories of the traditional left and right and in the policies of Labour and Conservative governments in power – gaps, silences and perversities. These positions identify structures which generate negative social outcomes – sexism and the disadvantage of women, militarism, racism, exploitation. These outcomes occur regardless of whether ostensibly 'right' or 'left', pro-capitalist or pro-labour, interests have governmental power.

In the 1980s, in Britain as elsewhere, two notable aspects of these interests and values salient to this discussion crystallized. First, a 'critique of politics' was articulated. Tendencies to perverse and unjust outcomes such as sexism and racism were identified in the very structures of partisan politics, parliamentary procedures and values, and the conventions and values of public life. This analysis generated a positive emphasis on efforts to make changes in social and cultural relationships beyond the ambit of conventional politics, with its structures of partisanship and emphasis on legislation. On the one hand, from these political efforts an *extension of the scope of politics* was derived. The concept and domain of politics was stretched beyond the bounds of state and governmental institutions, to encompass social institutions and interpersonal and intimate relationships. On the other hand, these analyses generated a *sceptical and critical approach to politics altogether*. Politics, in the sense of the conciliation of opposing interests through participation in public and representative institutions, is thought to be unable to do justice to the needs and aspirations of those individuals and those values that are at stake in unequal societies. This ambivalence about politics, interestingly, has its counterpart in more dominant discourses which, on the one hand, are forced to acknowledge the scope of politics beyond the state and conventional governing institutions but, on the other hand, reserve the term 'political' for rule and disputes about rule that are conducted through public and state institutions.

Second, oppositional values and analyses – pacifism, anti-nuclear power, feminism, anti-racism, social justice – were worked up into a range of teaching and educational programmes. These were successfully, albeit patchily, introduced into curriculum slots such as 'personal and social education', 'health education', 'general studies' and the like by enthusiastic teachers and some local education authorities (Davies, 1999). Hostility to these programmes and to their perceived political bias undoubtedly galvanized the Conservative government's proscription of partisan politics in schools. But more interesting for my argument here, this 'critique of politics' means that educators who are, or were, committed to the kind of critical social education enshrined in these programmes will no more be enthusiastic supporters of civic education, or the study of political institutions and constitution, than will the socialist and conservative parties and interests they criticize.

A further source of antipathy to politics stems from antipathy to government, and especially to government interference in education. Arguably, any socially or politically instrumentalist approach to education (the requirement, for instance, that education prepare children for 'economic realities', or for parenthood, or for a coming technological revolution) fundamentally undermines educational values, which should focus on the individual and her or his capacities and needs (Pring, 1999, pp. 74-5). Again, the burden of this argument is that governmental power is intrinsically oppressive, and it is important that social institutions, and individuals, are able to enjoy freedom from it. One important set of such social institutions are the educational institutions – these are the places where (ideally at least) individuals might be educated to become autonomous, to set their own goals for life, and to resist social and state power.

A final source of antipathy to politics looks back to the concern with 'values education' with which this essay opened. A number of strains of ethical theory emphasize the primary importance of moral values and human rights, uncontroversially enough, and link this commitment to a denial of the specificity or particular importance of political values, political relationships and political processes. If values like equality, tolerance of difference, political liberty or free speech are truly valuable, they are so because they are morally right, because they are values for human beings as such. Political processes and relationships cannot create values which do not already exist as moral values. This means that one important goal for education is the imparting of, and critical consciousness of, these values. But – it is inferred – this means that the study of 'politics' and discussion of explicitly political values is at best a diversion, or at worst positively undermines values education, because of the particular place of power and pragmatism in politics. The point, according to critics, is that if the perspective of politics is primary, then values such as autonomy, individual freedom, equality and justice might be compromised by the workings of power and the imperative of political stability. That is to say, the point of view of politics – teaching about particular state and institutional arrangements, and the values implicit and explicit therein – entails taking up the perspective of the state or collective, with obvious dangers to the liberty of individuals, not only dissenters (Pring, 1999, pp. 84-6). Another way of putting this argument is to say that the important thing is to get the values and morals right, then the politics will look after itself.

Recent debates about citizenship education in Britain are replete with protests that 'just' teaching young people about institutions, constitutions and democratic processes is 'not enough'. For example, the recent Scottish discussion paper (Review Group on Education for Citizenship, 2001) quotes the Scottish Consultative Council on the Curriculum:

> … an understanding of the political structures and processes, of rights, obligations, law, justice and democracy *will not be sufficient*. The curriculum *should go further* … by fostering a sense of active and responsible citizenship' [my emphasis].

Now every first-year university student should know that necessity does not entail sufficiency. The problem, in my reading of this and other documents referenced in this essay, is that their authors often seem to imply or conclude that insufficiency entails non-necessity. At least, one searches in vain in many of these discussion papers, and certainly in this one, for any clear recommendation that understanding of 'structures and processes, of rights, obligations, law, justice and democracy' is necessary or that, being necessary, clear plans have to be made for education in these fields.

The Scottish discussion paper, for instance, says, 'Finally, capability for citizenship, as envisaged here, *includes ideas about "political literacy"*' (my emphasis). 'Ideas about political literacy' seem very different, to me, from 'political literacy' itself, suggesting that the review group have neatly sidestepped the awkward possibility that children might have to be made politically literate. The recommendation of the Review Group is that it is inappropriate to think of a separate curriculum slot, because 'Education for citizenship is *more than* a simple expectation of political literacy. Civics lessons are *not enough*' (my emphasis). But the analysis and recommendations of the Review Group do not include any formal political education at all – not only is it insufficient, it has seemingly been rendered unnecessary. The emphasis on 'environment', 'thoughtful interaction' and involvement with 'the wider community' in this essay is not a supplement to an education which is clear about the specific nature of political relations. Instead, it is a substitute for it. The proposal to exploit the existing curriculum slots of 'personal and social education' or 'moral and spiritual' education is bound to dilute, rather than encompass, any possible emphasis on political values, political relationships and political skills.

Conclusion

Promoters of citizenship education, legal education and a greater emphasis on human rights, personal development and interpersonal skills, moral and spiritual education, health and parenting, preparation for economic realities, environmentalism, education for racial, sexual and international justice – can coherently enough share all or any of these antipathies to politics.

Real political societies are full of friction. Political actors play annoying games. Participants experience emotional difficulties and discomforts. The contest for political power is endless. Settlements of economic, social, ethnic and religious conflicts are impossible or elusive. No wonder, perhaps, that many ideal models of politics are focused on the goal of reasoned settlement, harmonious social relations, rational co-operation and the constraint of power by right. Yet this emphasis on non-violent conciliation can foster the illusion that politics is less antagonistic than it really is. Further, it can foster the illusion of the non-necessity of politics – the possibility of a society free of politics.

But politics is non-optional. In political societies we all have to encounter fellow citizens who are strangers (not liked, not loved, not known; also 'different' – with different voices, different values, different ways of life and modes of conduct). These strangers may be antagonists. The aim of political education must be to enable people to participate in these webs of political relations, to understand the formal institutions that structure them and, thereby, to be equal to the structures of power and authority which govern them. Of course values such as justice, non-violence, autonomy and democracy itself are a necessary background to such engagement. If the values are wrong, then the politics will, undoubtedly, be wrong. However, it is not the case that getting the politics right is simply a matter of getting the values right.

References

Advisory Group on Citizenship ('Crick Report') (1998), *Education for Citizenship and the Teaching of Democracy in Schools*, Final Report of the Advisory Group on Citizenship, 22 September 1998, Qualifications and Curriculum Authority, London.

Batho, G. (1990), 'The History of the Teaching of Civics and Citizenship in English Schools', *The Curriculum Journal*, Vol. 1, pp. 91-107.

Brindle, P. and Arnot, M. (1999), '"England Expects Every Man to Do His Duty": The Gendering of the Citizenship Textbook', *Oxford Review of Education*, Vol. 25, pp. 103-23.

British Youth Council (BYC) (1986), *The Voice of Young People*, BYC, London.

Citizenship Foundation (1997), *Colloquium on Education and Citizenship: Citizenship and Civic Education*, Citizenship Foundation, London.

Commission on Citizenship (1990), *Encouraging Citizenship*, Her Majesty's Stationery Office, London.

Conover, P.J., Crewe, I. and Searing, D. (1991), 'The Nature of Citizenship in the United States and Great Britain: Empirical Comments on Theoretical Themes', *Journal of Politics*, Vol. 53, pp. 800-32.

Crick, B. (1993), *In Defence of Politics*, 4th ed., Penguin, Harmondsworth.

Crick, B. and Porter. A. (eds) (1978), *Political Education and Political Literacy*, Longman, London.

Davies, I. (1999), 'What Has Happened in the Teaching of Politics in Schools in England in the Last Three Decades and Why?', *Oxford Review of Education*, Vol. 25, pp. 125-40.

Dunn, S. (1993), *The Common School*, University of Ulster, Coleraine.

Fogelman, K. (ed.) (1991), *Citizenship in Schools*, David Fulton, London.

Fogelman, K. (1997), 'Citizenship Education', in J. Bynner, L. Chisholm and A. Furlong (eds), *Youth Citizenship and Social Change*, Ashgate Publishing, Aldershot.

Freeden, M. (1996), *Ideologies and Political Theory*, Clarendon, Oxford.

Furnham, A. and Gunter, B. (1983), 'Political Knowledge and Awareness in Adolescents', *Journal of Adolescence*, Vol. 6, pp. 373-85.

Goldman, L. (1999), 'Education as Politics: University Adult Education Since 1914', *Oxford Review of Education*, Vol. 25, pp. 89-101.

Hahn, C.L. (1998), *Becoming Political: Comparative Perspectives on Citizenship Education*, State University of New York Press, Albany.

Hahn, C.L. (1999), 'Civic Education in the United States', in J. Torney-Purta, J. Schiville and P. Amadeo (eds), *Civic Education Across Countries: Twenty-four National Case Studies from the IEA Civic Education Project*, Eburon, Delft.

Harris, J. (1993), *Private Lives, Public Spirit: Britain 1870-1914*, Penguin, Harmondsworth.

H.M. Inspectors of Schools (1999), *Standards and Quality in Scottish Schools 1995-1998*, The Scottish Office, London.

John, G. (1991), *Education for Citizenship*, Charter 88, London, *http://www.charter88.org.uk/pubs*.

Johnson, N. (1977), *In Search of the Constitution: Reflections on State and Society in Britain*, Pergamon Press, Oxford.

Langton, K.P. and Jennings, M.K. (1968), 'Political Socialisation and the High School Civics Curriculum in the United States', *American Political Science Review*, Vol. 62, p. 857.

Lansdown, G. (1995), *Taking Part: Children's Participation in Decision Making*, IPPR, London.

Lister, I. (1973), 'Political Socialisation and the Schools: With Special Reference to the Knowledge of Political Concepts of English Sixth Formers', *Teaching Politics*, Vol. 2, pp. 2-9.

Lynch, J. (1992), *Education for Citizenship in a Multicultural Society*, Cassell, London.

Mercer, G. (1972), 'Political Interest Among Adolescents: The Influence of Formal Political Education', *Teaching Politics*, Vol. 1, pp. 8-13.

Mount, F. (1992), 'The Recovery of the Constitution', *Charter 88 Sovereignty Lecture*, *http://www.charter88.org.uk/pubs/sovlecs/mount.html*.

National Curriculum Council (1990), *Education for Citizenship*, Curriculum Guidance 8, NCC, London.

Niemi, R. and Junn, J. (1998), *Civic Education: What Makes Students Learn*, Yale University Press, New Haven, Conn.

Phillips, A. (1993), *Democracy and Difference*, Polity Press, Oxford.

Pring, R. (1999), 'Political Education: The Relevance of the Humanities', *Oxford Review of Education*, Vol. 25, pp. 71-87.

Review Group on Education for Citizenship (2001), *Education for Citizenship in Scotland: A Paper for Discussion and Consultation*, Learning and Teaching Scotland, Edinburgh.

Review Group on the Youth Service in England (1982), *Experience and Participation* ('The Thompson Report'), Her Majesty's Stationery Office, London.

Schools Curriculum and Assessment Authority (SCAA) (1995), *Spiritual and Moral Development*, Discussion Paper No. 3, SCAA, London.

Schools Curriculum and Assessment Authority (1996), *Education for Adult Life: The Spiritual and Moral Development of Young People*, Discussion Paper No. 6, SCAA, London.

Scottish Office (1998), *Taking a Closer Look at Promoting Social Competence*, The Scottish Office, London.

Secretary of State for Education and Employment (1997), *Excellence in Schools*, Cm3681, Her Majesty's Stationery Office, London.

Smith, D.I. (1989), *Taking Shape: Development in Youth Service Provision*, National Youth Bureau, London.

Smith, J., Southworth, M. and Wilson, A. (1985), *A Course in Political Education for 14-18 Year Olds*, Longman, London.

Stradling, R. (1977), *A Programme for Political Education: The Political Awareness of the School Leaver*, Hansard Society, London.

Torney-Purta, J., Schiville, J. and Amadeo, P. (eds) (1999), *Civic Education Across Countries: Twenty-four National Case Studies from the IEA Civic Education Project*, Eburon, Delft.

Wilkins, C. (1999), 'Making Good Citizens: The Social and Political Attitudes of PGCE Students', *Oxford Review of Education*, Vol. 25, pp. 217-30.

Williamson, H. (1997), 'Youth Work and Citizenship', in J. Bynner, L. Chisholm and A. Furlong (eds), *Youth, Citizenship and Social Change*, Ashgate Publishing, Aldershot.

5

Aims in Citizenship Education: Responsibility, Identity, Inclusion

Graham Haydon

In a plural and liberal society it should not be expected that there will be easy, universal or once-for-all agreement on the aims of citizenship education. In such a society – cross-cutting the categories in which issues of diversity and inclusion are usually addressed (class, gender, ethnicity, religion, abilities/disabilities, sexuality, age) – there is room for different understandings of what citizenship involves and diverse conceptions of the good citizen. So when the aims of citizenship education are discussed, there is always scope for different lists of aims, different interpretations of items on those lists, and different priorities between items.

If the aims adopted in programmes of citizenship education are themselves plural, it can at least be said that in any coherent programme the different aims must be mutually consistent. But whether a number of items on a list of aims are mutually consistent may, in turn, depend on the interpretations given to these aims. A number of aims which look consistent on the face of it when expressed as simple labels, may still turn out to be less than consistent when more fully interpreted.

In this essay I am interested in the consistency of one particular, plausible, list of aims: social and moral responsibility; community involvement; political literacy; national identity; and social inclusion. In arguing that the mutual consistency of these aims depends on their more detailed interpretation, I focus on how we are to interpret the aim of social and moral responsibility. It would be possible to give similarly detailed consideration to each of the other items on the list, but not in the space of one essay.

The first three items on this list are taken from the Crick Report,[1] which lists three strands of effective education for citizenship: social and moral responsibility; community involvement and political literacy. It seems reasonable to interpret

---

1 The Final Report of the Advisory Group on Citizenship, 22 September 1998, entitled *Education for Citizenship and the Teaching of Democracy in Schools*, is hereafter referred to as the 'Crick Report'. I am taking the Crick Report as a reference point in this paper, both because of its influence in England and Wales in largely informing the content of National Curriculum requirements for citizenship; and because its division of citizenship education into three strands has the advantage of clearly marking the overlap between citizenship education and moral education. On the latter point, see also Haydon (2000). References to the Crick Report give paragraph numbers.

these strands as setting aims in citizenship education, since they are all introduced as aspects of what pupils should learn. The next two candidate items on the list – the ideas that citizenship education should promote a sense of national identity, and that it should help to bring about social inclusion – are taken from the more diffuse source of political debate in Britain in the years following the Crick Report. The next section of this essay will say more about the status of these five ideas as aims for citizenship education. The third section will consider in more detail how the strand of social and moral responsibility can best be conceptualized, given that it has to be seen in relation to the other aims. The fourth section will draw some conclusions.

Five Candidate Aims

Of Crick's three strands, the third, political literacy, most obviously involves a content that can be taught, and learned, in schools. There are concepts, ideas and knowledge about traditions, principles and institutions which teachers can put across to students. In a different way, the second strand also invites practical initiatives which could complement the taught curriculum, while being just as concrete. Although 'community involvement' does not itself specify a content to be learned, Crick refers to students 'learning about and becoming helpfully involved in the life and concerns of their communities, including learning through community involvement and service to the community' (Crick Report, 1998, p. 12). But the first of the three strands, moral and social responsibility, is in certain ways more difficult for schools to address.

The idea of *teaching* moral and social responsibility may seem to many teachers to run the risk of indoctrinating students in society's values, or of imposing the teacher's own values. Once the suspicion of such a risk has arisen (whether well grounded or not), teachers will reasonably seek ways of avoiding the undesirable outcomes. Yet the routes to avoidance may consist, in effect, of allowing this third strand to collapse into the other two. For if teachers try to avoid didactically imposing certain values by confining their teaching to trying to ensure that students understand certain ideas and principles, then it becomes difficult to distinguish the teaching of moral and social responsibility from the teaching of political literacy. If on the other hand teachers try, in areas which seem to have moral import, to avoid teaching as such and concentrate on setting good examples and involving students in practical activities where they can exercise responsibility, development of moral and social responsibility becomes difficult to distinguish from community involvement.

So it does not appear that the strand of social and moral responsibility can be treated as separate – and Crick does not suggest that it can. Not only can it not be separated out from the other strands of citizenship education, as Crick acknowledges (Crick Report, 1998, Appendix A), it can also not be separated from other aspects of education. In particular, it clearly has a close relationship with what goes under the heading of PSHE (Personal, Social and Health Education). So schools may be forgiven some uncertainty about how to respond to the idea of social and moral responsibility as a strand of citizenship education. On the one hand they may want to claim, with good reason, that a lot that they are doing is already contributing to this strand. On the other hand they may find it difficult to articulate explicitly what it is that they are doing. In the next section I shall raise questions about the kind of language in which the aim of social and moral responsibility can best be articulated.

In considering the aims of citizenship education, a further complication arises from taking seriously two themes one might expect to be important in citizenship education, not least because they have been prominent in British political discourse in recent years: national identity and social inclusion. Recent political debate indicates the existence of a widely held view which would have it that (to use Crick's terminology) the promotion of a shared sense of national identity should itself be a major strand of citizenship education. Crick does not take that line – perhaps rightly, and certainly wisely from a political perspective – but the Crick Report does recognize the importance of questions of national identity (Crick Report, 1998, 3.13-3.16).

The Report does not deal with social exclusion and inclusion as a theme in its own right, but again it implicitly recognizes the importance of this. Citizenship is about effective participation in society. For many people who are effectively excluded from such participation, or who see themselves as excluded, citizenship is not a reality except in an attenuated sense. In what Crick calls 'a secondary sense', such people may have the rights and duties of citizenship, but they will not be active members of society. (See Crick Report, 1998, 3.6 on youth alienation.)

Can these two concerns – national identity and social inclusion – sensibly be construed as further aims of citizenship education? At first sight, Crick's own three strands can, with a relative lack of controversy, be taken as aims in the education of individual students. That is, it seems to make sense to say that three of the aims of educating the individual are that he or she should develop a sense of social and moral responsibility, should become involved in community life and concerns and should acquire the knowledge and skills which are part of political literacy. It may also seem at first sight to make sense to aim at individual students coming to have a sense of their national identity. All of these possible aims seem to make sense, because they all turn on something in the make-up of an individual: their attitudes, dispositions, knowledge and so on. Put another way, one can express these aims in terms of what an individual is supposed to be learning. Individuals can learn to see themselves as having responsibilities to others, they can learn to behave in various ways in their community, and they can learn the various ideas and concepts involved in political literacy.

Against this background, the idea of social inclusion seems to be on a rather different footing, because being socially included rather than excluded does not seem to be something that the individual learns. Whether or not an individual is effectively included in society is not primarily a matter of the individual's own state of mind – knowledge, dispositions or attitudes. However well an individual is educated, education alone cannot bring about his or her social inclusion. We might speculate that, while social inclusion is clearly important to Crick, it is because it cannot be taken as a direct aim in the education of any one individual that it almost disappears from view within the Report.

Further thought, though, suggests that the picture is more complicated for all of these strands, themes or aims. This is clearest in the case of involvement in the community. Such involvement is not possible if it is not allowed and accepted by others. The development of the skills involved in action within any community, and the disposition to put those skills to use – actually to get involved – will depend on the opportunities being there and indeed, beyond that, on active encouragement. If social exclusion, by definition, is a condition in which an individual is not involved in their community, then the condition of exclusion cannot be primarily the result of a failure in the individual's own learning.

By contrast, it might seem that the development of a sense of moral and social responsibility is an individual attainment, and that it is therefore something educators can aim at as they might aim at the development of skills and knowledge in curriculum subjects. But even this development cannot be the outcome exclusively of a relationship between educator and student. For this development to take place, there has to be some space in which responsibility can be exercised, but also space in which the young person can be supported in the initial exercise of responsibility. Other people have to be willing to see the individual as one who is an agent, capable of making decisions and of being aware of the consequences of his or her actions. For other people to see the individual as capable of social and moral responsibility, they have to see the individual as part of society. To the extent that an individual is excluded from society, he or she is prevented from developing moral and social responsibility.

Is political literacy, on the other hand, something that could be taught as a body of abstract knowledge, and which therefore does not depend on any particular social relationship for its development? Not as Crick defines political literacy, for his definition involves skills and values as well as knowledge. Skills for effective participation in public life cannot be developed unless the opportunity for participation is available. Here Crick's political literacy overlaps with community involvement, since it is hard to see how the values which go with involvement in public life could develop in someone with no experience of that involvement.

So the necessity for social inclusion rather than exclusion is an essential background to the whole of Crick's thinking about the strands of citizenship education. What of national identity? In a similar way, it is true that development of a sense of identity cannot be purely an individual achievement – an individual will not develop a sense of being a member of a particular group if others in that group do not recognize him or her as a member. Indeed, this interplay between identity and recognition is a common theme in recent political philosophy. But in the case of national identity, there is ample room for controversy between reasonable and politically literate people about how far a sense of national identity is a desirable attribute and, if it is to some degree desirable, how important it is. In recent years some politicians have made clear their view that citizenship education involves trying to ensure that all British citizens have a national identity, as British, as their primary identity. Crick allows for a more nuanced view. He recognizes, in addition to the possibility of national identity, the existence of ethnic and religious identities. Indeed, he claims 'citizenship education creates common ground between different ethnic and religious identities' (Crick Report, 1998, 3.14). He also says, clearly rightly, that 'these matters of national identity in a pluralist society are complex and should never be taken for granted'.

It is one thing to say that all citizens of Britain should be able to recognize and value a shared common British citizenship. It is going further to say that, for all citizens of Britain, their identity as British should dominate other aspects of their identity; and Crick – wisely, again – does not go as far as the second position. The sharing of common citizenship is, as we have seen, tied up with social inclusion: an active citizen is necessarily someone who, at least in certain important respects, sees himself or herself as (and is seen by others to be) involved in society. But a particular sense of identity is not in the same way tied to social inclusion. Someone who does not see himself or herself primarily as British over and above other identities is not thereby excluded from society, but may indeed be included and actively participating in many ways. Without further argument, the fact that someone does not have a sense that their primary identity is British is not a reason why they should enjoy anything less than full citizenship.

The upshot of this section is that we should not think of any of the aims of citizenship education – including the three strands picked out by Crick – in purely individualistic terms. If social and moral responsibility, involvement in society and political literacy are to be aims for any, they should be aims for all – not only on normative grounds of equality, but also because such aims cannot be realized for individuals in isolation. Further, once we acknowledge that the aims of citizenship education do not necessarily have to be confined to development of qualities or capacities in individuals, we can include promotion of social inclusion among them (where citizenship education itself is, of course, not just an activity of individual teachers, but a shared practice in a nation's schools). And it is also possible to include aims relating to a shared sense of identity, but it is especially important in this case to avoid oversimplified interpretations. The next section will show that there are links between the themes of identity and inclusion and the language we use when speaking of responsibility.

Interpreting Social and Moral Responsibility

Having indicated something of the way in which the five items on the initial list are interrelated, I want now to concentrate on unpacking what may be involved in Crick's strand of social and moral responsibility. In particular, I want to look at the kind of language in which educators and others express the detail of the content and aims within this strand.[2]

Clearly talk of social and moral responsibility overlaps with, even if it is not entirely reducible to, talk about moral education (I have commented in Haydon (2000) on the fact that the actual term 'moral education' has been little used in

---

2   Here I shall be taking further a theme which I touched on but did not develop in Haydon (2000).

recent discussions of citizenship education.) Discussion of moral education has a long history, not least within philosophy. And among the philosophers who have been discussing moral education in recent years, it is well known that there are two different and, to some extent, competing conceptions of what moral education is fundamentally about. One conception uses a language of individual autonomy, rational thought and the principled endorsement and following of norms. The other uses a language of the development of virtues, where a virtue is a valued personal quality which involves aspects of feeling and motivation as well as cognition or understanding.

It is well known, too, that 'virtue ethics' has had something of a vogue in recent years, and that this has indeed spilled over well beyond academic discussion. In the United States the idea of 'character education' – which has an obvious, though not unproblematic, affinity with the virtue conceptions of moral education (McLaughlin and Halstead, 1999) – is by now well established, and it is beginning to be heard about more in Britain too. But in connection with citizenship education, what is especially interesting is the recent tendency for the language of virtues to be used in discussion of the qualities citizens need if a liberal society is to flourish. The notions of 'liberal virtues' and 'civic virtues' are now much discussed (e.g. Galston, 1991; Macedo, 1990; White, 1996). The idea that the education of citizens has to be centrally concerned with the development of the right civic virtues is a strong strand within recent philosophical writing on citizenship education.

Thus the language of virtues provides a way of interpreting the strand of 'moral and social responsibility' to which Crick refers. But to the extent that the development of virtues is emphasized, the idea that moral and social responsibility, as a strand of citizenship education, might be about enabling citizens to subscribe rationally to a shared set of norms or principles becomes less visible, if it is not rejected altogether.

In the philosophical literature on moral education there are many arguments both for and against using and prioritizing the language of virtues. I want to consider, and to raise some questions about, its value in context of citizenship. My argument here – though it does not exhaust the arguments on the issue – turns on the importance, already noted, of the ideas of inclusion and identity.

First, more needs to be said about what it is for an individual to possess a virtue. Most modern philosophical writers on virtue ethics follow, to varying degrees, a model drawn originally from Aristotle. A virtue is a state of character. That already says that it is not a superficial characteristic of the person; a virtue goes quite deep. A person with a certain virtue is, in ways that matter, a different kind of person from someone without that virtue. This is because having a virtue is not like having some piece of knowledge which can be acquired and then forgotten, or like acquiring a skill which could go rusty through lack of use. Virtues have depth because they involve feeling and motivation. For instance, the person who has the virtue of compassion is someone who notices, and actively takes notice, when someone else is in difficulties. He or she is a person who cares about this, who is motivated to do something about it and who, at least on many occasions, will be able to put that motivation into practice.

So to try to develop particular virtues in people is to try to develop particular kinds of people. Within a liberal tradition of political thinking, this must immediately raise some questions about whether it is a proper role for a state education system to try and ensure that individuals grow up and leave school as one kind of person rather than another. Is there a model of 'the right kind of person' whom a society needs if it is to flourish? Or is a diversity of persons, different individuals having different virtues, actually more desirable? And even if there is some common set of virtues which it is necessary for all citizens to have if their society is to flourish, does it immediately follow that the education system within a liberal society should be trying to ensure that it produces people with those virtues?

These are not intended as rhetorical questions. They can be seriously debated within a liberal framework. It may well be possible to show that the idea of a state education system trying to develop virtues in its students is not in itself illiberal. But what I want to pursue here is a more specific question: in a society which is not only liberal but plural in its cultures and traditions, can the promotion of a set of virtues be compatible with inclusion and the proper recognition of diversity?

A familiar theme within recent philosophical virtue ethics is that the bare idea of any particular virtue needs to be filled out with a more substantive content (cf. MacIntyre, 1999). The notion of compassion as sketched above, for instance, was indeed the merest sketch. When it comes to filling in the sketch, giving its lines more precise definition, there is room for different cultures or traditions to do this in different ways. (At some times and in some places, for example, compassion could be attributed to someone without reference to anything outside a human social world. But today in some Western societies it would be hard for some people to call others compassionate if those others were in no way moved by the conditions of animals in factory farms or laboratories.) Compassion, justice, courage – all these virtues and many more can be understood in very different ways. Not only that, but different cultural and religious traditions can differ, not just in how they interpret particular virtues, but also in the virtues they give special prominence to, and in their order of priority among the virtues they recognize.

In a multicultural and multi-faith society, it is not accidental that there will be different understandings of the nature and importance of particular virtues. That there are different understandings of virtues and their importance must be true by definition of a multi-faith and multicultural society, since the differences between faiths and cultures do consist in part in differences about the qualities which are rated as important virtues. That is to say that different faiths and different cultures to a degree value different sorts of person.

Now the link with identity becomes clearer. It is a familiar theme that people identify themselves to a certain extent with what they see as their community of faith or of culture. There are many aspects to this, including sharing language, sharing a history, and sharing practices, manners and particular enthusiasms. But tied up with all of this, in identifying him- or herself as a member of a particular community, an individual sees him- or herself as having, or aspiring to have, the qualities recognized and valued within that community – that is, as having or aspiring to certain virtues and hence being, or aspiring to be, one sort of person rather than another.

Suppose, though, that we see the strand of moral and social responsibility within citizenship education as a matter of developing virtues. Which virtues are these to be?

There are several possible ways in which this question might, in practice, be answered. In one, those members of society who have the power to determine the direction education takes – or, if this sounds too strong, those who have the dominant influence in educational matters – will select the virtues to which they give priority, and seek to implement their understanding of those virtues. But this does not seem to be a route for inclusiveness in a plural society. If those who have the influence to determine the direction of citizenship education themselves come from a particular tradition and background then, even if they intend no bias, the virtues they favour cannot coincide with all the different sets of virtues favoured by the different traditions within the society. By this route it will inevitably turn out that the virtues which are to be promoted will be congenial to, and will appear natural and unproblematic to, some parts of society, but less so to others.

Then, in turn, members of groups to whom the favoured virtues do not appear natural and unproblematic will not be able to identify fully with the model citizen constituted by those favoured virtues. And to that extent, the aspiration that they be fully included as citizens will not be met.

The question 'which virtues?' might be answered in a second way – by attempting to find through consensus one set of virtues, and the understanding which accompanies them. But because different cultures can have different understandings even of virtues recognized by all under the same name, any consensus arrived at in this way risks being superficial. All may agree, say, that tolerance is an important virtue, but if different parties have different conceptions of what is involved in tolerance (and they are in fact very likely to have different understandings of where the limits to tolerance lie), then the consensus will be a thin one.

There is a third way in which the question may be answered – not by reading off some set of virtues, consciously or unconsciously, from one tradition, but by attempting to argue that certain virtues and not others are essential if society is to flourish. Some writers have attempted to justify a set of civic virtues, seen as necessary for a flourishing liberal democratic state, in this way.

The third approach has something in common with the second, in that any interpretation of the virtues it can work with will be a fairly thin interpretation. That is to say, any viable interpretation of a virtue such as tolerance or a sense of justice will not be able to say very much about the feelings which the just person, as such, must have, or about any distinctive motivation of this person. To attempt to say much would be to endorse one particular interpretation of the virtue of justice or tolerance which would not be shared by all. In fact the third approach, even though it may be framed in the language of virtues, may be difficult to distinguish from an approach which simply points to the importance of certain principles. Is praising the virtue of tolerance very different from saying that it is desirable for people to exercise tolerance towards each other? If the idea of tolerance is really cashed out in all the richness of interpretation virtue language calls for, so that praising tolerance is actually praising a particular sort of person (one marked by tolerance, with all the feelings and motivations that might involve), then there is certainly a difference. But if that richness of interpretation is avoided – if there is even a deliberate attempt to avoid it for the sake of marking out something all can subscribe to – then the idea of a civic virtue of tolerance collapses into no more than endorsement of a principle of tolerance. This is the same as the outcome likely with the second approach. The attempt to arrive at a consensus, not by arguing from first principles but by seeing what people can in fact agree on, will again necessitate giving up on rich interpretations for the sake of achieving agreement.

It might be suggested that there is nothing wrong with that. Does it matter if the only interpretations of virtues equally available to all are rather minimal interpretations? Has the argument not shown that if there is to be a shared sense of identity across a plural society, and if some groups are not to be excluded from that shared identity, then only a thin language of virtues will do?

This is partly right, but it raises the question of why the language of virtues should be used in such contexts at all. Precisely because the language of virtues will, for different groups, have differing connotations, the use of such a language risks obscuring what should, above all in democratic citizenship contexts, be transparent. People who share a common citizenship need to know what it is that they can agree on – at a level beyond simply agreeing that 'toleration' or 'justice' are good things. But the way to achieve such clarity, so far as it can be achieved at all, is surely to focus directly on the norms each citizen expects others to adhere to. For a specific understanding of a particular virtue a specific background, sometimes a specific faith or even metaphysic, may be required. By contrast, a norm or principle picks out what we expect people to do or to refrain from doing. In a sense, it focuses on externals. To moral philosophers, the focus on externals – on the principles people subscribe to, on the norms which govern their actions, rather than on underlying feelings or motivations – has often been seen as an undue narrowing of focus. But for theorists of citizenship, the focus on externals may pick out precisely what is wanted. Each of us, as a citizen, can reasonably expect, and demand, that our fellow citizens live by certain norms and principles. We cannot demand of each of them that they *be* a certain sort of person. For instance, we can demand that other people exercise tolerance of our own lifestyle choices, where they do no harm to others, for here tolerance is something that can be understood in terms of action. But we cannot demand that in every case this tolerance is exercised on the basis of some particular underlying motivation or metaphysic or world view.

It should be clear that in questioning the value, in the context of citizenship, of the language of virtues, I am not impugning at all the importance of the social and moral responsibility strand within citizenship education. On the contrary, the point is that the language of norms and principles bearing on behaviour is better suited to spelling out the kind of responsibility which can be required of citizens. We hold our fellow citizens responsible for their actions, to the point of imposing laws enforced through punishment. It is significant that what society seeks to enforce is not the possession of certain virtues. We do not punish citizens for failing to be sufficiently generous, courageous or whatever. We punish them for failing to adhere to certain specified norms. And one of the strongest arguments for insisting citizens are educated in moral responsibility is that we cannot reasonably and fairly punish people for failing to abide by society's norms if they have not received an education which fits them to be aware of these norms and understand the reasons for them (Haydon, 1979).

Conclusions

I have argued that moral responsibility, social inclusion and national identity can all, if carefully interpreted, be compatible aims for education for citizenship – as can Crick's other strands of community involvement and political literacy. But it might turn out that interpreting any one of these five strands in some particular way would lessen its compatibility with the others. I have argued in more detail that interpreting just one of these aims – moral responsibility – in terms of the development of virtues (even virtues labelled 'civic') will reduce its compatibility with the other aims.

National identity can be developed compatibly with the other aims if it means the shared recognition of citizenship of a particular nation. But this is not the national identity which consists in being a certain kind of person, in having a particular set of virtues – 'British' virtues, for instance. Identity and virtues do go together, but the possession of or aspiration towards particular virtues is part of people's more specific identities as members of, for example, a religious community or an ethnic tradition. Citizenship, though it requires moral responsibility and community involvement, does not demand a sense of national identity that outweighs other identities.

Social inclusion involves (though it is not exhausted by) mutual recognition of norms which are expectations of behaviour, rather than of feeling and motivation. If we think the norms which we apply among ourselves, within one community, do not apply to certain others – if we think we can do to others what we would not allow ourselves to do among ourselves – then we are excluding those others. If individuals perceive, correctly or not, that the norms of the wider community are not being applied to them – if, for instance, their rights are not recognized or their voice is not heard – then their condition is one of exclusion. None of this precludes the possibility of criticism of prevailing norms. A liberal citizenry will be a body within which criticism of prevailing norms is accepted and even encouraged. But it does emphatically mean that people should not suffer exclusion simply because they do not display the favoured virtues of the majority.

Moral responsibility, then, is best conceptualized in ways which avoid the divisive tendencies of the language of virtue ethics. Or so this paper argues. Since the language of virtues seems more adequate for the overall consideration of moral education than the language of norms and principles (Haydon, 2003), it follows that we need to make a distinction between citizenship education (even its moral and social responsibility aspect) and moral education in general. Intuitively, from a liberal point of view – though not from some other points of view – this seems right, but establishing it would take more space than is available here.

References

Advisory Group on Citizenship ('Crick Report') (1998), *Education for Citizenship and the Teaching of Democracy in Schools*, Final Report of the Advisory Group on Citizenship, 22 September 1998, Qualifications and Curriculum Authority, London.

Galston, W. (1991), *Liberal Purposes: Goods, Virtues and Duties in the Liberal State*, Cambridge University Press, Cambridge.

Haydon, G. (1979), 'Political Theory and the Child: Problems of the Individualist Tradition', *Political Studies*, Vol. 17(3), pp. 405-20.

Haydon, G. (1999), *Values, Virtues and Violence: Education and the Public Understanding of Morality*, Blackwell, Oxford.

Haydon, G. (2000), 'The Moral Agenda of Citizenship Education', in D. Lawton, J. Cairns and R. Gardner (eds), *Education for Citizenship*, Continuum, London.

Haydon, G. (2003), 'Moral Education', in R. Curren (ed.), *A Companion to the Philosophy of Education*, Blackwell, Oxford.

Macedo, S. (1990), *Liberal Virtues: Citizenship, Virtue and Community in Liberal Constitutionalism*, Oxford University Press, Oxford.

MacIntyre, A. (1999), 'How to Seem Virtuous without Actually Being So', in J.M. Halstead and T.H. McLaughlin (eds), *Education in Morality*, Routledge, London.

McLaughlin, T.H. and Halstead, J.M. (1999), 'Education in Character and Virtue', in J.M. Halstead and T.H. McLaughlin (eds), *Education in Morality*, Routledge, London.

White, P. (1996), *Civic Virtues and Public Schooling: Educating Citizens for a Democratic Society*, Teachers College Press, New York and London.

6

Citizenship Education and Multiculturalism

David Archard

States need citizens and citizens are created, not born. States can only survive if they have a citizenry adequate to their nature and ends, and education is the principal tool for the creation of citizens. Thus, education is a 'program for social survival' (Walzer, 1983, p. 197). Further, as Michael Walzer adds, education 'is always relative to the society for which it is designed'. Here Walzer self-consciously follows Aristotle, who observed:

> The citizen should be moulded to suit the form of government under which he lives. For each government has a peculiar character which originally formed and which continues to preserve it ... (Aristotle, *The Politics*, 1337,[a] 10-19).

Aristotle had in mind broadly characterized types of polity: 'The character of democracy creates democracy, and the character of oligarchy creates oligarchy'. But it is also possible to think of a civic education as serving the ends of an individual polity with its own particular political culture, history, set of institutions and national identity.[1]

The Crick Report[1] thus envisages a citizenship education designed not simply for a liberal democracy, but also one for the distinct society that is the United Kingdom. One crucial element of citizenship in any polity is a sense of being a member of that polity, of sharing with one's fellow-citizens a conjoint set of political purposes and ends. Importantly, therefore, the Report emphasizes the importance of finding or of restoring 'a sense of common citizenship, including a national identity that is secure enough to find a place for the plurality of nations, cultures, ethnic identities and religions long found in the United Kingdom' (Crick Report, 1998, 3.14). Again the Report gives the last word to the Lord Chancellor, who is quoted as insisting that an essential precondition of citizenship is that people should have 'a sense of belonging – of identity – with the community around them' (Crick Report, 1998, 11.1).

---

1   The Final Report of the Advisory Group on Citizenship, 22 September 1998, entitled *Education for Citizenship and the Teaching of Democracy in Schools*, is hereafter referred to as the 'Crick Report'. References to the Crick Report give paragraph numbers.

Contemporary liberal democratic societies are multicultural societies. This initially means no more than that they contain enduring, well-defined communities whose sense of collective identity derives from significant shared ethnic, linguistic, religious and cultural features. 'Multicultural' here designates a fact about societies. It is not a normative or evaluative term. However, modern liberal democratic societies also recognize the obligation to acknowledge the fact of multiculturalism and to frame laws, implement policies and design institutions that are an appropriate response to that fact. The obligation can be discharged in various ways which range from laws proscribing discrimination, through the inculcation of a public ethos tolerant of communal diversity, to the positive recognition of difference in the form of legal exemptions and special benefits.

The Crick Report recognizes the existence of cultural diversity within the United Kingdom. It identifies 'a commitment to equal opportunities and gender equality' as a key value to be acquired by the citizenship education it commends. Beyond that, it states only that 'we all need to learn more about each other'. More particularly, 'majorities must respect, understand and tolerate minorities and minorities must learn and respect the laws, codes and conventions as much as the majority' (Crick Report, 1998, 3.16). A citizenship education is thereby seen as creating 'common ground between different ethnic and religious identities' (Crick Report, 1998, 3.14). This is a very British approach. Tolerance of difference requires mutual understanding and knowledge. But it is difference within a commonality, that is, within a shared civic and national identity fostered by the education in citizenship.

It has already been said that different instances of citizenship education can aim to create different sorts of citizen. At its most basic and minimum, individuals can be taught to know what the essential law of the land is and to obey it. The Crick Report recommends that more than simple political obedience should be inculcated. It wants people to 'think of themselves as active citizens, willing, able and equipped to have an influence in public life' (Crick Report, 1998, 1.5). It follows the Greek political tradition wherein 'citizenship has meant involvement in public affairs' (Crick Report, 1998, 2.1), and insists that 'volunteering and community involvement are necessary conditions of civil society and democracy' (Crick Report, 1998, 2.5). It thus identifies a healthy civil society – one in which a 'rich variety of non-political associations and voluntary groups' flourish – as the basis of a flourishing democracy (Crick Report, 1998, 2.8). It is worth noting that communal diversity also finds its first and most obvious means of expression within civil society. It is, for instance, in churches, temples, mosques and synagogues that distinct communities worship together. Communities also identify themselves through distinctive modes of social organization, volunteering activity, cultural practices and private educational initiatives. Thus, a flourishing civil society is one which most likely promotes cultural diversity.

What follows in this essay is an exploration of the tension between the creation of an active citizenry sharing a common civic and national identity, and the persistence of communal diversity. One might imagine this tension as one between centripetal and centrifugal forces. On the one hand, diversity pulls citizens apart. My membership of a community – ethnic, religious or cultural – is that respect in which I think of myself as different from my fellow-citizens, as having in common with my community what I do not share with my co-nationals. On the other hand, a civic identity pulls individuals together. It is that respect in which we exhibit a commonality of political purpose and practice. I share with my co-citizens a commitment to making work a particular set of political institutions. Managing communal diversity within a political unity is thus a difficult and complex enterprise. It seems clear that a civic identity, if it is successfully to constrain and manage multiculturalism, must have a fundamental importance in people's lives. Individuals must be and, importantly, think of themselves as, above all else, citizens of the same polity.

What does the Crick Report envisage as the learning outcomes of its proposed citizenship education? It identifies four elements. They are concepts, values and dispositions, skills and aptitudes, and knowledge and understanding. Citizens should command an understanding of key concepts such as democracy, fairness, justice, and the rule of law, power and authority. Citizens should know and understand the 'particular aspects of their society with which citizenship education is concerned', along with 'the topical and contemporary issues, events and activities which are the lifeblood of citizenship education' (Crick Report, 1998, 6.8). Thus, for example, they should know and understand the economic features of their own society, its taxation and public expenditure structure. Further, they should recognize and appreciate the significance of any important Budget proposal, how it changes economic policy and what difference it makes to the taxation or expenditure system.

Turning now to values and dispositions, skills and aptitudes, I want to identify what is recognizably a virtue of rational or critical individual autonomy. The Report thinks that pupils 'should be helped, in particular, to reflect on and recognise values and dispositions which underlie their attitudes and actions as individuals and as members of groups or communities' (Crick Report, 1998, 6.8.3). The skills and attitudes appropriate to citizenship education should be developed and applied in certain contexts. These contexts should be chosen 'in order to allow pupils to reinforce and further deepen their understanding, think critically, develop their own ideas, respond in different ways to a diversity of views, defend or change an opinion, and recognise the contribution of others' (Crick Report, 1998, 6.8.3).

This fundamental civic virtue is emphasized throughout the Report. A key disposition is the 'willingness to be open to changing one's opinions and attitudes in the light of discussion and evidence'. A key skill and aptitude is 'a critical approach to evidence put before one and ability to look for fresh evidence' (Crick Report, 1998, p. 44, Fig. 1). At the heart of active citizenship are the 'critical capacities to weigh evidence before speaking and acting' (Crick Report, 1998, 1.5). The Report commends the White Paper, *Excellence in Schools*, for insisting that citizenship education should, besides understanding and respect for law, justice and democracy, encourage 'independence of thought. It should develop skills of reflection, inquiry and debate' (Crick Report, 1998, 2.7).

I have identified the virtue in question as one of rational or critical autonomy. It is the ability of an individual to subject to critical scrutiny – in the light of evidence, rational argumentation, analysis, and the resources of alternative competing values – his or her own beliefs, values, and dispositions. Autonomy is the 'capacity to rationally reflect on, and potentially revise, our conceptions of the good life. An autonomous person is capable of reflecting on her current ends, and assessing whether they are worthy of her continued allegiance' (Kymlicka, 1999, p. 24). Autonomy is also recognizably a liberal virtue. It is one esteemed in a liberal education and it is central to a liberal ideal of the good life.

Here, then, is a first source of tension between citizenship education and communal diversity. Citizenship requires autonomy, but some at least of the communities do not value autonomy. One of the most significant minority communities within the United Kingdom are the Muslims. Mark Halstead's summary of the aims of an Islamic education is worth quoting:

> The aim of education in Islam … is to provide children with positive guidance which will help them to grow into good adults who will lead happy and fruitful lives in this world and who will aspire to achieve the reward of the faithful in the world to come. The goodness of human beings lies in their willingness to allow the whole of their lives to be governed by Islamic principles. There is no question of individuals being encouraged through education to work out for themselves their own religious faith, or to subject it to detached rational investigation at a fundamental level. The divine revelation systematized in the *shari'a* (Islamic law) provides them with the requisite knowledge of truth and falsehood, right and wrong, and the task of individuals is to come to understand this knowledge and exercise their free will to choose which path to follow (Halstead, 1990, pp. 4-5).

It is not simply that a citizenship education teaches individuals to be autonomous, whereas the Muslim community does not regard autonomy with favour. It is also, and perhaps more crucially, that the exercise of autonomy may be subversive of a communal identity such as that of Muslims. After all, the Crick Report, as quoted earlier, recommended that individuals 'should be helped … to reflect on and recognise values and dispositions which underlie their attitudes … *as members of groups or communities* [my emphasis]'. An autonomous citizen can reflect on those ideals and beliefs that are constitutive of his or her membership of his or her community and decide, in Kymlicka's words, 'whether they are worthy of her continued allegiance' (Kymlicka, 1999). But the Islamic community will want those beliefs and values that it shares to be passed on to the next generation. That is just what it is for this community to endure. The constitutive values and beliefs are not to be subject to critical scrutiny and endorsed or rejected. They are inherited as the true faith and learnt as such.

How might defenders of citizenship education, such as the authors of the Crick Report, respond to the charge that this education teaches a disposition that is inconsistent with the preservation of a valued communal identity? Of course much depends on how that disposition is specified, something to which I will return in due course. Let us for the present grant that a minimal degree of autonomy is required of the active citizen. A first answer to the question posed is to insist that the acquisition of autonomy – where this means the ability to scrutinize and assess one's current ends, one's conception of the good life – is not a direct aim of citizenship education. Further, this education directly serves ends which all communities – even those that do not value autonomy – can recognize as worthy of pursuit. Let me take the two elements of this claim in reverse order.

The Muslim community wants its members to have the protected freedoms to pursue the religion of their choice, to engage in the cultural practices that are central to its shared identity, to associate together as Muslims in various voluntary activities, campaigns and groups, and publicly to defend and to make non-Muslims aware of Islamic ideas. These freedoms are precisely the liberal civic liberties of religion, association and speech. They are best secured and protected within a liberal political order. But a liberal democracy will only survive if it is supported by an active citizenry. Further – as has been already demonstrated – the production, and reproduction, of such a citizenry requires an education in citizenship (Macedo, 1995). Such an education must, at a minimum, teach those skills and aptitudes that allow, and indeed encourage, individuals to participate politically. What can these skills and aptitudes be, if they do not include critical scrutiny of political authority? Amy Gutmann believes that a 'democratic society should educate all educable children to be capable of participating in collectively shaping their society' (Gutmann, 1989, p. 77). She also thinks that children 'must learn not just to behave in accordance with authority but to think critically about authority if they are to live up to the democratic ideal of sharing political sovereignty as citizens' (Gutmann, 1987, p. 51).

The defender of a civic education has shown that this education directly serves the end of reproducing a liberal polity. This is an end which a community that does not value autonomy, but does value the protection of its civic freedoms, can acknowledge is worth having.

The other half of the response to the challenge posed for the defender of citizenship education is that this education does not directly aim at the production of autonomous individuals. Will Kymlicka, thus, sees 'the promotion of personal autonomy … as the indirect consequence of civic education, not as its direct or explicit purpose' (Kymlicka, 1999). Or consider the claims of John Rawls in this context. Rawls distinguishes his own 'political liberalism' from the 'comprehensive liberalism' of Kant and John Stuart Mill. A comprehensive liberal would design a public education so as 'to foster the values of autonomy and individuality as ideals to govern much if not all of life' (Rawls, 1993, p. 199). However political liberalism, by contrast, does not rest upon the assumed value of an autonomous life. It would not seek to educate children to live such a life. Yet the political liberal would teach children to be 'self-supporting'; that is, to be independent members of political society, able to understand and to be motivated by the ideals of a political conception of justice. As a result, a political liberal education would mean 'in effect, though not in intention, educating children in a comprehensively liberal conception of personal autonomy' (Rawls, 1993, pp. 199-200). Once again a civic education for a liberal democracy is described as securing, even whilst it does not aim at securing, autonomous individuals.

Amy Gutmann has described this by-product of a liberal civic education as its 'spill-over effect' (Gutmann, 1995, p. 571). Other writers have also noted its import (Coleman, 1998). The thought is that learning the skills and aptitudes necessary to be an independent citizen, and to scrutinize critically the exercise of political authority, cannot but spill over into a more general personal autonomy. If a person can learn how to reflect on the political conceptions of others, assessing whether they are worthy of their continued allegiance, why should he or she not be able to do the same with his or her own conceptions of the good life, as well as those of others? There is, of course, still some distance between a comprehensive liberal education in personal autonomy and a politically liberal civic education in active citizenship. Nevertheless, if the latter does not restrict itself – as the Crick Report does not suggest that it should – to the teaching of concepts and facts (such as the teaching of constitutional basics and the various doctrines espoused within society), then the gap remains largely one of explicit purpose. The gap is not one of actual consequences. It seems obvious that methods of rational critical enquiry cannot be restricted in their scope, and thus that a capacity to examine, and challenge, values and beliefs in one sphere of one's life – the political – will extend more generally.

However, what is true is that the capacity of autonomy can be defined more or less narrowly. At one extreme an individual is able at any moment of his or her life to subject each personal belief and value to critical scrutiny. A person's conception of the good life is original, unique, and his or hers alone. The individual alone devises and endorses, but revises where appropriate, the plan of life by which he or she lives. Few of us do, or perhaps could, conform to such a stringent ideal. For very many of us autonomy is a weaker, less comprehensive, trait of character. According to this conception, an autonomous person can think critically about some, but perhaps not all, of his or her beliefs and ideals. We each live by standards not entirely our own, but which we nevertheless do not unreflectively endorse. Each of us will relinquish those values that we come to recognize as mistaken.

Stanley Benn has suggested a somewhat similar distinction between an autarchic and an autonomous life. The autarchic life is self-directed, that is, led according to commitments which, in turn, derive from beliefs subject to a general concern for the truth. An autonomous life is autarchic but, in addition, the beliefs underlying the commitments are coherent, and their coherence is the outcome of a continuing self-directed process of critical scrutiny and adjustment. The autonomous person lives according to principles or a law that one gives to oneself. Benn thinks that autarchy is the normal condition of human beings and that autonomy is, by contrast, an excellence of character (Benn, 1988, chs 8 and 9).

Now there is every reason to think that the species of personal autonomy which is a 'spillover' from the citizenship education that the Crick Report commends is much closer to autarchy, or to the weaker version of autonomy, than to autonomy in the full and strong sense of the term. A person with fundamentalist religious beliefs, such as a Muslim, can lead his or her life according to these beliefs, which he or she judges – and holds it to be important that they are – true. Individuals scrutinize legislation and public policy in the light of these beliefs, and are to this extent active citizens, participating in the public life. They do not rationally deliberate upon their underlying deep convictions, which are taken as truths. The believer is not in Benn's sense autonomous, but his or her political life is nevertheless autarchic.

Recognizing all of the above serves to weaken the sharp contrast between the liberal autonomous life and the non-autonomous life espoused within some minority communities. Moreover, there is a danger of oversimplifying the contrast here, and it is one some writers make for rhetorical purposes. Arneson and Shapiro, for instance, contrast a 'religious traditionalist' and a 'secular worldly' way of life. They characterize education for the former as one of 'withdrawal' from the world, whereas an education for the latter is a preparation for an open future, and for different ways of life (Arneson and Shapiro, pp. 401-2). Others, similarly, are inclined to set the liberal ideal of personal autonomy against 'blind reliance on authority' (White, 1982, p. 5). But it is not only, as has already been argued, that autonomy comes in varying degrees, and not as a single organizing trait of character excluding all others. It is also that what is set against the liberal way of life is more complex than is often rhetorically depicted. Of course some ways of life practised in minority communities do leave no space for anything but the narrowly defined traditional values inherited from the past, and unthinkingly transmitted to the next generation. But it is also true that many religious traditions foster and encourage criticism, rational deliberation and an independence of mind (Burtt, 1996). Admittedly, they do so within the terms of that tradition. But again, if an individual learns, albeit as a member of the faith and within the terms of that faith, to scrutinize and to evaluate the meanings of a canonical text or the pronouncements of a religious elder, why should not the acquired skills 'spill over' into a more general capacity of critical review?

There is a further point. Autonomy is misleadingly characterized if, as sometimes appears to be the case with its liberal defenders, it is seen chiefly or exclusively in terms of a capacity to change or to revise one's way of life. Autonomy is also about a certain independence of character, and that may most centrally be realized in adhering to a way of life (Callan, 2002). Autonomy requires steadfastness of character, strength of resolve and the ability to execute one's considered choices. Being educated to esteem a way of life, to value an identity, can anchor an individual in a way that exposure to many different ways of life or a resolution not to value any one way of life – both not grossly unfair characterizations of a liberal education – cannot.

Thus, to sum up, the first source of tension between citizenship education and communal diversity – namely that citizenship requires autonomy, but some at least of the communities do not value autonomy – need not be as problematic as it might seem. However, there is a problematic – and straightforward – conflict between the value of equality and the beliefs of some minority cultures. A key, indeed constitutive, value of any liberal democracy is the equality of citizens. We have noted that the Crick Report identifies a 'belief in human dignity and equality' and a 'commitment to equal opportunities and gender equality' as essential values and dispositions to be acquired in citizenship education. A minority culture that professes and practises a belief in gender *inequality* espouses a way of life which directly contradicts the required civic ideal. It professes that belief if it is explicitly expounded by elders and leaders and within canonical texts of the culture. The belief is practised if, as a matter of fact, it organizes the domestic and private lives of the culture.

Certainly the depiction of the Muslim community as oppressive of its female members, whom it treats as unequal subordinates, may well display a mixture of prejudicial assumption and misleading oversimplification. Muslim women may willingly support supposedly patriarchal and enforced practices such as arranged marriages and the wearing of Islamic dress. It is also true that a belief in separate education for boys and girls need not be inconsistent with a commitment to gender equality. There are reasons to support such an education that do not derive from a belief that girls are inferior to boys. These points are all well made by Mark Halstead (Halstead, 1991). Nevertheless, he himself summarizes Islam as proclaiming the absolute equality of worth of men and women, at the same time as it would encourage separate treatment of the genders in recognition of their different natures. In particular it sanctions differentiated social roles, with women fulfilling the traditional function of domestic carers (Halstead, 1991).

Now it is certainly true that Muslim women may choose to be just wives and mothers. In non-Muslim households an unequal division of domestic labour can be willingly and deliberately practised, with either adult partner assuming the major domestic role and with a view to maximizing overall familial income. This is an economic or pragmatic reason for a partition of domestic labours. However, many non-Muslim women also embrace a traditional understanding of their gender's role as domestic helpmate to the male. Liberalism, at its core, insists that individuals should be as free as possible to pursue the good life as they understand and endorse it, within the overall structure of a just society. Why, then, should not those within traditionalist cultures be free to organize and live their family life as they see best? (Russell, 1995, pp. 397-426) Moreover, liberals are, in general, also favourably disposed towards a pluralism of lifestyles. A flourishing civil society, which the Crick Report sees as the foundation of active citizenship, is also the site of diversity. To insist that all families conform to a feminist template of familial justice would be to impose one doctrine of the good life on those who do not subscribe to it (Lloyd, 1994). Finally, it will be said that practices within civil society – especially those that are voluntarily entered into – are independent, strictly speaking, of the political sphere. Muslims of both genders are equal as citizens in the public realm even if there is inequality in private. A wife and a mother has the same vote, the same legal and civic rights, as her husband, even if she is his subordinate within the household.

However things are not that simple. Set against the view that the practising of traditional gender roles is chosen, and entirely consistent with both the liberal valuation of freely chosen, diverse modes of private life and the equality of civic status, are the following two considerations. The first is that the choice may not be that free. The second is that inequality within the private sphere may subvert equality in the public sphere. First, then, it is important to recognize the pressure that communal membership – especially when realistic alternatives to membership are few or absent – can exert on members. There are real costs of exit from a community. This is especially true in the broader context of public attitudes. Members of minority cultures suffer racism, both personalized in their everyday lives and institutionalized. Over two-thirds of British Muslims believe that the rest of the population do not see Islam as part of mainstream British culture. More than one in three say that they have experienced hostility and abuse directed towards them personally or at a family member because of their religion (*Guardian*/ICM opinion poll, 2002). Events such as the 1991 and 2003 Gulf Wars and September 11th can exacerbate Islamophobia. Thus, two-thirds of British Muslims think relations between Muslims and non-Muslims have deteriorated since September 11th (*Guardian*/ICM opinion poll, 2002). Membership of the culture provides a haven, a secure identity and a basis of self-respect. Leaving a place where one is esteemed, understood and valued for the uncertain, unfamiliar and hostile environment beyond is not an attractive proposition. The freedom to enter and to leave an association may be seen as the core liberal principle by which the permissibility of cultural membership is appraised (Kukathas, 1995). But it is important that the freedom in question is not understood in purely formal terms. There is no real freedom to leave a culture, even in the absence of any legal or institutional bar, if the personal costs of doing so are simply too high.

Second, inequality in the private sphere subverts public, civic equality. In the first place, if women are largely confined to the fulfilment of their disproportionately burdensome domestic labours, then they are to that extent less able than men to act as citizens (James, 1992). The thought is this. The freedoms to vote, to stand for political office, publicly to speak one's mind, are in the first instance negative liberty rights. This means that they are freedoms that the state secures by refraining from obstructing or interfering with individuals – not, for instance, preventing them from speaking their mind. But individuals are able to exercise these rights to varying degrees. They may take up a greater or lesser public role. To the degree that women are occupied within the family home playing the role of wife and mother, they are less able to play the public role. It is also the case that preparation for this role is at the expense of an extended education and pursuit of a career, and can deprive a woman of her financial, and thus social, independence.

In the second place, familial inequality may subvert civic education in political equality in the following way. Families play an important role alongside any citizenship education in transmitting values and capacities to the young. There is an argument to the effect that children can only learn the values of justice and equality in families that are themselves just and equal. John Stuart Mill provided an admirably clear and direct statement of the view that families are 'schools of justice'. Critical of existing nineteenth-century familial structures, characterized by the subjection of women, he argued that

> ... citizenship, in free societies, is partly a school in equality; but citizenship fills only a small place in modern life, and does not come near the daily habits or inmost sentiments. The family, justly constituted, would be the real school of the virtues of freedom.

He concluded that

> The moral training of mankind will never be adapted to the conditions of the life for which all other human progress is a preparation, until they practise in the family the same moral rule which is adapted to the normal constitution of human society (J.S. Mill, 1984, pp. 294-5).

The key claim – that families 'school' future citizens in the values by which they live – is an empirical one (Okin, 1994), and as such it is open to refutation. A common-sense rejoinder is that many feminists were themselves brought up in traditional families with a gender-based division of domestic labour (Okin, 1994). Indeed, it might make more sense to suggest that we learn the value of justice from unjust families, by identifying a private injustice which the public rules of one's society ought to forbid, and by sympathizing with the position of the unjustly treated family member. One's sense of justice and commitment to it might be the stronger, the closer one's personal familiarity with injustice.

For all of that, there is something jarring about the contradiction between the public profession of equality and the private practice of inequality. Any plausible liberal theory of the just society also requires an account of its good order. A well-ordered society is not only one that is just, but one whose citizens have a sense of justice, and accept the principles of justice (and know that everyone else accepts the principles) which regulate the society (Rawls, 1993). If citizens are thus motivated by an effective sense of justice, it makes sense to think it should motivate them in all areas of their lives. There is something anomalous about citizens who accept that the basic social and political institutions of society should be regulated by a principle of justice which nevertheless is not taken to govern their roles within their family or community.

This essay is, as stated earlier, an exploration of the tension between the creation of an active citizenry sharing a common civic and national identity, and the persistence of communal diversity. Insofar as the education in citizenship teaches the capacity to be autonomous, I have argued that this need not be as much in conflict with the maintenance of a particular communal identity as some think. However, insofar as the education in citizenship teaches the values of justice and equality, then there is a real tension with the maintenance of a particular communal identity.

There is a final source of tension. As stated at the outset the Crick Report regards a citizenship education as appropriate not only for a liberal democracy, but also for the particular society that is the United Kingdom. A key element of citizenship is a sense of belonging to *this* polity. Thus, to repeat, the Report emphasizes the importance of inculcating 'a sense of common citizenship, including a national identity that is secure enough to find a place for the plurality of nations, cultures, ethnic identities and religions long found in the United Kingdom' (Crick Report, 1998, 3.14).

Now in part this is achieved within the citizenship education itself. As the Report envisages it, pupils acquire knowledge of the UK as a political entity, its changing constitution, its multinational character, its relations with the Republic of

Ireland, the European Union and the Commonwealth, and its place within the global community (Crick Report, 1998, 6.12-6.14). But, as the Report also acknowledges, the education in citizenship is one element in a broader curriculum. Moreover, this education in citizenship overlaps with, and is reinforced by, the teaching of other subjects such as History, Geography and English. Thus, '[f]or example, the history of Parliament is at the heart of British history and can readily lead into discussion of present day electoral arrangements' (Crick Report, 1998, 7.4). Geography's understanding of 'how people and places are inextricably linked and interdependent' permits an extended knowledge of politics, both local and global (Crick Report, 1998, 7.5). In English, books, plays, poems and newspapers, as well as non-print sources (television, radio, the Internet), provide links to elements of the citizenship education (Crick Report, 1998, 7.6).

These other subjects in the curriculum do not function merely as another mode in which the basic lessons of citizenship are registered, and thus only as a supplementary pedagogic tool. For what all the subjects reinforce is the sense of a particular identity. The education of British children teaches a national, albeit not necessarily a nationalist, curriculum. The history is the history, most centrally, of Britain, of the lives of British people, and of the key events and major figures within its formation. Geography teaches about the particular and localized environment the children inhabit, its defining features, natural resources, climate, and the distribution of its population and principal economic activities. In English pupils are taught principally about their own language and culture, their literary heritage. This heritage is one of writers – novelists, poets and dramatists – who have themselves celebrated and recorded the history and environment of their society. Think only of Shakespeare's history plays.[2]

What education does in this regard is not that remarkable. Our acquisition of a particular national identity is achieved by our immersion in the many ordinary, day-to-day features of our general environment. Each of us is constantly reminded of Britishness by numerous quotidian events and the circumstances of our everyday lives: what is given priority on the news in the press and media, the performance of 'our' sporting representatives, the prevalence of flags, symbols and emblems of nationality in public spaces, the often barely noticed rituals and ceremonies of Britishness. We live, breathe and unconsciously assimilate a national identity. It is one that is 'flagged' in numerous very ordinary ways each day. The nationalism in question is 'banal' (Billig, 1995).

Will this education in the particularities of one's own society be enough to secure a 'sense of common citizenship?' William Galston thinks, at least from an American perspective, that civic education requires more. He advocates a 'noble, moralizing history' containing a 'pantheon of heroes who confer legitimacy on central institutions and constitute worthy objects of emulation' (Galston, 1991, p. 244). Galston believes that a more sceptical, questioning approach to the teaching of one's society's history will be insufficient to ensure that individuals embrace the core commitments of a liberal society. Eamonn Callan thinks that

---

2   See, for instance, the sections on English and History in the *National Curriculum*.

Galston's moralizing civic education is 'sentimental' and one that sustains fictions at the expense of a 'coarsening of moral vision' (Callan, 1997, pp. 105-8). Moreover, the dispositions acquired through such a sentimental education are incompatible with the civic virtues underpinning liberal democracy. A flourishing democracy whose citizenry are active requires that 'civic virtues informed by critical reason ... be widely and deeply diffused among the citizenry' (Callan, 1997, pp. 111-12).

Nevertheless, Callan sees what Galston, and the Crick Report, view as necessary: the grounds for engagement in this, our community. That does not preclude, as Callan acknowledges and the Crick Report presumably also would, a role for rational scrutiny of that engagement. Callan's own solution is to see citizens as the inheritors of a particular political project or tradition who, at the same time, are enjoined to 'make the best of this tradition'. Making the best of one's tradition involves a critical, but optimizing, engagement with one's own country's past and projected future. This stands between a detached 'implacable scepticism' and Galston's politically debilitating 'sentimentalism' (Callan, 1997, p. 113).

I leave to one side what sense can be made of the notion of 'making the best' of a tradition. What is notable in the present context is the talk of '*a*' or '*this*' tradition. The Crick Report speaks of '*a* national identity that is secure enough to find a place for the plurality of nations, cultures, ethnic identities and religions long found in the United Kingdom' (my emphasis). This is a hard trick to make. National identity may be fractured and internally contested in virtue of its finding a place for a plurality of constituent identities. Our nature as individual citizens is marked by a simultaneous fragmentation and proliferation of identities. The point is elegantly expressed by Michael Walzer: 'There are still boundaries, but they are blurred by all the crossings. We still know ourselves to be this or that, but the knowledge is uncertain, for we are also this *and* that' (Walzer, 1997, p. 90).

It is notable then that the majority of Muslims in Britain see themselves first and foremost as 'British Muslims' rather than as 'British' or 'Muslim' (*Guardian*/ICM opinion poll). This is a complex identity to embrace, especially in a Britain that two-thirds of British Muslims regard as failing to see Islam as a part of its mainstream culture. In this context what is the tradition of which the best should be made? Following Galston's prescription, what 'noble, moralizing history' should be taught of this culture? These kinds of question have evident educational import. The Crick Report is optimistic that a national identity which is secure enough to find a place for the plurality of its constituent identities can be taught. However, if that plurality is constitutive of, rather than simply inhabiting, the common identity, then we may face hard choices about how to teach this identity. A civic education could teach, in the face of difference, that there is a single national identity and common tradition. Or it could accommodate difference by representing the United Kingdom's tradition, culture and history in pluralistic terms. Insofar as separate schools still have to teach a common curriculum, that could only mean introducing heterogeneity into the curriculum.

The Crick Report does not acknowledge these difficulties. They might, anyway, seem to be overstated. Forty-one per cent of the Muslim community in

Britain thinks it needs to do more to integrate into the mainstream British culture, as opposed to the 33 per cent who think it has got it about right, and 17 per cent who think it has integrated too much already. Forty per cent approve, as opposed to 39 per cent who disapprove, of the recently proposed new citizenship ceremonies, with a modern oath of allegiance to Britain. Sixty-five per cent approve of a requirement to demonstrate a certain standard of the English language and knowledge of British society (*Guardian*/ICM opinion poll). All of this suggests a willingness by Muslims to be engaged in British society as active citizens. However, it also remains true that British Muslims are unwilling for this integration into society to be at the price of abandoning or diluting their distinctive identity. Moreover, especially for the younger generation of British-born Muslims, being British requires acceptance of their Islamic identity by the dominant mainstream culture (Khan, 2000). Muslims are thus unwilling to compromise on those values which they hold to be central to their identity. For this reason education remains a key area of potential conflict between the British state and the Muslim community. Education is the domestic issue about which Muslims feel most concerned (*Guardian*/ICM opinion poll), and the content of any compulsory sex education has already been the subject of considerable dispute (Khan, 2000).

The Crick Report is to be commended for recognizing that a healthy democracy needs good citizens and that these are not born, but created by an appropriate education. Its outline of that education is laudably commonsensical, tolerant, fair-minded and practicable. However, the Report does not mention or seriously address the issues of multiculturalism. As indicated, it only alludes to the problem by endorsing the values of equality and mutual toleration, and emphasizing the necessity of creating 'common ground between different ethnic and religious identities'. It would be smug to think simply that this is something that Britain does well, as it always has done. In many ways the problems of contemporary multiculturalism are *sui generis*. I have suggested that there are tensions between the creation of an active citizenry, sharing a common civic and national identity, and the persistence of communal diversity. Some of these are less pronounced than thought by others. Some, however, are significant. The Report is most welcome for providing a context within which these can be broached and seriously discussed.

References

Aristotle, *The Politics* (1984), translated by J. Solomon in J. Barnes (ed.), *The Complete Works of Aristotle: The Revised Oxford Translation*, Vol. 2, Princeton University Press, Princeton, N.J.

Arneson, R.J. and Shapiro, I. (1996), 'Democratic Autonomy and Religious Freedom', in I. Shapiro and R. Hardin (eds), *NOMOS 38: Political Order*, New York University Press, New York, pp. 401-2.

Benn, S.I. (1988), *A Theory of Freedom*, Cambridge University Press, Cambridge.

Billig, M. (1995), *Banal Nationalism*, Sage, London.

Burtt, S. (1996), 'In Defense of Yoder: Parental Authority and the Public Schools', in I. Shapiro and R. Hardin (eds), *NOMOS 38: Political Order*, New York University Press, New York, pp. 416-17.

Callan, E. (1997), *Creating Citizens: Political Education and Liberal Democracy*, Clarendon Press, Oxford.

Callan, E. (2002), 'Autonomy, Child-Rearing and Good Lives', in D. Archard and C. Macleod (eds), *The Moral and Political Status of Children*, Oxford University Press, Oxford, pp. 118-41.

Coleman, J. (1998), 'Civic Pedagogies and Liberal-Democratic Curricula', *Ethics*, Vol. 108(4), p. 748.

Department for Education and Employment/Qualifications and Curriculum Authority (1999), *Citizenship. The National Curriculum for England*, DfEE/QCA, London.

Galston, W. (1991), *Liberal Purposes: Goods, Virtues and Diversity in the Liberal State*, Cambridge University Press, Cambridge.

Guardian/ICM opinion poll (2002), *The Guardian*, 17 June 2002, p. 4.

Gutmann, A. (1987), *Democratic Education*, Princeton University Press, Princeton, N.J.

Gutmann, A. (1989), 'Undemocratic Education', in N. Rosenblum (ed.), *Liberalism and the Moral Life*, Harvard University Press, Cambridge, Mass., p. 77.

Gutmann, A. (1995), 'Civic Education and Social Diversity', *Ethics*, Vol. 105(3), p. 571.

Halstead, J.M. (1990), 'Muslim Schools and the Ideal of Autonomy', *Ethics in Education*, Vol. 9(4), pp. 4-5.

Halstead, J.M. (1991), 'Radical Feminism, Islam and the Single-sex School Debate', *Gender and Education*, Vol. 3(3), pp. 263-78.

James, S. (1992), 'The Good-Enough Citizen: Female Citizenship and Independence', in G. Block and S. James (eds), *Beyond Equality and Difference*, Routledge, London, pp. 48-65.

Khan, Z. (2000), 'Muslim Presence in Europe: The British Dimension – Identity, Integration and Community Activism', *Current Sociology*, Vol. 48(4), pp. 32, 41.

Kukathas, C. (1995), 'Are There Any Cultural Rights?', in W. Kymlicka (ed.), *The Rights of Minority Cultures*, Oxford University Press, Oxford, pp. 228-56.

Kymlicka, W. (1999), 'Education for Citizenship', *The School Field International Journal of Theory and Research in Education*, Vol. 1/2, pp. 9-36.

Lloyd, S.A. (1994), 'Family Justice and Social Justice', *Pacific Philosophical Quarterly*, Vol. 75, pp. 356-7.

Macedo, S. (1995), 'Liberal Civic Education and Religious Fundamentalism: The Case of God v. John Rawls?', *Ethics*, Vol. 105, pp. 485-6.

Mill, J.S. (1984), *The Subjection of Women*, in J.M. Robson (ed.), *Collected Works of John Stuart Mill, Vol. XXI: Essays on Equality, Law and Education*, pp. 294-5.

Okin, S.M. (1994), 'Political Liberalism, Justice and Gender', *Ethics*, Vol. 105, p. 38 and pp. 364-5.

Rawls, J. (1993), *Political Liberalism*, Columbia University Press, New York.

Russell, J.S. (1995), 'Okin's Rawlsian Feminism? Justice in the Family and Another Liberalism', *Social Theory and Practice*, Vol. 21(3), pp. 397-426.

Walzer, M. (1983), *Spheres of Justice*, Basil Blackwell, Oxford.

Walzer, M. (1997), *On Toleration*, Yale University Press, New Haven, Conn.

White, J. (1982), *The Aims of Education Restated*, Routledge and Kegan Paul, London.

7

Citizenship Education and Gender

Madeleine Arnot

Introduction

Women, children and the family dwell in the 'ontological basement', outside and underneath the political structure. This apolitical status is due not to historical accident or necessity, but to arbitrary definition .... Since the subject matter of political theory is politics and since reproductive processes have traditionally been assigned to women and have taken place within the family, it follows that women and the family are excluded from the very subject matter of the discipline (Roland Martin, 1994, pp. 107-8).

The aim of the citizenship education initiative in the UK has been signalled as 'no less than a change in the political culture of this country both nationally and locally' (Crick Report,[1] 1998, p. 7). In this essay I shall argue that such a goal does not necessarily entail any attempt to transform the gendered basis of contemporary political culture. Indeed, one could go further and argue that, if we politically educate the nation's children along the lines suggested by the Qualifications and Curriculum Authority, the next generation may sustain established gender conventions in the political sphere and confirm women's position in the 'ontological basement' that Jane Roland Martin refers to above.

The gender implications of the citizenship education programme recently introduced into English and Welsh primary and secondary schools provide the focus of this essay. Gender as a citizenship issue is not easily separable from human rights, diversity, racism or more general questions of discrimination – themes well covered by other commentators.[2] Perhaps because of this, there has been a dearth of commentary on the gender implications of this significant departure in the English curriculum.[3] Or perhaps such a lack of critical analysis is a result of the fact that the Crick Report is noticeably and strangely silent on

---

1   The Final Report of the Advisory Group on Citizenship, 22 September 1998, entitled *Education for Citizenship and the Teaching of Democracy in Schools*, is hereafter referred to as the 'Crick Report'. References to the Crick Report give paragraph numbers.
2   See Osler and Starkey (1996) for an analysis of race issues and Osler, Rathenow and Starkey (1995) on European issues.
3   See Arnot and Dillabough (2000).

questions of gender (Osler and Starkey, 1996).[4] Any discussion of the gender implications of the Crick Report (1998) and the *Citizenship Order* therefore clearly needs to explore the implicit as well as the explicit stances on this issue.

As Chair of the Advisory Group, Bernard Crick was not unaware of gender issues. Recently, when reprinting his early articles, he admitted that he had been 'irritated' and 'a little ashamed' to discover how casually in the past he himself had used the normative 'he' to represent both men and women.[5] Nevertheless he believed that 'progress' had been made since the days when such conflation of the female with the male was the norm. Sadly, precisely such a conflation characterizes the new citizenship education programme and the guidance offered to schools. These materials signally fail to address masculine associations of the concept of citizenship and the different relationships of men and women to it. The new body of political educators appear to have been negligent in not engaging with a major body of Western political thought – feminist political theory; and feminist educationalists seem to have lost an important opportunity to achieve national recognition for gender equality as a guiding principle of citizenship education. As the European Commission argued in 1995, a high priority should be the integration of women into the processes of political, cultural and economic decision-making, over and above their educational success in various European school systems.[6] Yet as I shall show, the new models of political education in schools fail to ask schools to address this agenda.

I shall develop three linked arguments about the possible gender implications of this curriculum reform. The first thread of my argument focuses on the consequences for gender equality policies in schools of the covert but nevertheless relevant tensions between egalitarianism, civic republicanism and liberalism underlying the citizenship education proposals. These tensions are problematic for those wishing to address gender inequalities of power and the consequent discriminatory practices, not least because of the failure to include social equality as a goal of citizenship education.

The second strand of my argument focuses on the important distinction between the public and private spheres, implicit and left unchallenged by these political compromises. I suggest that the masculine marking of the public sphere, which is not even hinted at in the *Citizenship Order*, points to the likely failure of schools to address the specificity of female citizenship and women's association with the private sphere. Here my discussion draws on research my colleagues and I conducted on the gendered discourses of citizenship employed by student teachers

---

4   James Tooley (2000) accused the Crick Report of focusing too heavily on the 'institutionally racist, sexist and no doubt homophobic society we live in'. According to Tooley, this agenda setting report had too strong an awareness and commitment to equal opportunities and gender equality encouraging teachers to bias because they have failed to notice that there is a 'political creed exploding on every page' (p. 145). This claim is dismissed by Crick (2000c).

5   He continued to use this normative gender assumption when reprinting those early essays to sustain the 'integrity of the text'.

6   European Commission's Third Term, Medium Term Action Programme.

in five European countries. Failure to encourage schools to deconstruct such gendered languages and models of citizenship could well render ineffective the advice to schools about including 'equal opportunities' in their citizenship pedagogy.

The third line of my argument takes this analysis one step further and explores the relationship between gender, sexuality and citizenship. Of particular concern here is the assumption of the norm of heterosexuality and its exclusionary consequences. The normative prescriptions about family life in the new curriculum (which are contrasted with a recognition of change in lifestyles) suggest confusion about the values associated with the relationship between the sexes. Here another opportunity for developing more sophisticated contemporary understandings about the relationship between gender, sexuality and citizenship was lost.

Underlying the discussion about what should or should not be taught about gender are assumptions about the relationship of schooling to the promotion of social reform. Before embarking on a discussion of the specificity of gender, I shall therefore first consider the relationship between egalitarianism and citizenship education represented by the Crick Report and the *Citizenship Order*.

Egalitarianism and Citizenship Education

Egalitarianism, and possibly democracy, were to some extent the greatest losses of this curriculum reform. The new model of citizenship education has indeed transformed the English historical tradition of crude 'dead safe, old rote-learning', content-led civics teaching (Crick, 2000a, p 119), not least by extending the sphere of politics into community involvement, and towards active citizenship. However, it has not done so in the name of promoting greater social equality. The schemes of work which the Qualifications and Curriculum Authority is now producing for schools provide ample evidence of the failure to address issues of equality. Materials for the study of business and enterprise, the world of work, and even discussion of human rights and global issues, whilst providing some excellent resources, noticeably fail to refer to the impact of structural social inequalities. The Commission for Racial Equality and the Equal Opportunities Commission are excluded from the list of relevant or useful contact organizations involved in citizenship issues. There is no specific encouragement for teachers to refer to sex or race discrimination legislation other than the Human Rights Act 1998.

In effect, the development of citizenship education represented in the Crick Report, the *Citizenship Order*, curriculum guidance and schemes of work suggests an ambivalence, if not discomfort, about the place of egalitarian goals within the frameworks of political literacy. Garmarnikow and Green (1999, p. 120) comment that the Crick Report includes

> an almost total absence of concern for structured inequalities, especially economic ones; a misrecognition of the political, social and educational hierarchies embedded in social relationships, networks and associations; and the invisibility of inequalities of power as an issue for social justice.

Their analysis of the Crick Report suggests that what has disappeared from the social democratic agenda put forward by T.H. Marshall is

> any notion of serious struggle for rights in relation to both the state and other structures of power; citizenship as changing relations of power; and citizenship as fundamentally compromised by systemic, structured inequalities (Garmarnikow and Green, 1999, p. 120).

Garmarnikow and Green imply that Crick's concepts of the 'empowered' or 'educated' citizen replace – or displace – any central social justice concerns. Citizens, rather than the state, are therefore called on to take responsibility for economic renewal and for building social cohesion. In this analysis, the Crick Report is conceptualized as part of Third Way politics and recent and somewhat diverse theories of social capital. This contextualizing exposes the Report to Garmarnikow and Green's criticism that its liberal progressive tendencies are likely to sustain rather than challenge globalized and dehumanizing economies and 'polarising social inequalities' (Garmarnikow and Green, 1999, p. 121) in ways which, paradoxically, could even lead to authoritarian populism.

Crick's (2000c) response to this critique is not only to deride the authors for their unproblematic location of the *Citizenship Order* in the context of the Third Way (especially given Home Office Minister David Blunkett's rather different ideological approach), but also for misreading the assumptions underlying the *Citizenship Order*. Rather than the Report demonstrating a loss of passion, or indeed displaying timidity in combating social inequalities, Crick argues that its great achievement (the 'gold', as it were) is precisely its success in offering individuals an appropriate form of political literacy, a full sense of civic (moral and social) responsibility and duty, and a commitment to becoming active participants in the society in which they belong. If citizenship education was meant to implement a programme of political reform, to which Crick implies he might have been sympathetic, then there would have been little chance of succeeding in the political climate of the late 1990s. The compromise reached, he argues, ensured that British teachers would teach all viewpoints – they would be balanced and uncontroversial in their pedagogy. However, once young people became active citizens, they might then achieve the egalitarian reforms required in the name of social justice. One of the key means of attaining this goal would be what he termed the 'sceptical' citizen – the development of an intellectually informed scepticism (Crick, 2000c, p. 71).

This tension between egalitarianism and political education raises fundamental questions about the purposes of citizenship education and its relationship to democratic agendas. It points less to the limitations of the Third Way and social capital theory, and more towards other political philosophies, such as civic republicanism and liberalism, both of which are represented in the new curriculum subject. As Quintin Skinner (1998) describes so well, such polarization is about the relationship of the citizen to the state and, more fundamentally, about what constitutes civil liberty. It is a tension which has shaped Anglophone political philosophy over the last three centuries. Neo-Roman political philosophy rose to prominence in England in the seventeenth century, with the English revolution. It was used to attack the English monarchy and to defend American colonial revolution. Skinner argues, however, that by the nineteenth and twentieth centuries it was swept aside by the 'ideological triumph of liberalism', which claimed hegemonic status. Whilst civic republicanism promoted the concept of the individual's duty to the state, liberalism focused on the rights of the individual, which were to be guaranteed by the state.

These different concepts of rights and duties were clearly in Crick's mind when he chaired the Advisory Group on Citizenship. He has now publicly revealed how he found himself cautiously steering a course away from the liberal concept of 'the good citizen', towards the duties of the active citizen required by notions of a civic republic. He reveals this shift in the following comment:

> I often wonder how many of my group realised that they were signing up to the radical agenda of civic republicanism rather than the less demanding 'good citizen' and 'rule of law' imperatives of liberal democracy. The 'citizenship order' for schools provides instrumentalities for this more radical agenda: discussion of controversial issues; participation in school and community affairs; learning skills of advocacy; the idea of 'political literacy' as a blending of skills, knowledge, and attitudes; learning awareness of cultural diversities – the different nations, religions, and ethnic groups within the United Kingdom; all this and more where there was no national curriculum for citizenship before (Crick, 2002, p. 114).

Nevertheless, when challenged on whether citizenship education implied more democratic schools and greater recognition of the rights of pupils within schools, Crick (2000a) responded stoutly that he was proud to be called 'a liberal'. The 'strong bare bones' of the *Citizenship Order*, with its 'light touch order' (Crick, 2000a, p. 66) from central government to schools, was in his view fully justified. Minimal government prescriptions, balanced 'non controversial' teaching, and no pressure on schools to deliver social reform of society were the conditions which were needed to create knowledgeable, skilled and committed citizens. Further, the diversity of school responses to citizenship education would cater for pluralism and social difference.

Crick also developed a line of pedagogic thinking (not all of which was adopted by the Advisory Group) which he considered to be an appropriate form of political education for the future citizen. In this framework, interestingly, he recognized the concepts of *equality*, *democracy*, *tradition* and *custom* as important, but also as too-complex topics for school-based education. Citizenship education, in his view, must provide a basic vocabulary so that the politically literate person can be clear about 'what he or she means by "democracy" or "equality"' (Crick, 2000a, p. 79). From this pedagogic perspective, concepts such as 'equality', 'tradition', 'custom', and 'democracy' itself, are understood as compounds of the more basic concepts of liberty, welfare, representation, rights and justice. These latter concepts, in turn, can be delivered to children through the notion of *government* (power, force, authority, order and relationship); the concept of *law* (justice, representation and pressure); and the concept of *people* (nationality, individuality, freedom and welfare). According to this model, 'equality' as a concept could be taught at an advanced level of political education. However, the concept of 'equality', although initially included in the guidance to schools (QCA, 2000), does not appear even to be mentioned in any later documentation, nor indeed is the concept encouraged as a more advanced second order construct.

Crick suggested almost hopefully that the new citizenship education, defined by its liberal 'softly, softly but gently' approach to the conduct of government and its potentially powerful pedagogy of civic republicanism, might open Pandora's box. The 'irritatingly more unpredictable' free citizens (Crick, 2002, p. 114) 'might become more demanding and more knowledgeable about how to achieve their demands' as a result of 'the more disruptive, unpredictable civic republican theory'. One could not preclude ensuing development of a struggle for greater rights and power. Young citizens would be empowered by scepticism on the one hand, and knowledge and strategic thinking on the other. They would not, in the event, be 'fobbed off' with just 'volunteering' (Crick, 2002, p. 115).

Even so, it is unlikely that this curious mix of liberal and civic republican values in citizenship education will encourage schools to challenge the gendering of public life which still lies at the heart of contemporary society. The continuing association between masculinity and the political sphere, privileged in this curriculum subject, suggests that the impact of this new initiative on gender inequalities in civic life is likely to be minimal. It is to this critique that I now turn.

Masculinity and the Public Sphere

It is not insignificant that the motto of the second wave of the women's movement was that 'the personal is political'. Of central importance to feminist political theorists is the arbitrary construction of 'the political', and its association with the public realm. As Derek Heater (1999, pp. 91-2) rightly observed, the failure of civic republicanism to include, in any substantial way, civic society and the quality of life, as well as a tendency to elitism implied by the high levels of participation required in formal politics, militate against feminists aligning themselves with this approach. On the whole, such a model of the citizen is associated with the involvement of men in formal politics, and their association with the civic virtues of military valour and political activism. 'The civic republican tradition was built on the assumption of practice that being a citizen is a uniquely male function' (Heater, 1999, p. 92). Although 'mellowed' by liberalism, the neo-republican concept of the citizen is still masculinized.

Skinner's (1998) intellectual history of English political philosophy hints at some of the limitations of civic republican (neo-Roman) traditions:

> When the neo-roman theorists discuss the meaning of civil liberty they generally make it clear they are thinking of the concept in a strictly political sense. They are innocent of the modern notion of civil society as a moral space between rulers and ruled ... and *have little to say about the dimensions of freedom and oppression inherent in such institutions as the family or the labour market* [my emphasis]. They concern

themselves almost exclusively with the relationship between the freedom of subjects and the powers of the state. For them the central question is always about the nature of the conditions that need to be fulfilled if the contrasting requirements of civil liberty and political obligation are to be met as harmoniously as possible ... (Skinner, 1998, p. 17.)

As Hannah Arendt (1958, p. 24) points out, the classic Greek philosophers' concepts of a man's (*sic*) private life and a second life (*bio politikos*), built into the concept of *The Republic*, represented an axiomatic distinction between these two spheres – between the world of politics and the family and household. The public world symbolized freedom, and the social inequalities associated with the private familial realm were taken for granted. Arendt argues that equality here meant free from being ruled or being a ruler, as in the household. Modern notions of the distinctions between public and private have transformed these classical traditions. Instead of allocating economic activities to the private sphere, they are now part of the public sphere, as are many other private human activities which are now under closer surveillance by the state. The modern age, Arendt argues, has instead constructed a new concept of a private/intimate sphere outside the much-extended public realm. This separation between the political realm where citizens have a duty to be active, responsible and full members of government, and the private sphere in which individuals are ruler or ruled, in which they might yet live in servitude, is arguably still being sustained. This is precisely the point of conflict for feminist political theorists.

As Pateman (1988) so adeptly analyses, the form of social contract which was defined as the basis of liberal democratic society was also premised upon this public-private distinction. The social order of men was constructed over, and above, the alleged 'disorder of women' implied by their emotionality, subjectivity and closeness to nature. Associated with the social contract was a second exploitative contract – what she called the *sexual contract*. Whilst the social contract formed the basis of a brotherhood of man, a political fraternity which controlled the political order, the sexual contract assigned men the right to women through marriage and control over the household. This latter contract controlled what was represented as the 'disorder' of women with their naturalistic, emotional and subjective qualities. Such a philosophy, although signalling the centrality of citizens' rights, nevertheless constructed marriage and motherhood outside the sphere of such rights, and hence of citizenship. Women were allocated second-class citizenship, with the prospect that their entry into the public, civic world could only be achieved at the expense of massive disruption of this public-private division. The concept of the citizen in this model becomes abstract – an imaginary construct which is premised upon the male models of the citizen worker, the soldier and the voter. Male privileges of citizenship, particularly their power within the public realm, are increased through such an apparently neutral concept of citizenship.

Following from such abstraction, the 'silence' about gender relations in the new English *Citizenship Order* is relevant. References to gender are well hidden in a text which employs the language of 'discrimination', 'human rights' and 'equal opportunities' without any specific reference to under-representation of women in public life, the need to encourage female leaders, the importance of engaging women in civic decision-making or the encouragement of men's civic duties in relation to private life and fatherhood. There is a silence about the importance of challenging a historical legacy which has marginalized the sphere of everyday family life in discussions about rights, duties, justice and freedom. These forms of gender power, which are detrimental to and obstruct the very forms of political, civil and social power encouraged by the *Citizenship Order*, are unlikely to be questioned. Without specific advice to schools to address such political biases, it is likely to be assumed that women's historic struggle for citizenship has been resolved by female suffrage. Contemporary languages of citizenship and their strongly gendered representations of male and female citizens will be left unchallenged.

Let me draw on the findings of a European research project, Promoting Equality Awareness: Women as Citizens, funded by the European Commission, to illustrate the relevance of this last point. Research I conducted with colleagues in Spain, Portugal and Greece in 1995 explored student teachers' conceptualizations of citizenship.[7] The qualitative data generated in this project uncovered some of the different political discourses employed by male and female student teachers. A strong political discourse of duty based on civic republicanism and classical Greek theory was found in countries which had experienced dictatorship, and had provided civic education programmes in schools (Greece, Spain and Portugal). Indeed, these continental political philosophical traditions supported notions of the citizen's duty to encourage democracy above and beyond the action of the state. By contrast, student teachers in the UK (not surprisingly, given their lack of civic education) made reference only to limited political activities such as voting. However, in those countries where a strong civic republican discourse of duty was found, there was a tendency for it to be used mainly by male teachers in the sample. Women appeared neither to use the discourse of civic republicanism, nor to find a position for themselves in it. Female teachers in all national samples were more likely to employ Judaeo-Christian discourses of morality – emphasizing the ethics of care and community involvement – or contemporary egalitarian discourses around social rights and social justice provided by the state. For them the 'good citizen' was more often than not the grandmother, the mother or the carer in the private sphere, rather than the civic leader, representative or voter.

The new generation of teachers we researched saw as important the aims of promoting greater harmony between different social groups, and of encouraging individual responsibility and active participation in society. However, the version of the 'sceptical citizen' described by English and Welsh teachers was supported more by disillusionment with politics than by insightful political agendas (Arnot et al., 1996). The data from this project also suggested that Crick was right to move

---

7   Questionnaire data were collected from approximately 300 secondary student teachers in Greece, 375 in England and Wales, 103 in Catalonia, Spain and 180 in Portugal. Eight single-sex focus groups of male and female student teachers were set up in England, five groups in Greece and two groups in Spain.

the committee away from the notion of 'the good citizen', since this concept tended to elicit (as recently as 1995) class-biased caricatures of bowler-hatted 1950s gentlemen, with associated images of male respectability, employment and 'normal' but 'exceptionally boring' family life. Typical representations of the 'good citizen' by Welsh male student teachers were:

> A middle-aged balding fellow with a nice garden and semi-detached house.

> A citizen is necessarily a nice man in a bowler hat who has a job of work in the city and then comes back to his nice semi-detached house with a wife and 2.5 kids.

The dominance of men in the public sphere was central to the view of citizenship held by most of the student teachers in the countries involved. They appeared to find it hard to conjure up any positive involvement of women in the public sphere. Men were perceived as having most control over policy decisions and public appointments, and an especially strong influence over economic and foreign policy. Women, on the whole, were perceived as having negligible influence on policy and public appointments. Gender and generational differences were noticeable in the UK, although young student teachers seemed less likely than their college lecturers to regard it as important that women should occupy public positions.

This association of public/private with the sexual division of labour was also carried through to the representations of men and women in each sphere. We could not identify any consensus about the image of women in public life in any of the five countries. More than 62 per cent of the student teachers in the UK sample selected the word 'competitive', and 51 per cent chose the image 'powerful', to describe men in public life. By contrast, the representations of women in public life were weaker. Thirty-four per cent of student teachers described women as 'efficient', 27 per cent as 'competitive' and 25 per cent as 'independent', rather than 'powerful'. Conversely, the images of women in private and domestic life were strong ('caring' and 'efficient'), whilst images of men in this sphere were absent or, if present, rather negative. Forty-three per cent of the English and Welsh student teacher sample described men in private and domestic life as 'disorganized', 'hesitant' (31 per cent) and 'dependent' (18 per cent). If left unchallenged, this absence of a collective representation of women in the public civic sphere, and of men in the private sphere, could have major implications for the education of both girls and boys, especially in relation to their adult lives and their future roles as citizens.

Particularly relevant to this analysis is that there were few indications that student teachers felt the masculinization of public life and citizenship could be changed, and that women would be needed to help transform such structures. The source of male power in the public realm was partially taken for granted, in spite of a strong awareness of sex discrimination. Male student teachers in different European countries appeared to collude with differentiated gender roles, and expressed little personal commitment to challenging the masculine associations permeating the public realm. There was apparently a naturalness about male power based on gender role difference. The juxtaposition of power and femininity represented by women in public life disturbed traditional notions of femininity and was expressed as a kind of corruption – women in public life were seen either as over-assertive (autocrats) or as sexually predatory. There appeared in some instances to be a deep anxiety among men about their loss of control over the public sphere, which led to polarized constructs of femininity. For example, men used the distinction between reproduction and sexuality to categorize women in public domains as either mothers and madonnas or whores/sluts/bimbos (Arnot et al., 2000). Women were therefore not represented as legitimately successful and autonomous in public life.

Given these findings, it is noticeable and rather sad that a new curriculum initiative of such historic significance was not backed by major government support for curriculum development work, professional training of teachers (many of whom will contribute to cross-curricular citizenship activities), or extensive, mandatory initial training on citizenship. This lack of government support suggests the processes of deconstructing the old, and constructing new, political discourses around citizenship will not happen. Instead there is the danger of reproducing conventional male and female citizenship identities.

Gender, Sexuality and Citizenship

Thus far, I have argued that liberal and civic republican traditions of thinking not only fail to commit themselves to gender equality, or to challenge gender power, but arguably also fail to give sufficient attention to the masculinization of the public sphere. I wish, however, to advance this argument further. This neglect of gender power has arguably also meant that citizenship status has become closely associated with the institutionalization of heterosexual privilege (Richardson, 1998, p. 83). Feminists have argued that public-private sphere dualism implicitly works with sexualized notions of citizenship which are grounded in hegemonic notions of heterosexuality. This is seen particularly in the celebration of marriage and the nuclear family, and in the social exclusion of lesbian women and gay men. The extent to which the *Citizenship Order* challenges these assumptions and works instead with contemporary social understandings of sexual diversity is disappointing, especially since sexual politics is often indicative of the directions of social/cultural change.

Sue Lees (2000) offers a valuable analysis of the consequences for gender relations of the model of citizenship education being developed in the UK. Her analysis of references to gender, marriage, sexuality and the family in the Advisory Group Report and the *Citizenship Order* demonstrate a failure to take on board the interconnections between the personal and the political. These documents also lack a recognition of the interconnections between sexuality education and citizenship education (although the latter links to personal and social education). Shifts in family life which are very relevant to the civic activity and social rights of both female and male citizens have been well documented. Lees quotes, for example, the facts that by the early 1990s, 27 per cent of births were to unmarried mothers, and that women were marrying later and getting divorced earlier. Divorce has increased sixfold over the last 30 years. Citizenship rights for women as heads of households and single parents are nevertheless limited. Indeed, female single parents are now classified as 'an excluded group' (Lees, 2000, pp. 261-2). The extent to which the *Citizenship Order* recognizes such processes of social change is found in the passing reference to the need for young people, particularly at Key Stage 4, to be taught about changes in personal relationships – they should be taught 'about the impact of separation, divorce and bereavement on families' (QCA, 2000, p. 193). However, the normative stance taken by the *Citizenship Order* in relation to the family and marriage is also problematic, not least because of its confusions and obfuscations. For example, the Statement of Values produced for the Conservative government by the National Forum for Values in Education and the Community (reprinted in the QCA's initial guidance) encourages schools to engage with the diversity of moral values, but at the same time support family and marriage, on the basis that there is a 'general agreement' in schools about such pro-family values (QCA, 2000, p. 195).

Agreement on these values is compatible with different interpretations and applications. It is for schools to decide – reflecting the range of views in the wider community – how these values should be interpreted and applied. For example, the principle 'we support the institution of marriage' may legitimately be interpreted as giving rise to the positive promotion of marriage as an idea of the responsibilities of parenthood, and of the duty of children to respect their parents (QCA, 2000, p. 195).

In the event, pupils at Key Stage 4 should know about 'the nature and importance of marriage for family life and bringing up children' and 'the role and responsibilities of a parent and the qualities of good parenting and its value to family life'[8] (QCA, 2000, p. 193). Employing the notion of 'we' to assume consensus, the document declares:

> We value truth, freedom, justice, human rights, the rule of law and collective effort for the common good. In particular, we value families as sources of love and support for all their members, and as the basis of a society in which people care for others (QCA, 2000, p. 196).

On this basis pupils should be encouraged not just to 'support families in raising children and caring for dependents', but also to 'support the institution of marriage' (QCA, 2000, p. 196).

As Richardson (1998) points out, national security is often sustained by a form of citizenship education which protects a stable model of good citizenship based upon heterosexual (married) nuclear families. As a result, lesbians and gay men have an uncomfortable relationship with the 'nation' to which they belong, but to which they are considered a threat. The restraints on teachers under Section 28 of the 1988 Local Government Act which prevent the schools promoting alternative lifestyles is symptomatic of such a moral panic. Tolerance of gay and lesbian

---

8   Teachers are encouraged to discuss such relationships in single- and mixed-sex groups.

groups is only on condition that they remain within the boundaries defined by society. Richardson (1998) argues that lesbians and gay men are only 'partial citizens', as they are often excluded from civil, political and social rights, left unprotected by the law and the police from discrimination and harassment on grounds of sexuality, and experience prejudicial treatment in relation to social rights of welfare. Richardson argues that lesbians and gay men are thus 'dehumanized' by a 'disembodied' concept of citizenship.

Such contemporary debates about sexuality and citizenship, while often openly discussed in government, have nevertheless not framed the conventional political view of citizenship captured in the Crick Report and QCA's *Citizenship Order*. Citizenship education sustains conventional models of heterosexuality. Had it not done so, the curriculum reform might not have been acceptable to government or to particular constituencies. The compromise which was reached linked citizenship education to personal, social and health education, yet here again we find the failure to engage in questioning gendered power relations. Key Stage 4 pupils are to be taught to be 'aware of exploitation in relationships' and:

- To challenge offending behaviour, prejudice, bullying, racism and discrimination assertively and take the initiative in giving and receiving support ...
- To be able to talk about relationships and feelings
- To deal with changing relationships in a positive way, showing goodwill to others and using strategies to resolve disagreements peacefully (QCA, 2000, p. 193).

However, this neutral language may well not signal to schools the importance of relating issues such as domestic violence, rape and sexual assault and abuse to issues of citizenship. Also, as Hanson and Patrick (1995) suggest, citizenship education should arguably encourage young people to develop

> an understanding of their sexuality, the choices that flow from it and the knowledge, understanding and power to make those choices positive, responsible and informed (Hanson and Patrick, quoted in Lees, 2000, p. 262).

It is here that citizenship education in the broad sense could become an invaluable tool, by offering a set of rights by means of which young men and women could be taught about the way sexual identities are constructed, and how they shape sexual behaviour and orientation. Elucidating these rights would be just as important as explaining the mechanics of contraceptive devices. Extensive sociological research is now available for teachers and schools to draw on to demonstrate how young people construct femininity and masculinity, and relate to each other. Institutional and cultural constraints which shape sexual identities, and the role of sexual performance in relation to normative notions of compulsory heterosexuality, need to be addressed. This kind of education could relate the 'issues of responsibility and moral choice' mentioned in the government reports on citizenship education not just to rights, but also to questions of sexual power relations, the different forms of male and female moral reasoning, and conflicting male and female responsibilities in society. Lees concludes her analysis of the

Citizenship Orders by asking an important question which underlies this whole debate: should citizenship education provide a forum for contesting gender power relations? I describe below what such a critical engagement with gender might look like.

The Pedagogy of Citizenship and Female Agency

There are a number of different pedagogic approaches to gender and citizenship. For example, Patrick Brindle and I found that from 1940 to 1960 most of the citizenship education textbooks adopted minimalist, exclusionary approaches to female citizenship (Brindle and Arnot, 1999). By contrast, civics texts published for girls during this period explored the notion of women's rights and the extent of women's access to, and exclusion from, the public sphere and the exercise of power. The present *Citizenship Order* offered to schools encourages the former exclusionary – rather than the latter inclusionary – approach to citizenship pedagogy. It is much less likely to encourage schools to promote the level of *critical engagement* we found in a small selection of postwar textbooks. Curiously, the Army Board of Current Affairs produced these texts in the 1940s for schools and adult community groups. Similar in politics to the maximal models of citizenship described by McLaughlin (1992), these civic textbooks expected participants to subject every opinion, 'regardless how conventional and seemingly axiomatic', to critical questioning in group discussion. Here was a radical engagement with the social construction of gender in citizenship education. Participants were asked: 'Is the woman's place in the home?' If so, 'Who says so? Women themselves? Men? Society as a whole?'

If we say that woman's place is in the home, do we mean the home is her only province? Do we intend to exclude her from participation in government, public life and social welfare activities? (Williams, 1947, p. 4, quoted in Brindle and Arnot, 1999, p. 116).

Critical engagement with gender issues requires citizenship education programmes which consider what it would mean to have equal partnerships between men and women, equal pay, and a concept of male duty in relation to domestic work. Will schools today really take such questions on board? Will they problematize, as the Army Board did so courageously in the 1940s, not just the distinction between public and private spheres and its implications for women's citizenship, but also the exertion of male hegemonic status in society? Civic education programmes in schools could do worse than bring out into the open, illustrate and discuss these political and gender tensions for a new generation of both male and female young people. Attention could be focused on developing, particularly, what it would mean for girls to acquire a sense of their own agency (Dillabough and Arnot, 2002).

The exclusion of women from public democratic discourses does not necessarily imply the failure of women to engage with politics. The research I reviewed earlier from the European project suggests that female student teachers actively explore hegemonic representations of public and private life, and the forms of femininity associated with each. The way they talked about these issues gave us reason to think that there was an emerging critical consciousness – whether articulated as 'blaming themselves', or as the problem of 'womanhood', or in references to personal struggle. Their comments and observations suggest that, for many women, what is at stake in the political realm of civic life are personal struggles. Women are not represented as powerless – in fact, student teachers identified three sources of female power:

1.   the power of women as mothers and heads of household;
2.   female sexual power; and
3.   feminism as power, that is, feminist challenges to male dominance.

The promotion of female agency and power is a task which has hardly been discussed. Encouragement by schools of female participation in school councils is only the tip of the iceberg. Recent research has shown that, although there are some spaces in schools in which agency, negotiation, avoidance, opposition and resistance can be developed, these pedagogic spaces are limited, especially for girls (see contributors in Arnot and Dillabough, 2000). Often the spheres in which female agency can be developed are constrained by conventional definitions of femininity and by the regulation of girls' sexuality. The rhetoric of equal and democratic participation which characterizes much of citizenship education adds to this by placing girls in a contradictory relationship to civic activity. The model of the 'active citizen' employed is apparently neutral – while sustaining masculine conceptions of citizenship premised upon the subordination of women. If politics were construed not in an instrumental or pragmatic sense, but as a horizon which 'opens up the possibilities of human action and which is a contested symbolic, material and factual terrain', political education would offer the opportunity to create new social identifications and forms of action (Morrow and Torres, 1998, p. 22).

Conclusion

There are still serious disparities between the experiences of men and women in European societies. As the Council of Europe seminar on 'A New Social Contract between Men and Women' argues, these disparities

> … compromise human rights for both men and women, including the right to participate fully as equal partners in all aspects of life. These disparities also have consequences for our societies, which are consequently too often deprived of women's contribution in the public arena and men's contribution in the private sphere. These disparities eventually result in various forms of dysfunction that impact on men and women's lives and will tend to be perpetuated unless we succeed in bringing about a change in the relationship between women and men and in involving men in the struggle (Council of Europe, 2000, p. 2).

Looked at from this perspective, the *Citizenship Orders* are very weak examples of what could have been achieved. The radical agenda of civic republicanism, the humanistic and individualistic agenda of liberalism and the *realpolitik* enjoying the patronage of David Blunkett and New Labour have fashioned a concept of citizenship which does not address the serious disparities between men's and women's lives with respect to citizenship. Citizenship is constructed through normative or exclusionary principles, rather than sensitized to its masculine focus. More often than not, the concept of 'equal opportunities' is used as a pedagogic mechanism for ensuring participation for all in the teaching sessions (DfEE/QCA, 1999, p. 19), rather than as substantive content.

What might the way forward then be? A number of possible ways forward have already been referred to in this brief essay. Any list would need to encourage: integration of sexuality education into citizenship programmes; recognition of community and family as citizenship spheres; recognition of the contribution of women educators in the development of citizenship identities as mothers, teachers and teacher educators; and involvement of women in all economic, political and cultural decision-making. Data derived from empirical research also indicate that the conditions for inclusion of women in public life cannot be separated from the development of male civic roles/virtues in private and domestic life.

If gender equality is to become more than just a silent dimension of citizenship education, official support must be given to developing an appropriate egalitarian agenda for schools. The starting point for this could be any or all of the following initiatives:

1. formation of appropriate networks for the development of citizenship education in relation to gender equality;
2. the development of, and cross-fertilization of, research studies on gender and citizenship education;
3. the promotion of appropriate forms of citizenship education for trainee teachers and educational practitioners, as a means of highlighting and addressing contemporary gender concerns; and
4. the development of appropriate citizenship education curricular guidance and material, to which gender equality is integral.

References

Advisory Group on Citizenship ('Crick Report') (1998), *Education for Citizenship and the Teaching of Democracy in Schools*, Final Report of the Advisory Group on Citizenship, 22 September 1998, Qualifications and Curriculum Authority, London.

Arendt, H. (1958), *The Human Condition*, Chicago University Press, Chicago.

Arnot, M., Araujo, H., Deliyanni, K. and Ivinson, G. (2000), 'Changing Femininity, Changing Concepts of Citizenship in Public and Private Spheres', *The European Journal of Women's Studies*, Vol. 7, pp. 149-68.

Arnot, M., Araujo, H., Deliyanni-Kouimtzi, K., Rowe, G. and Tome, A. (1996), 'Teachers, Gender and the Discourses of Citizenship', *International Studies in Sociology of Education*, Vol. 6(1), pp. 3-35.

Arnot, M. and Dillabough, J. (eds) (2000), *Challenging Democracy: International Perspectives on Gender, Education and Citizenship*, Routledge Falmer Press, London.

Brindle, P. and Arnot, M. (1999), '"England Expects Every Man to Do His Duty": The Gendering of the Citizenship Textbook 1940-1966', *Oxford Review of Education*, Vol. 25(1&2), pp. 104-23.

Council of Europe (2000), *A New Social Contract between Women and Men: the Role of Education*, Seminar Proceedings, Council of Europe, EC/ED(2000)10, Strasbourg.

Crick, B. (2000a), *Essays on Citizenship*, Continuum, London.

Crick, B. (2000b), 'The Citizenship Order for Schools', in N. Pearce and J. Hallgarten (eds), *Tomorrow's Citizens*, Institute of Public Policy Research (IPPR), London, pp. 77-83.

Crick, B. (2000c), 'The English Citizenship Order: A Temperate Reply to Critics', *The School Field*, Vol. 9(3/4), pp. 61-72.

Crick, B. (2002), *Democracy*, Oxford University Press, Oxford.

Department for Education and Employment (DfEE)/Qualifications and Curriculum Authority (QCA) (1999), *Citizenship: The National Curriculum for England, Key Stages 3-4*, Her Majesty's Stationery Office, London.

Dillabough, J. and Arnot, M. (2002), 'Recasting Educational Debates about Female Citizenship, Agency and Identity', *The School Field*, Vol. 8(3/4), pp. 61-90.

Garmarnikow, E. and Green, A. (1999), 'Social Capital and the Educated Citizen', *The School Field*, Vol. 10(3/4), pp. 103-26.

Hanson, B. and Patrick, P. (1995), 'Towards Some Understanding of Sexuality Education', in S. Inman and M. Buck (eds), *Adding Value? Schools' Responsibility for Pupils' Personal Development*, Trentham Books, Exeter.

Heater, D. (1999), *What is Citizenship?*, Polity Press, Cambridge.

Lees, S. (2000), 'Sexuality and Citizenship', in M. Arnot and J. Dillabough (eds), *Challenging Democracy: International Perspectives on Gender, Education and Citizenship*, Routledge Falmer Press, London, pp. 259-76.

Marshall, T.H. and Bottomore, T. (1950, 1992), *Citizenship and Social Class*, Pluto Press, London.

McLaughlin, T.H. (1992), 'Citizenship, Diversity and Education: A Philosophical Perspective', *Journal of Moral Education*, Vol. 21(3), pp. 235-50.

Morrow R. and Torres, C. (1998), 'Education and the Reproduction of Class, Gender and Race: Responding to the Postmodern Challenge', in C. Torres and T.R. Mitchell (eds), *Sociology of Education: Emerging Perspectives*, State University of New York Press, Albany.

Osler, A., Rathenow, H. and Starkey, H. (eds) (1995), *Teaching for Citizenship in Europe*, Trentham Books, Exeter.

Osler, A. and Starkey, H. (1996), *Teacher Education and Human Rights*, David Fulton, London.

Pateman, C. (1988), *The Sexual Contract*, Polity Press, Cambridge.

Qualifications and Curriculum Authority (QCA) (2000), *Citizenship at Key Stages 3-4: Initial Guidance for Schools*, QCA Publications, Sudbury, Suffolk.

Qualifications and Curriculum Authority (2002), *Citizenship: A Scheme of Work for Key Stage 4*, QCA Publications, Sudbury, Suffolk.

Richardson, D. (1998), 'Sexuality and Citizenship', *Sociology*, Vol. 32(1), pp. 83-100.

Roland Martin, J. (1994), 'Excluding Women from the Educational Realm', in L. Stone (ed.), *The Education Feminism Reader*, Routledge, New York.

Skinner, Q. (1998), *Liberty before Liberalism*, Cambridge University Press, Cambridge.

Tooley, J. (2000), *Reclaiming Education*, Cassell, London.

8

The Political Status of Children and Young People

Andrew Lockyer

Under the heading 'What we mean by citizenship', the Advisory Group on Citizenship began their Final Report, entitled *Education for Citizenship and the Teaching of Democracy in Schools* (1998) (hereafter the 'Crick Report'[1]), by setting their view of democratic citizenship in an historical context:

> In the political tradition stemming from the Greek city states and the Roman republic, citizenship has meant involvement in public affairs by those who had the rights of citizens: to take part in public debate and, directly or indirectly, in shaping the laws and decisions of the state. In modern times, however, democratic ideas led to constant demands to broaden the franchise from a narrow citizen class of the educated property owners, to achieve female emancipation, to lower the voting age, to achieve freedom of the press and to open up the processes of government. We now have the opportunity for a highly educated citizen democracy (Crick Report, 1998, 2.1).

The opening reference to the republican tradition is more than a scholarly gesture; it identifies some of the core values that inform the Crick Report. The conception of citizenship it embraces derives from an ideological tradition which begins with Aristotle's *The Politics*, where 'sharing in rule as well as in being ruled' is the essential characteristic of democratic citizenship.

Aristotle recognizes that there are two relevant questions in defining citizenship: who are entitled to be citizens, and what function do they perform? The latter he famously saw to be more fundamental, because what the state asked of its citizens determined who was able to act the part. In democracy 'free birth' was the formal qualification – it was an inherited status – but in practice only the free-born who had the opportunity and inclination to share in public life were functioning citizens. Those who lacked either 'leisure' or right 'habits and training' were citizens 'in name only' (*The Politics*, 1948, Bk III).

The Advisory Group recognize that in classical times a large proportion of the population of states was excluded from sharing in public affairs, and they note with approval the extension of the franchise in modern democracies. However, it is not

---

1 The Final Report of the Advisory Group on Citizenship, 22 September 1998, entitled *Education for Citizenship and the Teaching of Democracy in Schools*, is hereafter referred to as the 'Crick Report'. References to the Crick Report give paragraph numbers.

quite the case that all those whom Aristotle assumed to be excluded from political life are now included. Whether citizenship is viewed as a body of legal rights and duties, or as a set of activities bearing on public affairs, the questions of who qualifies and what functions citizens perform remain critical.

In this essay I discuss the citizenship status of 'the child', and the rights and duties of young people in relation to civil and political activity, in the light of the recommendations of the Crick Report. My use of the term 'child' adopts the definition embodied in the *UN Convention on the Rights of the Child* – the nearest there is to an internationally recognized legal definition: 'A child means every human being below the age of 18 years unless, under the law applicable to the child, majority is attained earlier' (UNCRC, 1989, Article 1). Since the age of majority is taken to be the age at which nationals may vote in state elections, children are defined by their lack of enfranchisement.[2]

Citizenship Status

There is a central ambiguity at the heart of the Crick Report as to whether those subject to education for citizenship are currently citizens, or only citizens-to-be. The question of the citizen status of young people is glossed over not only in the Report, but in much of the writing on citizenship education.

The concept of education *for* democratic citizenship is itself ambiguous. It may refer to the education citizens do or should receive; or it may refer to that which prepares the way for becoming a citizen. There is no suggestion that citizen status is conditional on educational attainment – not, at least, for those with rights to inherit the status.[3] So we can take it either that those being educated are assumed to be citizens now, or that they will be citizens in the future. The focus here is Aristotelian – not on formal entitlements, but on creating actively functioning citizens. This permits some lack of precision.

There are places where the Report seems to endorse the view that those subject to education for citizenship are already citizens. For instance, the Report says that 'It is difficult to conceive of *pupils as active citizens* if their experience of learning in citizenship education has been predominantly passive' (Crick Report, 1998, 6.3.2) (my emphasis). It also cites approvingly, and at length, the views of the British Youth Council – 'so well do they sum up the common ground of many submissions and what we hope to achieve by our recommendations'. The BYC submission says: 'We believe that the most important issue facing young people as citizens is their lack of knowledge about society, its democratic process and their actual rights and responsibilities as citizens' (Crick Report, 1998, 3.20).

---

2   When I speak of 'young people' I am normally referring to secondary school-age children in their teens, without invoking their non-voting status.

3   This qualification is required since the Nationality, Immigration and Asylum Act 2002 in the UK makes the achievement of linguistic competence in English a prerequisite for granting citizenship.

However, the more common mode in the Report is to talk of young people as future rather than current citizens. The curriculum should 'enable young people to participate effectively in public life and prepare them to be future citizens ...' (Crick Report, 1998, 6.9.1). The focus is on preparing young people to 'develop into' or 'become active citizens' (Crick Report, 1998, 2.4); the implication is that during their school years young people are not yet 'fully citizens', either by function or entitlement.

The BYC want 'children and young people's rights and responsibilities as citizens' to be made known to them. They accept that not all citizens have the same rights and responsibilities – 'these change as they grow older' (Crick Report, 1998, 3.19). Clearly, for school-age children, not all the legal entitlements of adult citizens are already in place. Citizenship is not conceived of here as a legal threshold crossed at a specified age; rather it is a series of rights and responsibilities achieved and acquired by degrees. However, the Youth Council's desire for clarity about rights and responsibilities, especially in relation to the 'democratic process,' remains unmet in the Report.

The aim and purpose of citizenship education is said to be the acquisition of 'knowledge, skills and values relevant to the nature and practices of participative democracy'. Education for democratic citizenship is expected to 'enhance the awareness of rights and duties, and the sense of responsibilities needed for the development of pupils into active citizens' (Crick Report, 1998, 6.6).

While the Report incorporates the values of autonomy and respect for individual rights, associated with liberal education, the main emphasis is on preparing young people for active participation in democratic life. This involves more than understanding the practices and purpose of democratic institutions at local and national level (including how political activity relates to 'world affairs and global issues'). It extends to acquiring 'skills and aptitudes', and the appropriate 'values and disposition' associated with active citizenship (Crick Report, 1998, 6.7.1-6.8.4).

Clearly, awareness of rights and duties is not enough. Being able and motivated to perform as a responsible citizen is the intended learning outcome. Viewing citizenship in this way not only leaves open when (at what age or stage of development) particular rights and responsibilities become operative, it also invites would-be citizens to demand recognition of their status, and to act with regard to their rights and responsibilities.

The Crick Report requires preparation for more than the attainment of personal goals and the respect for the rights of others associated with liberalism. It seeks to inculcate a commitment to civic values that goes beyond social awareness, to activate engagement in civil society and political affairs. In accordance with the values of civic republicanism young people must be prepared for, and disposed to participate in, democratic life, and to serve the public good. The critical issue is how far this is possible while young people are conceived to be and are treated as 'children'.

Politically Active Citizenship

Social responsibility, community involvement, and political literacy are the three essential strands of the concept of citizenship (Crick Report, 1998, 1.8). Each involves acquiring knowledge, developing skills and attributes, and embracing relevant values. Social responsibility and community involvement are themselves closely linked – the latter provides a forum for learning about and demonstrating the former. Being 'responsible' means engaging with society's problems, adopting caring attitudes, and being willing and able to behave appropriately 'in and beyond the classroom' (Crick Report, 1998, 2.11).

Beyond the classroom are both the school and the local community. Social responsibility is fostered by 'community-centred learning activities'. These may include the community of the whole school, perhaps communities within the school, and communities beyond the school. The Report suggests the possibility of an 'interactive role between schools, local communities and youth organizations'; and that pupils should engage with the institutions of civil society. This could even 'help to make local government more democratic, open and responsive' (Crick Report, 1998, 1.11).

The third strand of citizenship education, 'political literacy', is seen as inseparable from the other two. In 'a parliamentary democracy', we are told, 'responsibility is an essential political as well as moral virtue' (Crick Report, 1998, 2.12). Here we encounter a major theme long associated with the Advisory Group's Chair, one which makes political education a central plank of citizenship education. It is not enough to teach students about political institutions. They must learn about and be able to engage in politics, which requires deploying the language of political discourse. Professor Crick tells us elsewhere (Crick, 2000, p. 61) that political literacy is itself a 'compound of knowledge, skills and attitudes': it crucially involves both understanding and applying the key value-relevant concepts in political life. The politically literate person is not merely an 'informed spectator', but an 'active participant' able to engage in politics in an effective and responsible manner (Crick, 2000, p. 63).

The Report also makes Crick's point that a good citizen is not the same as a good subject (Crick Report, 1998, 2.2; Crick, 2000). There is a 'secondary sense' of citizenship associated with the rise of nation states, concerned with the conferring of the legal status of subject, but this is an essentially passive conception which does not differentiate democratic citizens from citizens of autocratic regimes. Good citizens in a democracy must be publicly aware and where necessary politically active. They must have respect for the rule of law, but not offer uncritical obedience; they should be able to distinguish between 'law' and 'justice'; and they must acquire the political skills required to seek, where necessary, 'to change the laws in a peaceful and responsible manner' (Crick Report, 1998, 2.4).

There are many reasons that might be canvassed for introducing citizenship education into the school curriculum in Britain now. But the primary aim declared by the Advisory Group is 'to change the political culture of this country both nationally and locally: for people to think of themselves as active citizens, willing, able and equipped to have an influence in public life ...' (Crick Report, 1998, 1.5). In Aristotle's words, citizens equipped for democracy must know how to 'share in rule as well as in being ruled'.

The impetus for this comes from expressions of concern, largely by politicians and academics, about the health of political life in contemporary Britain. The Report speaks of 'the worrying levels of apathy, ignorance and cynicism about public life'. It quotes the Lord Chancellor: '... we dare not be complacent about the health and future of British democracy. Unless we become a nation of engaged citizens, our democracy is not secure' (Crick Report, 1998, 1.5).

While not all the evidence cited is equally pessimistic, there is a substantial body of research which indicates at least 'a weakness in civic discourse', and at worst a disengagement of young people from politics, which schools are currently doing little to combat. The high abstention rate of 18- to 24-year-olds from voting in general elections is one of the indicators giving most cause for concern, even if it is not necessarily a predictor of a trend of 'historic political disconnectedness'. As a manifestation of youth alienation it is nonetheless disquieting – 'things may not be getting dramatically worse, but they are inexcusably and damagingly bad and could and should be remedied' (Crick Report, 1998, 3.1).

The importance of citizenship education as a political initiative does not of course imply that its political and democratic character will be uppermost. The Report cites with initial approval the House of Commons Commission on Citizenship, *Encouraging Citizenship* (1990), for its endorsement of T.H. Marshall's 'three elements' in citizenship – the civil, the political and the social. The Report says that the Commission 'rightly puts greater stress on the reciprocity of rights and duties' than did Marshall. However, 'it had less to say' on Marshall's second element – the right to participate in the exercise of political power. Here the critical tone of the Chairman's voice comes through – 'perhaps' *Encouraging Citizenship* 'took political citizenship for granted (which historically it has never been safe to do)' (Crick Report, 1998, 2.3).

Actually *Encouraging Citizenship* puts its main emphasis on the obligation to contribute to the common good by voluntary public service. Its silence on the political rights of young people is not difficult to understand. Although it cites with approval Aristotle's definition of citizenship, it entirely overlooks the central democratic principle of sharing in rule when it specifies the 'rights, duties and obligations of citizenship' (Commission on Citizenship, 1990, p. 6). The Speaker of the House of Commons prefigures this in his 'Foreword' when he enjoins school teachers to 'tell students about the freedoms we enjoy'. Schools should encourage young people to acquire and practise basic skills of citizenship, including 'the ability to argue a case fairly and calmly, to represent others, to work in a team and plan together'. Young people should also be offered 'the experience of working with others to tackle real problems in their local environment' (Commission on Citizenship, 1990, p. vi). But it is not quite clear whether this 'tackling' should extend to tackling those with political power. It is therefore unclear whether young people are themselves yet to share in all the freedoms 'we enjoy'.

While community involvement and voluntary service may provide experiences which both form responsible attitudes and develop basic skills of democratic practice, it is a further step to suggest that school-age children might learn from political experience. The Crick Report in places tentatively suggests this further step, but whether it carries through fully the implications of this suggestion is questionable. This depends in large measure on whether either the school itself, or the opportunities it affords for community involvement, can provide a genuine forum for the exercise of politically active citizenship. This is doubtful.

School as a Political Experience

The notion that the school either can, or should attempt to, provide a forum for the development of politically active citizenship is seriously contentious.

To take the issue of propriety first, the Crick Report acknowledges at the outset that 'parents and public may be worried about the possibility of bias and indoctrination in teaching about citizenship' (Crick Report, 1998, 1.9). This is a cause of concern in relation to the teaching of controversial issues generally, without giving particular attention either to what is overtly political, or to the notion that political literacy might involve political activity.

The 1996 Education Act, which forbids the promotion of partisan political views by teachers and 'the pursuit of partisan political activities by pupils under 12 while in school' (Crick Report, 1998, 10), is recognized as providing the legal framework within which schools must function. Concerns about leftist agitators indoctrinating young minds (Scruton et al., 1985; Lewis, 1986; Flew, 2000) – which largely led to prohibitions first embodied in the 1986 Education Act (No. 2, sections 44 and 45) – were always exaggerated, but the existence of this legislation has significantly inhibited the teaching of politics (Frazer, 2000).

The Advisory Group's response is threefold. First, the danger of political bias in teaching is not confined to political education. It may equally occur in subjects such as History, Geography and English literature. Second, and most importantly, controversial issues ought not to be avoided. They are part of life, for which children must be prepared – indeed, they 'constitute the essence of worthwhile education', as distinct from training (Crick Report, 1998, 10.4). Finally, and here is a hostage, the professionalism of teachers is to be trusted, although perhaps not taken for granted (Flew, 2000). There are ways in which teachers 'unwittingly or otherwise' might impose their own views on pupils, and the Report offers advice on how this might be avoided (Crick Report, 1998, 10.9).[4]

There is a recurring message that the proposals for citizenship education will make significant demands on the class conduct skills of teachers. With the right teaching approach, pupils will be equipped to debate contentious issues, appreciate different points of view and exercise their own critical judgement. Open class discussion will serve to inculcate what Crick calls procedural values – 'tolerance,

---

4 The issues of identifying and avoiding political bias in teaching are illuminated in the essay 'On Bias' in Crick and Heater (1977) (republished as Essay 3 in Crick 2000), which adds a 'postscript' discussion of some helpful literature on the distinction between education and indoctrination.

fairness, respect for the truth, and reasoned argument' (Crick, 2000, p. 68). These values are more than procedural; they in part constitute, as well as facilitate, liberal education. But they are consistent with ethical pluralism, and appropriate for a multicultural society. Even if such teaching can never be entirely neutral in relation to different conceptions of the good, it can afford equal respect to those who hold differing reasonable views. On the other hand, ethical procedures do not of themselves resolve disputed issues, especially not where they arise from a conflict of fundamental values. Nor is there an easy prescription about what, if anything, to do about genuinely held illiberal or unreasonable views. It is especially problematic when illiberal views are associated with core values which challenge the procedural values, and derive from a young person's familial acculturation.

Moreover, what cannot be assumed is that reasonable classroom discussion is sufficient to promote active political engagement, even if it may assist personal development and provide some relevant skills and attitudes for discursive democracy. Political education (of the sort under discussion) requires experience and action, as well as knowledge and understanding; it is not obvious that schools can provide this.

As we have noted, the concept of political literacy embedded in the Report is a broad one, which takes much of its inspiration from Bernard Crick's well-canvassed view of politics. Politics is concerned with the conflict of ideals and interests and the peaceful resolution of conflict (Crick, 1962). Politics is to be found not only in political institutions, among those overtly engaged in politics, but also in everyday life – in the action and interaction of groups, wherever there are relationships of power and decisions to be made (Crick, 2000, pp. 64-6).

The education process endorsed by the Advisory Group requires in the first place the school, and secondly the locality in which it is situated, to provide part of the learning environment. A crucial aspect, it seems, for learning the lessons of active participation.

Here the 'ethos and organisation' of the school becomes critical to the promotion of active citizenship – 'whether pupils are given opportunities for exercising responsibilities and initiatives or not', and 'whether they are consulted' on matters which affect them collectively, such as 'the efficient running of a school' (Crick Report, 1998, 5.3.2).

Under what are called 'whole-school approaches', schools are enjoined to promote an ethos which encourages pupil participation:

> ... schools should make every effort to engage pupils in discussion and consultation about all aspects of school life on which pupils might reasonably be expected to have a view; and wherever possible to give pupils responsibility and experience in helping to run parts of the school (Crick Report, 1998, 6.3.1).

This may be facilitated through 'informal channels', or by having school or class councils consider matters like 'school facilities, organisation and rules' and (more boldly) even 'matters relating to teaching and learning'. The recommendation to establish schools councils is given major significance by the claim (which some might consider overblown) that they give 'practical first-hand experience of decision-making and democratic process' (Crick Report, 1998, 3.19). If it is to be taken seriously, this explicit linkage of active citizenship with democratic participation in school business has far-reaching implications for the ethos and organization of schools (Griffiths, 1996; Holden and Clough, 1998; Alderson, 2000).

The school is certainly one on the institutions of everyday life where the 'action and interactions of groups' is to be encountered; for school-age children it is likely to be the most important arena of such experience. As a forum for political action, or as a sharing in the exercise of power, the experience is likely to be somewhat limited.

The organization and management of schools in Britain (and elsewhere) have been decidedly undemocratic (Wringe, 1984, 1992; Jeffs, 1996). In the words of Roger Hart (1992):

> Many western nations think of themselves as having achieved democracy fully, though they teach the principles of democracy in a pedantic way in classrooms which are themselves models of autocracy. (Quoted in Holden and Clough, 1998, p. 20.)

Although the ethos in which learning takes place may be more or less autocratic, it is widely acknowledged that what state and most private schools in Britain have traditionally taught best is obedience and social conformity. Young people have been largely prepared for an adult life in which they take their place in the hierarchical organizations and associations of civil society (Adams, 1972; Wringe, 1984; White, 1994). How far this can, or should, be changed is equally questionable.

Even if schools remain a long way from being democratic institutions, they may be better or worse at providing opportunities for the acquisition of politically relevant experience. Pupils can be encouraged to take an interest in the school as a corporate entity and an interactive community, or discouraged from doing so. Genuine pupil-teacher consultation, extracurricular collective projects, participation in effective schools councils, or having meaningful representation on school boards can all be seen to engender positive results (Holden and Clough, 1998; Alderson, 2000).

Where schools take serious account of the views of young people, this is reflected in the self-confidence of pupils and their identification with the school's goals and purposes (Fielding, 1996; Ruddock et al., 1997). Equally, where pupil consultation is minimal or token, they generally recognize this, and it has the opposite effect (Alderson, 2000; Wyse, 2001).[5] However, despite the variations of regime and ethos, what the politically literate pupil will learn, which the illiterate might not, is the relative powerlessness of those like themselves in unequal political relationships.

---

5   Alderson reports that where schools councils are seen by students as tokenism, this may have a more negative impact than having no council at all. Her findings are based on a survey conducted between 1996 and 1999, covering 250 schools in England and Northern Ireland and based on 2,272 questionnaires completed by 7-17-year-olds.

The school itself must be a severely limited arena of democratic practice, but we should consider to what degree schools might promote democratic 'community involvement'. Schools are enjoined by the Crick Report to promote various forms of 'community-centred learning'. We noted that there was particular enthusiasm in official circles for young people having voluntary experience in the community. The concept of 'service learning' has been a much-favoured means of engendering civic consciousness in the US (Annette, 1999); its closest parallel in Britain has been 'work experience'. Doubtless, there is potential here for increasing young people's understanding of society and communities beyond the school, and this might contribute something to political awareness.

Projects which involve the whole class studying matters of local concern (the favoured example is environmental issues) and then making representations to local government (for example, by writing to councils or meeting councillors) may even provide some direct experience of issue-based politics (see Clough in Holden and Clough, 1998, ch. 4). The Advisory Group cite instances of such school initiatives. Presumably community involvement of this sort is behind the claim that it might 'help to make local government more democratic, open and responsive' (Crick Report, 1998, 1.11).

Valuable though some individual voluntary community work may be, especially if it is *voluntary*, and rewarding as some engagement with civic and local political life should be, it is hard to believe that this will enable many young people to feel significantly part of the democratic process. The same may be said of the growing number of projects, fostered by government and voluntary agencies, to enable young people's voices to be heard on matters which affect them (Hodgkin and Newell, 1996). Youth parliaments and councils, focus groups and elected and representative forums may well give school-age children a glimpse or taste of genuine political participation. The more successful these are in motivating young people to become politically literate, the less satisfactory young people are likely to find their lack of political rights.

Reciprocity of Rights and Duties

The Advisory Group, as we noted, commends the Commission on Citizenship for 'rightly' emphasizing 'the reciprocity between rights and duties' (Crick Report, 1998, 2.3). It does so with the suggestion that the liberal approach to citizenship inherent in the work of T.H. Marshall is prone to place too much emphasis on individual rights, rather than on duties and obligations. The form of 'reciprocity' endorsed by the Advisory Group is not self-evident.

In fact, the Commission say that the relationship between rights and duties is 'far from simple'. They do not 'accept there is a simple quid pro quo relationship – a bargain – between entitlements and duties for each individual citizen'. They go on to say both rights and duties have 'validity,' or in other words 'both exist in their own right' (Commission on Citizenship, 1990, p. 7). This suggests that having at least some rights is not conditional upon fulfilling duties, and perhaps vice versa.

It might help to clarify what relationship is believed to exist between rights and duties, when it is said approvingly that they are 'reciprocal'.

At the centre of rights discourse is a claim about the logical symmetry between rights and duties. That is, claiming that X has a moral or legal right, means Y (someone or all others) has a concomitant duty, to act or refrain from acting. According to this view it makes little sense to speak of 'rights' (as Hobbes notoriously does) for which there are no corresponding duties (Hobbes, 1960, ch. XIV). However, there is a separate moral doctrine of reciprocity which claims that for X to be a right-holder – a beneficiary of others' duties – he or she must also be a bearer of duties. It is a further, but related, moral claim that those with duties, or responsibilities, should also have rights. There is nothing illogical about right-holders and duty-bearers being different classes of persons. But where there is respect for human equality, any departure from the moral symmetry of possessing both rights and duties requires justification.

Some entitlements and obligations will legitimately differentiate between citizens and non-citizens; others (human rights) will not. Also, not all subjects or citizens will have the same rights and responsibilities; some, for example, will depend on particular roles or offices. One of the generally accepted grounds for differentiating among rights-holders and duty-holders is their varying capacities for deriving benefit from rights and fulfilling duties. For instance, young children may be attributed non-optional rights – rights to receive benefits which promote their welfare – that others have a duty to meet, without their being deemed able (yet) to fulfil any duties.[6] Only when children become capable of acting as moral agents and thought capable of exercising optional rights (or liberties) might they also be capable of bearing duties or exercising responsibilities.

It is reasonable to argue that the obligations that we have to others are, at least in part, to reciprocate for rights enjoyed (in the sense of benefits received) prior to our being capable of bearing responsibilities. Some liberals may doubt that we can incur such moral debts without contracting to; most will allow, as John Locke does, that children acquire some sort of obligations to a parent who has (with care) nurtured them, if not to the state.[7]

The general thrust of the Crick Report (and the Commission on Citizenship) is that a balance should be struck between teaching about individual rights and learning to carry out duties and responsibilities. The latter are not merely the duties which the rights of other individuals logically entail, they are morally reciprocal with being a recipient of rights. Moreover, the moral and legal duties which citizens have may go beyond what is due to other individuals, to include what is owed to the democratic polity as a whole. This might be expressed as an abstract universal duty (to humanity) to promote 'democratic institutions;' or implicitly, as

---

6   Here I implicitly reject the extreme version of the will theory of rights, which has it that all rights entail the right-holders being capable of choice. See Alan Milne (Milne, 1968; 1973) and H.L.A. Hart in some moods (Hart, 1982).

7   Locke says children have a duty to honour their parents after they have reached the age of majority, though they no longer have a duty to obey them (Locke, 1963, ch. VI).

Burke put it, an obligation to 'a particular nation' of past and future citizens (Burke, 1993).

What is clear is that teaching about human rights is an important part of the citizenship-promoting curriculum, and this embraces learning about individual responsibility and the ethic of service to communities – local, national and international. There is a message conveyed within the Advisory Group's programme for democratic citizenship education – that liberal education needs some communitarian and republican values added.

However, the moral reciprocity of rights and duties in relations between adults and children, pupils and teachers, or young people and society at large, may be neither equitably balanced, nor justifiably unbalanced. The idea that non-optional rights, which are paternalistic, should be the sort 'enjoyed' by those incapable of choice is non-controversial. But that they should be the principal or predominant rights when a young person is deemed capable of having duties, or bearing responsibility, is not so self-evidently justifiable or fair.

Although the official discourse surrounding citizenship education contains much talk of rights and duties, pupils exercising autonomy (or liberty rights) is relatively rarely mentioned. The Crick Report insists that education for democratic citizenship is a statutory requirement, both because of its necessity for the health of democratic institutions, and because it is 'part of the entitlement of all pupils' (Crick Report, 1998, 1.1). It is of such importance it is non-optional. Compulsory education in general is a pupil's non-optional right, insofar as he or she is a beneficiary of it, but it is also a pupil's duty to receive it, insofar as it is for society's benefit. It is both a non-optional right and a duty.

The concept of rights is one of those key terms which politically literate pupils are supposed to have grasped increasingly firmly in the course of citizenship education.

By the end of Key Stage 2, pupils will have an understanding of the term 'rights', along with 'responsibilities, right, wrong, fair, unfair, rule, law and forgiveness'. This will be linked with understanding crime and punishment and the vocabulary associated with criminal justice. They will also have learned about the principal local and national political institutions and understand 'voting and elections'. They will know about 'human rights' in connection with global issues associated with poverty, famine, charity and aid (Crick Report, 1998, 6.12.2). They should acquire the knowledge and vocabulary to discuss human rights in an international context.

By the end of Stage 3, pupils will focus on the rights that affect them more directly. They must understand 'at a basic level, the legal rights and responsibilities of young people with particular reference to the UN Convention on the Rights of the Child, particularly the right to be heard' (Crick Report, 1998, 6.13.2). They will know about 'discrimination', 'equal opportunities,' 'age-related laws' and the 'rights and responsibilities underpinning a democratic society'. They will also know about the European Convention on Human Rights and the UN Declaration of Human Rights, and be able to express and justify their opinions, take part in debates and vote on topical issues and events (Crick Report, 1998, 6.14.1).

It is easy to imagine that pupils who are appropriately skilled and, to some degree, politically literate will want to debate the relationship between their own rights and duties. This may even lead to their reflecting upon their citizenship status. They may notice that young people are sometimes, and for some purposes, considered citizens and at other times not. They may observe that such legal rights as they have are predominantly non-optional and directed towards their future, rather than their current, interests. The optional or liberty rights they do have are, for the most part, conditional or qualified by the rights of supervisory adults. The sharpest pupils may even notice that, among avowedly universal human rights, some apply to all persons at all times, and others only to all persons when they are adults.[8]

Those modestly versed in history and politics will realize that declarations of rights, and enacted legislation, are the products of political processes over which young people have to date had very little influence. Even in the process of the adoption of the *UN Convention on the Rights of the Child*, young people's views were not canvassed (Detrick, 1991). This need not further feed the cynicism of the young. Some may be encouraged by the knowledge that the UNCRC in 1989 was the first international declaration which gave some recognition to the rights of young people to participate in decisions that affect them. They might be seriously encouraged if the growing impact of the adoption of Article 12 could readily be seen within their particular school and wider community.

The sentiments I suggest above may arise not simply as a consequence of talk about rights and duties in the classroom, but from the range of topics which the programme of education for democratic citizenship prescribes. The process of becoming educated in the central ideas of liberal democracy, if it works, means pupils will become increasingly knowledgeable, confident and able to deploy key moral and political concepts. It is unimaginable that the issue of their own political rights will not arise.

Those out-of-class activities may give some taste of politics inside and outside the school, but I suggested they do not satisfy the conditions of democratic engagement. The more successful citizenship education is, the more likely it is to lead to young people asking difficult questions. Foremost among them, sooner or later, will be the question of their inferior citizenship status. It is nothing new that some non-citizens will wish to challenge the status quo; they will have the linguistic means, though not the legitimate political power, to do so.

My point thus far is that the element of 'political literacy' in citizenship education is a bold requirement which it is going to be difficult for the formal education system, as it is currently organized, to meet. To the extent that active political participation is fostered in school or out of school, it is hard to see it satisfying pupils who are becoming politically literate. In the next section I will consider what implications the proposals for education in democratic citizenship might have for familiar arguments surrounding the political status of young people.

---

8   For instance, the 1948 UN Declaration of Human Rights speaks of 'universal and equal suffrage', and 'everyone has a right to take part in the government of his country' (UDHR, 1948, Article 21(1)).

Citizen Status and Voting Rights

Where there is democratic rule, citizenship status is closely linked to the entitlement to vote in state elections. Modern democracies, like classical democracies, exclude sections of their resident populations from sharing in rule. Children are legally defined and socially regarded in part by their lack of political standing. While the temporary status of childhood is not intended to convey the absence of civic identity, the evidence suggests that the early exclusion of young people from acculturation into political life is a condition which many fail to transcend. In the language of classical liberal democratic theory, when they reach the age of majority and are deemed able rationally to consent to membership of the polity, many elect to remain citizens in name only.

To define citizen status in terms of voting rights, and childhood by their absence, is to start with an unhelpful syllogism. Unhelpful, that is, unless it causes us seriously to rethink our conception of the relationship between childhood and citizenship. We might start by viewing young people as already being citizens, with an existing series of rights and duties – not identical with those of adult citizens, but there is a presumption of equality which requires differences to be justified. Then the point at which citizens should be vested with political rights becomes an open question.

There is no space here to rehearse all the arguments for and against extending the franchise to young people. Most contributors to the debate since the mid-1970s (crudely characterized as liberationists or protectionists) have focused on the issue in relation to the general justification of paternalism (Farson, 1972; Holt, 1975; Houlgate, 1979; Scarre, 1980; Purdy, 1992). Those who have recognized its significance from the perspective of democratic theory have been inclined either to view voting as an instrument for registering young people's interests (Schrag, 1975; Cohen, 1975; Harris, 1982; Franklin, 1986, ch. 2), or from the perspective of political legitimacy (Easton and Dennis, 1969; Haydon, 1979; Lindley, 1989). The wider implications of their engagement in civil and public life has not usually been considered. My particular focus here is to examine the significance of the adoption of the Advisory Group's proposals – especially its emphasis on the acquisition of political literacy – for the arguments surrounding the voting age.

First, we must acknowledge that the importance attaching to voting varies substantially according to different views of democracy. In the 'realist' or 'revisionist' account of democratic rule, voting in local and national elections is the principal form of political activity for most citizens – albeit a minimal form of civic engagement. Voting is characterized as exercising the right to choose between the political programmes of competing party élites (Shumpeter, 1943). According to this theory of democracy, voting is a prerequisite of individuals having their interests count. Children's interests cannot be incorporated into the interests of their parents since (by the Benthamite formula) 'each is to count as one and nobody more than one', and the common good is an aggregate sum of each individual's utility. (See Plamenatz, 1973.)

In practice, of course, individual votes are of such small consequence (especially in a first-past-the-post election) that it is hard to see why any rational person should incur the opportunity cost of exercising their vote, let alone incur the cost of informed voting (Downs, 1957; Duncan, 1983). There is little need to worry about voter competence. This view is reinforced by the empirical facts which the realist theorists have long brought to our attention – namely, the low level of political knowledge and interest of the average voter, and the apparent stability and effective functioning of representative government in these circumstances (Shumpeter, 1943). On this minimalist view, education for democratic citizenship can afford to be almost indifferent to politics, including the actual exercise of the franchise.

However, even if voting is only regarded as the periodic registering of a self-regarding preference, it should not be considered inconsequential. While voting in state elections is only a minimum exercise of power, it is arguably sufficient to require those who rule to take seriously the interests of groups who have the vote. (See J.S. Mill's *Representative Government*, 1964.) Moreover, voting contributes to a fair decision procedure, and lends some legitimacy to political institutions and the democratic process (Singer, 1973). From an individual perspective, voting may be regarded both as a symbolic endorsement of the principles of democracy and as an act of civic identification with the ends and purposes of a particular polity (Weale, 1999).

The exercise of the franchise goes beyond both its directly instrumental and its expressive functions. Within the conception of citizenship endorsed by the Advisory Group, voting must be seen as integral to political activity and civic engagement. It must be grounded in a full (or thick) conception of democratic participation. On this model, voting is not the registering of a private preference, but the exercise of a public judgement as to what serves the common good (Thompson, 1970; Barber, 1984). So while voting in elections is itself a limited engagement, it provides the focus for a range of political activities – deliberating, debating, persuading, organizing, lobbying, canvassing, and perhaps declaring partisan allegiance. It therefore supplies the rationale for developing the knowledge, skills and attributes which constitute political literacy. It is the culmination of civic and political engagement.

Thus, as John Stuart Mill insists in *Representative Government*, the right to vote carries the duty to exercise the vote in an informed and independent manner (J.S. Mill, 1964, ch. 8). The arguments Mill deploys for extending the vote to women – even if they have shown no previous inclination to have an informed political opinion – can equally be applied (which Mill fails to do) to those who are currently below the voting age. To give the vote to those previously denied it, is to provide the best motive for leading them to acquire the experience and interest to use it wisely (J.S. Mill, 1964, pp. 290-2). It is in the light of this insight into political education that withholding the franchise alongside promoting education for active citizenship must be viewed.

However, if we regard voting as exercising a judgement about the common good (or 'national interest') rather than registering a private preference, the competence requirement looks a good deal more stringent. There is a plausible case for arguing that participation in the exercise of public power requires the highest level of maturity, worldliness and responsibility (Hughes, 1989). By this standard, it may be a sound intuition to expect personal autonomy to be granted before political power is experienced. It is reasonable to suggest that practical and moral judgement should be developed and exercised in private, and extended to the limited associations of civil society, before being acted upon in the public domain. Yet this exaggerates both the extent of individual responsibility demanded by democratic participation, and the potential for public harm in naïve political engagement.

Education for citizenship requires learning from experience. The empirical findings of the realist theorists have to be acknowledged, even though we might follow Crick in rejecting their complacent inference. The point remains that irrational, immature and ill-informed voting is a common characteristic of modern democratic practice (Harrap and Miller, 1987). The undoubted political illiteracy of many fully entitled adult citizens suggests at least a weakness in denying young people political entitlement on the grounds of their lack of mature capacity. Moreover, if political literacy ought to be considered a prerequisite for democratic citizenship, and if political competence can be acquired to a significant degree by schooling, then the coming generation will be entitled to believe that they are better equipped to exercise political rights than many of their politically uneducated parents. We must at least concede the aim that more school-age children will be better prepared for democratic participation in the future than in the past.

On the face of it, there is a less strong case for denying young people the vote on the grounds of their lack of political judgement than for relying on a claim about their general incapacity (compared with adults). This is not because we can clearly identify a relevant characteristic which all children lack and all adults possess. The facts of human development mean that whatever characteristic we hit upon – 'maturity', 'experience', 'rationality', 'ability to form life plans' – and wherever we locate the relevant age threshold, there will be some 'children' below this age who possess the relevant characteristics, and some 'adults' above it who lack them (Schrag, 1977; Harris, 1982). But a good utilitarian case can be made for having a general age of presumed capacity (Archard, 1996).

Denying young people the franchise is not convincingly grounded on the direct harm that might be a consequence of their voting (however we conceive of this activity). The view that it would change the democratic system for the worse is equally implausible, if extending the franchise is considered as an accompaniment of the receipt of effective political education. The strongest case for withholding the vote from young people is that granting full political rights may be incompatible with treating them with privileged paternalism. It may be deemed inconsistent to grant the franchise without also granting full adult autonomy. As Laura Purdy argues, if children were 'equal citizens' they could not be compelled to attend school, or be subject to protective parental supervision, or enjoy those other non-optional 'benefits' which we assign to them (Purdy, 1992).[9]

Although the prerequisites for the exercise of competent choice in domestic and political life are different, as are the ill-effects of incompetence, there is a

---

9   Whether such paternalism does in fact serve the young people's interests rather than those of adults is, of course, what liberationists challenge.

plausible case for linking personal autonomy and political rights. Leaving aside the minimal effect of voting, it is theoretically sound to argue that if someone is not permitted to be the best judge of their own interests, they ought not to be considered capable of exercising a judgement which affects others, or bears upon the common interest. This suggests that there is something to be said for linking political rights and autonomy rights with a shared presumption (or fiction) of competence and incompetence.

There are some grounds for setting different age thresholds for different entitlements and activities. For instance, the minimum age of criminal responsibility may perhaps justifiably be below the age of consent to marry; and there is a case for setting different age thresholds for political capacity – distinguishing, for example, between the ages for voting and holding office. This said, there are overwhelming practical and symbolic reasons for having a single age of general capacity – an age of majority – when full legal capacity, personal consent and political consent, as registered by the right to vote, coalesce.

Conclusion

Teaching citizenship will have to address the issue of the inferior status of young people. There is no good reason to define citizenship by the attainment of the age of majority, so children may be regarded as citizens with some rights and responsibilities before they can exercise political rights.

However, I have argued that political literacy, which is a central plank of citizenship education, requires political participation. Politically active citizenship is inadequately experienced without the recognition afforded and the incentive provided by having the right to vote.

There is already a growing demand, among young people's representatives and agencies concerned with encouraging political participation, that the voting age in Britain should be reduced to 16. The Electoral Commission are currently considering the general case. The Commission on Local Governance has already proposed voting at 16 in local elections, and reducing the minimum age for standing as a local councillor from 21 to 18 (Commission on Local Governance, 2002). The Electoral Reform Society are leading a 'Votes at 16 Campaign', with extensive support from groups which represent young people.[10]

Surveys suggest that the majority of young people believe that if they are old enough to leave school, leave home, pay taxes and serve in the armed forces, they ought to be entitled to vote. Moreover, there is evidence that many young people want to be more involved in public affairs (White et al., 2000; Combe, 2002; NYA, 2002), and that acquiring the vote would induce others to interest themselves in its use (Lister et al., 2001; Eden and Rocker, 2002). The case made that those who are old enough to fight for their country and pay taxes to support international wars

---

10 These include the British Youth Council, the YMCA, the National Youth Agency, the Children's Rights Alliance for England, and Article 12 in Scotland, amongst others (NYA, 2002; CRAE, 2002; CYPU, 2002; Tammi, 2000).

should be entitled to vote on political issues, including matters of war and peace, invokes a concept which of late has acquired increasing salience.

I have focused on political literacy, but the citizenship programme is committed to other aspects of both community involvement and personal development. The exercise of responsible judgement, in all spheres, is learned by being practised. Introducing citizenship education into the school curriculum will not guarantee a participatory democracy, but it may just create a climate in which young people themselves will influence the future of democratic institutions – including the democratic franchise.

References

Adams, P. (1972) (ed.), *Children's Rights: Towards the Liberation of the Child*, Panther Books, London.

Advisory Group on Citizenship ('Crick Report') (1998), *Education for Citizenship and the Teaching of Democracy in Schools*, Final Report of the Advisory Group on Citizenship, 22 September 1998, Qualifications and Curriculum Authority, London.

Alderson, P. (2000), 'School Students' Views on School Councils and Daily Life at School', *Children and Society*, Vol. 14, pp. 121-34.

Annette, J. (1999), 'Education for Citizenship, Civic Participation and Experiential and Service Learning in the Community', The School Field: Theorising Citizenship Education II, *International Journal of Theory and Research in Education*, Vol. X (3&4), pp. 85-102.

Archard, D. (1996), 'The Age of Majority', in I. Hampser-Monk and J. Stanyer (eds), *Contemporary Political Studies Vol. 1*, Political Studies Association, Exeter, pp. 520-28.

Aristotle (1948), *The Politics*, ed. Ernest Barker, Oxford University Press, Oxford.

Barber, B. (1984), *Strong Democracy: Participatory Politics for a New Age*, University of California Press, London.

Burke, E. (1987), *Reflections on the Revolution in France*, ed. J. Pocock, Hackett Publishing Company, Cambridge.

Burke, E. (1993), *Reflections on the Revolution in France*, ed. L.G. Mitchell, Oxford University Press, Oxford.

Children and Young People Unit (CYPU) (2002), *A Report on Yvote?/Ynot? Project*, CYPU, London, *www.cypu.gov.uk*.

Children's Rights Alliance for England (CRAE) (2002), *The REAL Democratic Deficit*, CRAE, London, *www.crights.org*.

Cohen, C. (1975), 'On the Child's Status in the Democratic State. A Response to Mr Schrag', *Political Theory*, Vol. 3, pp. 458-64.

Combe, V. (2002), *Up For It: Getting Young People Involved in Local Government*, The National Youth Agency, Joseph Rowntree Foundation, London, *www.jrf.org.uk*.

Commission on Citizenship (1990), *Encouraging Citizenship*, Her Majesty's Stationery Office, London.

Commission on Local Governance (2002), *Free to Differ: The Future for Local Democracy*, LGIU, London, *www.lgiu.gov.uk*.

Crick, B. (1962 and 4th ed., 1992), *In Defence of Politics*, Penguin, London.

Crick, B. (2000), *Essays on Citizenship*, Continuum, London.

Crick, B. and Heater, D. (1977), *Essays on Political Education*, Falmer Press, Lewes.

Detrick, S. (1991) (ed.), *The United Nations Convention on the Rights of the Child – A Guide to the 'Travaux Préparatoires'*, Martinus Nijhoff, Dordrecht.

Downs, A. (1957), *An Economic Theory of Democracy*, Harper and Row, New York.

Duncan, G. (ed.) (1983), *Democratic Theory and Practice*, Cambridge University Press, Cambridge.

Easton, D. and Dennis, J. (1969), *Children in the Political System: Origins of Political Legitimacy*, McGraw-Hill, New York.

Eden, K. and Rocker, D. (2002), *'...Doing Something': Young People as Social Actors*, Youth Work Press, Leicester.

Farson, R. (1972), *Birthrights*, Macmillan, London.

Fielding, M. (1996), 'Beyond School Effectiveness and School Improvement: Lighting the Slow Fuse of Possibility', *The Curriculum Journal*, Vol. 8(1), pp. 7-27.

Flew, A. (2000), *Education for Citizenship*, Institute of Economic Affairs, London.

Franklin, B. (1986), 'Children's Political Rights', in B. Franklin, *The Rights of Children*, Blackwell, Oxford.

Frazer, E. (2000), 'Citizenship Education: Anti-political Culture and Political Education in Britain', *Political Studies*, Vol. 48(1), pp. 88-103.

Griffiths, R. (1996), 'New Powers for Old: Transforming Power Relationships', in M. John (ed.), *Children in Our Charge: The Child's Right to Resources*, Jessica Kingsley, London.

Harrap, M. and Miller, W. (1987), *Elections and Voters*, MacMillan, Basingstoke.

Harris, J. (1982), 'The Political Status of the Child', in K. Graham (ed.), *Contemporary Political Philosophy*, Cambridge University Press, Cambridge.

Hart, H.L.A. (1982), 'Legal Rights', in H.L.A. Hart, *Essays on Bentham: Jurisprudence and Political Theory*, Clarendon Press, Oxford.

Hart, R. (1992), *Children's Participation: From Tokenism to Citizenship*, UNICEF International Child Development Centre, Florence.

Haydon, G. (1970), 'Political Theory and the Child: Problems of the Individualist Tradition', *Political Studies*, Vol. 17(3), pp. 405-20.

Hobbes, T. (1960), *Leviathan*, ed. M. Oakeshott, Blackwell, Oxford.

Hodgkin, R. and Newell, P. (1996), *Effective Government Structures for Children: The Report of a Gulbenkian Foundation Inquiry*, Calouste Gulbenkian Foundation, London.

Holden, C. and Clough, N. (1998), *Children as Citizens: Education for Participation*, Jessica Kingsley, London.

Holt, J. (1975), *Escape from Childhood: The Needs and Rights of Children*, Penguin, Harmondsworth.

Houlgate, L. (1979), 'Children, Paternalism and Rights to Liberty', in O. O'Neill and W. Ruddick, *Having Children: Philosophical and Legal Reflections on Parenthood*, Oxford University Press, Oxford.

Hughes, J. (1989), 'Thinking About Children', in G. Scarre (ed.), *Children, Parents and Politics*, Cambridge University Press, Cambridge.

Jeffs, T. (1996), 'Children's Educational Rights in a New Era', in B. Franklin (ed.), *The Handbook of Children's Rights*, Routledge, London.

Lewis, J. (1986) (ed.), *The House of Lords Debate: Educational Indoctrination*, Policy Research Associates, London.

Lindley, R. (1989), 'Teenagers and Other Children', in G. Scarre (ed.), *Children, Parents and Politics*, Cambridge University Press, Cambridge.

Lister, R., Middleton, S. and Smith, N. (2001), *Young People's Voices: Citizenship Education*, Youth Work Press, Leicester.

Locke, J. (1963), *Two Treatises on Government*, ed. P. Laslett, Cambridge University Press, Cambridge.

Mill, J.S. (1964), *Utilitarianism, On Liberty and Representative Government*, ed. A. Lindsay, Everyman, Dent, London.

Milne, A. (1968), *Freedom and Rights: A Philosophical Synthesis*, Allen and Unwin, London.

Milne, A. (1973), 'Philosophy and Political Action: The Case of Civil Rights', *Political Studies*, Vol. 21(4), pp. 453-80.

National Youth Agency (NYA) (2002), 'Lowering the Voting Age', *Spotlight Issues*, Vol. 5: July, NYA, Leicester, *www.nya.org.uk*.

Plamenatz, J. (1973), *Democracy and Illusion*, Longman, London.

Purdy, L. (1992), *In Their Best Interests: The Case against Equal Rights for Children*, Cornell University Press, New York.

Ruddock, J., Wallace, G. and Day, J. (1997), 'Student Voices: What They Can Tell Us As Partners in Change', in K. Scott and Z.N. Trafford (eds), *Partners in Change: Shaping the Future*, Middlesex University, London.

Scarre, G. (1980), 'Children and Paternalism', *Philosophy*, Vol. 55, pp. 117-24.

Schrag, F. (1975), 'The Child's Status in the Democratic State', *Political Theory*, Vol. 3, pp. 441-56.

Schrag, F. (1977), 'The Child and the Moral Order', *Philosophy*, Vol. 52, pp. 167-77.

Scruton, R., Ellis-Jones, A. and O'Keefe, D. (1985), *Education and Indoctrination*, Education Research Centre, London.

Shumpeter, J. (1943), *Capitalism, Socialism and Democracy*, Allen and Unwin, London.

Singer, P. (1973), *Democracy and Disobedience*, Clarendon Press, Oxford.

Tammi, L. (2000), *The Voting Age in Scotland ... Young People Have Their Say* (Article 12 in Scotland), *www.article12.org*.

Thompson, D. (1970), *The Democratic Citizen*, Cambridge University Press, Cambridge.

Trafford, B. (1997), *Participation, Power Sharing and School Improvement*, English Heretics, Nottingham.

UNCRC (1989), *United Nations Convention on the Rights of the Child*, UNICEF, Calouste Gulbenkian, UNA.

Weale, A. (1999), *Democracy*, MacMillan, Basingstoke.

White, C., Bruce, S. and Ritchie, J. (2000), *Young People's Politics: Political Interest and Engagement amongst 14-to 24-Year-Olds*, York Publishing Service, York.

White, P. (1994), *Beyond Dominion: An Essay in the Political Philosophy of Education*, Routledge, London.

Wringe, C. (1984), *Democracy, Schooling and Political Education*, Allen and Unwin, London.

Wyse, D. (2001), 'Felt Tip Pens and Schools Councils: Children's Participation Rights in Four English Schools', *Children and Society*, Vol. 15, pp. 209-18.

9

Community, Politics and Citizenship Education

John Annette

Introduction

Why is there an increasing interest in community and community involvement? In contemporary political thinking it has become both philosophically and 'politically' significant. Community has increasingly become the focus of government policy in the UK and the USA. From the 'Third Way' communitarianism of New Labour to the emergence of Compassionate Conservatism, the idea of community is now seen as a key to rethinking the relationship between civil society and the state. Government social policy concerning neighbourhood renewal and urban renaissance stresses the role of citizens in inner-city areas in designing and rebuilding their communities (Sirianni and Friedland, 2002; Taylor, 2003). The Neighbourhood Renewal Programme of the Office of the Deputy Prime Minister is calling for new ideas on community enterprise, community safety, healthy communities, sustainable communities and learning communities. According to Home Secretary David Blunkett, 'Our challenge today is to provide a meaningful sense of belonging and community engagement, which can be both robust and adaptable in the face of wider change' (Blunkett, 2001, p. 22). Linked to this challenge is the perceived sense of loss of community in contemporary British society. This has been associated with the idea of social capital, popularized by Robert Putnam in his study of the decline of civic engagement and social capital in the USA (Putnam, 2000). The concept of social capital has provided a theoretical basis for understanding the importance of community which, according to the neo-Tocquevillian analysis of Robert Putnam and his colleagues, has important consequences for citizenship and political participation.

In contemporary political and sociological theory there has been a renewed interest in the idea of community (Bauman, 2000; Delanty, 2003). The concept of community is elastic, allowing for an enormous range of meanings. From virtual communities to imaginary communities, conceptual understandings of community are to be found in a wide range of traditions of thought and academic disciplines. (A number of contemporary writers offer alternative ways of representing the varying understandings of the meaning of community – cf. Delanty, 2003; Frazer, 1999; Nash, 2002; Taylor, 2003.) I would argue that there are at least four main ways of conceptualizing community. The first way is to consider community descriptively as a place or neighbourhood. Thus the government's Neighbourhood Renewal Strategy talks about revitalizing communities primarily in terms of neighbourhoods. The second approach – discussing community as a normative ideal linked to respect, solidarity and inclusion – can be found in the now well-established debate between liberalism and its communitarian critics (Mulhall and Swift, 1996). The third way of understanding community is based on the construction of cultural identities, can be found in communities of 'interest' and is based on a politics of identity and recognition of difference. The fourth is to regard community as a political ideal which is linked to participation, involvement and citizenship, especially at the level of the community. It is this final way of understanding the meaning of the concept 'community' that I want to explore in this essay. It is the case, of course, that these conceptual understandings of community are often elided and combined to produce hybrid conceptualizations of contemporary community. Thus a political understanding of community may be based in a specific neighbourhood where there are public places, and may include a variety of communities of identity or interest. It is the case, of course, that political communitarianism can be understood by analysing the politics of community in terms of liberalism, communitarianism or civic republicanism. For example, in her important critique of political communitarianism Elizabeth Frazer recognizes that it is informed by philosophical communitarianism and its critique of liberal political theory. She also considers the philosophical and social-psychological basis of political communitarianism in terms of its social constructionism (Frazer, 1999, ch. 4), which involves questions of interpreting the meaning of communities of identity.

In considering community in terms of political and civic engagement, I want to analyse what role it plays in developing an education for democratic citizenship. This will also involve examining whether or not 'service learning', or learning through volunteering or community involvement, can provide a basis for constructing an education for democratic citizenship. I will argue that there is a significant difference between learning through volunteering with social capital as a learning outcome of citizenship education, and learning through community involvement with democratic citizenship, which involves an understanding of the political basis of community as a learning outcome.

Community, Communitarianism and Politics

The concept of community is central to the now-disappearing debate between liberal political thinkers and their communitarian critics. This debate has come to lose its focus. We now have liberal political thinkers integrating communitarian criticisms into their liberal political theory – or liberal communitarians like Michael Sandel, Charles Taylor, Michael Walzer or Alastair MacIntyre rejecting the label of communitarianism and responding (with the exception of MacIntyre) to liberal concerns. According to David Miller (Miller, 2000, ch. 6, 'Communitarianism: Left, Right and Centre'), it is unclear what actually constitutes the political theory of communitarianism, as distinct from a rhetorical concern about the decline of family and community. Andrew Mason (2000), in his study of the different levels of community and their normative significance, looks from a liberal perspective at the need for communities to be pluralistic and inclusive. He takes issue, for example, with David Miller's argument that a politics of the common good requires a shared national identity. While recognizing the need for a shared political identity, he analyses the limitations these overarching political identities have at lower levels of community. In a more recent study of the 'politics of community', Adrian Little attempts to consider the political implications of the theorization of community, and in doing so sketches out an agenda for a 'radical communitarianism' (Little, 2002). This is in some ways analogous to David Miller's attempt to theorize a 'left communitarianism', as distinct from a neo-conservative communitarianism. In particular, this radical communitarianism is seen in contrast with the prescriptivism of the neo-conservative communitarianism of Amitai Etzioni (1995) and some of his followers. The ideological division between civic republican communitarianism and neo-conservative communitarianism is not always clear-cut, and there is often an elision between the two positions in popular political discourse. New Democrat and New Labour policy statements often elide both ideological positions – voluntary and community sector involvement is seen both as limiting the sphere of the state and also as a way of working in partnership with the state. This has led conservative critics like Bruce Frohnen to view communitarianism as inherently a cover for community-based social democratic politics (Frohnen, 1996; Carey and Frohnen, 1998), while some left critics view communitarianism as inherently neo-liberal.

Community, Politics and Civic Republicanism

Following Elizabeth Frazer's distinction between a 'philosophical communitarianism' and a 'political communitarianism' (Frazer, 1999), Adrian Little raises some important questions about the apolitical conception of community in communitarianism. He writes:

> As such, the sphere of community is one of contestation and conflict as much as it is one of agreement. Thus, essentially, it is deeply political. Where orthodox communitarians see politics as something to be overcome to the greatest possible extent, radicals argue that the downward devolution of power will entail more politics rather than less (Little, 2002, p. 154).

In their studies of political communitarianism, both Little and Frazer regard the revival of civic republicanism as emerging from the debate between liberal and communitarian conceptions of the politics of community. In civic republicanism (see Oldfield, 1990; Maynor, 2003) freedom consists in active self-government, and liberty is not simply negative liberty, but active participation in a political community. According to Home Secretary David Blunkett:

The 'civic republican' tradition of democratic thought has always been an important influence for me … This tradition offers us a substantive account of the importance of community, in which duty and civic virtues play a strong and formative role. As such, it is a tradition of thinking which rejects unfettered individualism and criticises the elevation of individual entitlements above the common values needed to sustain worthwhile and purposeful lives. We do not enter life unencumbered by any community commitments, and we cannot live in isolation from others' (Blunkett, 2001, p. 19).

It is this civic republican conception of politics which, I would argue, animates the Crick Report[1] on education for citizenship, the new curriculum for citizenship and some aspects of New Labour's strategy for revitalizing local communities.

Community, Community Involvement and Local Political Participation

Elizabeth Frazer's analysis of political communitarianism examines the importance of, and difficulties associated with, locality in understanding community and political communitarianism. While some political communitarians have a nostalgic view of community, many of the philosophical communitarians (e.g. MacIntyre, Walzer and Taylor) have a more ambiguous view of the importance of local communities. This parallels the importance given to community involvement in the debate about how we can understand the usage of the concept of social capital and its supposed decline.

An increasing number of political scientists, for example Robert Putnam, are noting the decline of 'social capital' – represented by a decrease in participation in public affairs and voluntary and community activity – and are expressing a growing concern about the vitality of civil society (Putnam, 2000; Hall, 2002). The evidence in the UK is complex, and a recent study indicates that while 'social capital' is still strong, there is also a serious decline in public 'trust' (Hall, 2002). The Tocquevillian assumptions underlying Putnam's analysis of social capital presuppose a correlation between social capital and active citizenship. However, without levels of political understanding and a learning framework for the development of active citizenship (including non-formal and informal learning), it is not clear how social capital necessarily produces active citizenship (Edwards et al., 2001). A 'strong democrat' like Benjamin Barber argues for the importance of civil society in maintaining a participatory community by the maintenance of public spaces for civic participation (Barber, 1984; 1998a; 1998b). According to Barber:

---

1   The Final Report of the Advisory Group on Citizenship, 22 September 1998, entitled *Education for Citizenship and the Teaching of Democracy in Schools*, is hereafter referred to as the 'Crick Report'. References to the Crick Report give paragraph numbers.

We live today in Tocqueville's vast new world of contractual associations – both political and economic – in which people interact as private persons linked only by contract and mutual self-interest, a world of diverse groups struggling for separate identities through which they might count for something politically in the national community (Barber, 1998a, p. 42).

For Barber, the fundamental problem facing civil society is the challenge of providing citizens with the requisite skills:

... the literacy required to live in a civil society, the competence to participate in democratic communities, the ability to think critically and act deliberately in a pluralist world, the empathy that permits us to hear and thus accommodate others, all involve skills that must be acquired (Barber, 1992, p. 128).

As we will see later, Benjamin Barber and other political analysts see education for citizenship through civic participation as a key factor in maintaining civic virtue and active citizenship.

What is the role of community involvement and local political participation in an education for democracy in the UK? According to J.S. Mill, local democratic government not only creates the opportunity for political participation, it also provides the basis for an education for citizenship. It is a concept of citizenship based on a civic republican model of active or participatory citizenship, in contrast with the liberal individualist or communitarian conceptions (Faulks, 2000). Gerry Stoker writes: 'Local government should not be defined by its task of service delivery; rather it should be valued as a site for political activity' (Stoker, 1996, p. 194). While research has highlighted the problem of addressing the 'democratic deficit' in the UK nationally, there is also a growing literature on the 'crisis of local democracy' in the UK (e.g. King and Stoker, 1996; Pratchett and Wilson, 1996). Recently the Local Government White Paper, *Modern Local Government: In Touch With the People* (DETR, 1998), called for a democratic renewal which would include enhancing political participation and extending local authority and community leadership to promote the economic, social and environmental 'well-being' of local areas. These ideas are embedded in the Local Government Act 2000. Local authorities are currently facing up to the challenge of developing new ways of involving communities in local governance.

I would like briefly to explore how enhancing political participation in local and regional governance through community involvement could make a contribution to the renewal of democracy in the UK, and provide an education for active citizenship. The main challenge to implementing such developments is the question of whether local political authorities are willing and able to move beyond a politics of consumer satisfaction and public consultation, to a more deliberative and participatory democratic politics. Lawrence Pratchett argues for 'a new democratic polity which not only improves the effectiveness of existing practices but also draws upon different components of direct, consultative, deliberative and representative democracy to create a new democratic order' (Pratchett, 2000, p. 9).

The new democratic politics would include referendums, consultative activities and deliberative participation.

There is increasing interest in the deliberative democracy activities which have been advocated by the Local Government Association and follow on from the work of the Commission for Local Democracy, 1993-1995 and the ESRC research programme on 'Local Governance', 1992-1997. The evidence indicates that local governance now includes a growing repertoire of approaches which can encourage public participation. As Pratchett notes, these activities in themselves cannot establish a more deliberative democracy, but as part of a wider reform package they can provide the basis for realizing such a deliberative form of democratic politics (Pratchett, 2000). As local authorities establish 'local strategic partnerships' as part of their statutory obligation to involve local communities in developing 'community strategies', and also for areas which receive neighbourhood renewal funding, they can adopt an enormous variety of innovative approaches (Taylor, 2003). This reflects a gradual shift from local government to governance, and includes participation by a range of social networks which can generate both social capital and active citizenship.

Apart from the problem of the levels and forms of participation, another of the key issues underlying development of a deliberative democratic politics is the problem of social exclusion. To what extent do these new forms of deliberative democratic politics address the need to take into account an identity politics based on education, class, gender, race, ethnicity and disability? (Lister, 2003). Other important questions at the local level of governance are 'How do we define political participation?' and 'What should the role of the voluntary and community sectors in local democratic politics be?'

The 'politics' of urban regeneration, and the growing importance of the 'voluntary' and 'community' sectors as well as residents' groups, provide the context for growth in the European Social Fund (ESF), the Single Regeneration Budget (SRB) and New Deal for Communities (NDC) programmes, and now Neighbourhood Renewal-funded community development and partnership working in the UK. This gives another focus to studying 'political' participation in the UK, and to the creation of new opportunities for lifelong learning for active citizenship. The concept of 'community leadership' from below is based on a partnership between local government and residents' associations as well as voluntary and community sector organizations (see Taylor, 2003). This partnership working entails creating new forms of consultation and involvement of local people. (Of particular note is the work of the Community Development Foundation.) More recently, the Urban Forum has supported community involvement in Local Strategic Partnerships funded by the community empowerment fund of the Neighbourhood Renewal Programme. It is too soon to have any reliable information on the overall nature of the neighbourhood renewal programme and the success of local strategic partnerships. We know, for example, that electoral turnout has been greater for the election of New Deal for Community Boards in some areas than ward results for local elections. There seems to be some evidence of greater involvement, beyond the usual suspects, in area-based regeneration, but there is no clear evidence base yet to support this view. We are only beginning to have a fuller understanding of the important role of Black and minority ethnic voluntary and community organizations in urban regeneration, and no full understanding of its wider 'political' implications. The role of faith-based community organizations in regeneration, and their wider political significance, is another area where there is now some understanding, but still a lack of a clear evidence base.

Community, Politics and Service Learning for Active Citizenship

One area where there is a unique opportunity to increase political participation through community involvement is among young people, given the introduction of the new citizenship curriculum in England and other developments in the rest of the UK (Annette, 2000). What about active citizenship and citizenship education? The Crick Report (1998), *Education for Citizenship and the Teaching of Democracy in Schools*, resulted in the Secretary of State's proposals for the National Curriculum. There is also recognition in the Crick Report of the importance of service learning or active learning in the community which is based upon the principles of experiential learning. This kind of learning is based on reflection on student volunteering or civic engagement activities. Community Service Volunteers (CSV) and other voluntary sector organizations highlight the importance of encouraging awareness of political participation through service learning. Many schools in the UK and the United States provide school students with opportunities for engaging in service learning or (in the UK) 'active learning in the community' (Wade, 1997; for the UK see Annette, 2000; Potter, 2002). In schools, the problem for teachers will be integrating education for citizenship, including opportunities to engage in service learning, into an already overcrowded National Curriculum. Provision of the opportunity for students to participate in service learning also requires partnerships with the university's local communities. This consideration about teaching democratic values in schools and the place of service learning in the community is one which also raises some important questions about teachers' understanding of what constitutes the 'political', instead of a more communitarian concern for the political socialization of young people.

Benjamin Barber, in a number of influential articles and books, advocates education for active citizenship by engaging in critical thinking about politics and civil society, and through the medium of community service learning. There has been a tradition of community-based internship and experiential education since the 1960s, but the new emphasis in the USA since the 1990s has been on the link between citizenship education and service learning (Rimmerman, 1997; Reeher and Cammarano, 1997; Guarasci and Cornwall, 1997). There is also increasing emphasis on the requirement that service learning programmes should meet the needs of local community partners (Cruz and Giles, 2000). Service learning can not only help build a kind of 'bridging as well as bonding social capital' (Putnam, 2000), it may also develop capacity-building for democratic citizenship in civil society (Kahne et al., 2000; Battistoni and Hudson, 1997; Battistoni 2002). An important research question which needs examination is 'What are the necessary elements of a service learning programme which can build not just social capital, but also active citizenship?' (Kahne et al., 2000; Campbell, 2000).

Conclusion

In a now well-known passage, the Crick Report argues:

> We aim at no less than a change in the political culture of this country both nationally and locally: for people to think of themselves as active citizens, willing, able and equipped to have an influence on public life and with the critical capacities to weigh evidence before speaking and acting; to build on and to extend radically to young people the best in existing traditions of community involvement and public service, and to make them individually confident in finding new forms of involvement and action among themselves (Crick Report, 1998, p. 7; cf. Crick 2000 and 2002).

I am concerned that community involvement in the citizenship curriculum will be interpreted in terms of a conception of community as simply a place or neighbourhood, and that this will result in forms of volunteering which fail to challenge students to think and act 'politically' (see Crick, 2002, p. 115). I have tried to review how the debate on the significance of community for political thinking and citizenship education has emerged out of the liberalism versus communitarian debate and the revival of a civic republican conception of politics. This raises the issue of how we develop – through community involvement, especially at local level – a more deliberative and democratic politics which can also provide a more political framework for citizenship education.

I have explored how developments in the modernizing of local governance, and in community involvement in regeneration and neighbourhood renewal, can provide the basis for a lifelong learning for active citizenship. As Bernard Crick argues:

> Tocqueville was right. A high degree of autonomy for localities and groups within the state is essential for freedom within a democracy. So thought the civic republicans, remembering the Greeks and the Romans: within sub-groups and localities wherever possible and as far as possible participative democracy should be practised (Crick, 2002, p. 120).

Thus community involvement in the new citizenship curriculum based on the pedagogy of service learning must address the question of how the learning experience can best be structured to challenge students to become 'political' – and aware of the political significance of civic engagement in *local* communities (either linked to local government or through community development). This conception of citizenship education is based on a liberal and pluralist civic republican conception of politics (Dagger, 1997; Maynor, 2003). It reflects, I would argue, the spirit of the Crick Report and the vision of the then Secretary of State for Education and Employment, David Blunkett.

References

Advisory Group on Citizenship ('Crick Report') (1998), *Education for Citizenship and the Teaching of Democracy in Schools*, Final Report of the Advisory Group on Citizenship, 22 September 1998, Qualifications and Curriculum Authority, London.

Annette, J. (2000), 'Citizenship Education and Experiential and Service Learning in Schools', in D. Lawton, J. Cairns and R. Gardner (eds), *Education for Citizenship*, Continuum, London.

Barber, B. (1984), *Strong Democracy*, University of California Press, Berkeley.

Barber, B. (1992), *An Aristocracy of Everyone*, Oxford University Press, Oxford.

Barber, B. (1998a), *A Passion for Democracy*, Princeton University Press, Princeton, N.J.

Barber, B. (1998b), *A Place for Us: How to Make Society Civil and Democracy Strong*, Hill and Wang, New York.

Battistoni, R. (2002), *Civic Engagement across the Curriculum*, Campus Compact, Cambridge, Mass.

Battistoni, R. and Hudson, W. (eds) (1997), *Experiencing Citizenship: Concepts and Models for Service Learning in Political Science*, American Association for Higher Education, Washington, D.C.

Bauman, Z. (2000), *Community*, Polity Press, Cambridge.

Blunkett, D. (2001), *Politics and Progress: Renewing Democracy and Civil Society*, Politicos Publishing, London.

Campbell, D. (2000), 'Social Capital and Service Learning', *Political Science and Politics*, Vol. 33(4), pp. 122-36.

Carey, G. and Frohnen, B. (eds) (1998), *Community and Tradition*, Rowman and Littlefield, New York.

Crick, B. (2000), *Essays on Citizenship*, Continuum, London.

Crick, B. (2002), *Democracy*, Oxford University Press, Oxford.

Cruz, N. and Giles, D. Jr. (2000), 'Where's the Community in Service-learning Research?', *Michigan Journal of Community Service Learning*, Fall, pp. 28-35.

Dagger, R. (1997), *Civic Virtues: Rights, Citizenship and Republican Liberalism*, Oxford University Press, Oxford.

Delanty, G. (2003), *Community*, Routledge, London.

DETR (1998), *Modern Local Government: In Touch with the People*, Her Majesty's Stationery Office, London.

Edwards, B., Foley, M. and Diani, M. (2001), *Beyond Tocqueville: Civil Society and the Social Capital Debate in Comparative Perspective*, Tufts University Press, Hanover.

Etzioni, A. (1995), *The Spirit of Community*, Fontana Press, London.

Faulks, K. (2000), *Citizenship*, Routledge, London.

Frazer, E. (1999), *The Problems of Communitarian Politics*, Oxford University Press, Oxford.

Frohnen, B. (1996), *The New Communitarians and the Crisis of Modern Liberalism*, University of Kansas Press, Lawrence.

Guarasci, R. and Cornwall, G. (eds) (1997), *Democratic Education in an Age of Difference*, Jossey-Bass, San Francisco.

Hall, P. (2002), 'The Role of Government and the Distribution of Social Capital', in R.D. Putnam (ed.), *Democracies in Flux*, Oxford University Press, Oxford.

Kahne, J., Westheimer, J. and Rogers, B. (2000), 'Service-Learning and Citizenship: Directions for Research', *Michigan Journal of Community Service-learning*, Fall, pp. 42-52.

King, D. and Stoker, G. (eds) (1996), *Rethinking Local Democracy*, MacMillan, Houndsmill.

Lister, R. (2003), *Citizenship: Feminist Perspectives*, 2nd ed., Palgrave, London.

Little, A. (2002), *The Politics of Community*, Edinburgh University Press, Edinburgh.

Local Government Association (1998), *Modernising Local Government*, Local Government Association, London.

Mason, A. (2000), *Community, Solidarity and Belonging*, Cambridge University Press, Cambridge.

Maynor, J. (2003), *Republicanism in the Modern World*, Polity Press, Cambridge.

Miller, D. (2000), *Citizenship and National Identity*, Polity Press, Cambridge.

Mulhall, S. and Swift, A. (1996), *Liberalism and Communitarianism*, 2nd ed., Blackwell, Oxford.

Nash, V. (2002), *Reclaiming Community*, IPPR, London.

Oldfield, A. (1990), *Citizenship and Community*, Routledge, London.

Potter, J. (2002), *Active Citizenship in Schools*, Kogan Page, London.

Pratchett, L. (ed.) (2000), *Renewing Local Democracy? The Modernisation of British Local Government*, Frank Cass, London.

Pratchett, L. and Wilson, D. (eds) (1996), *Local Democracy and Local Government*, MacMillan, Houndsmill.

Putnam, R.D. (2000), *Bowling Alone in America*, Simon and Schuster, New York.

Reeher, G. and Cammarano, J. (eds) (1997), *Education for Citizenship*, Rowman and Littlefield, Lanham, M.D.

Rimmerman, C. (1997), *The New Citizenship*, Westview Press, New York.

Sirianni, C. and Friedland, L. (2001), *Civic Innovation in America*, University of California Press, Berkeley.

Stoker, G. (1996), 'Redefining Local Democracy', in L. Pratchett and D. Wilson (eds), *Local Democracy and Local Government*, MacMillan, Houndsmill.

Taylor, M. (2003), *Public Policy in the Community*, Palgrave, London.

Wade, R. (ed.) (1997), *Community Service-learning: A Guide to Including Service in the Public School Curriculum* (Suny Series in Democracy and Education), University of New York Press, New York.

10

Teaching Controversial Issues in Citizenship Education

Terence McLaughlin

Any conception of citizenship education which seeks to go beyond the '... safe and dead, dead-safe, old rote-learning civics' to which Bernard Crick stands opposed (Crick, 2000, p. 119) is bound to engage students in learning about matters which are, in some significant sense, controversial. The inescapability and necessity of 'teaching controversial issues' in any form of citizenship education which seeks to transcend the merely informative has long been recognized by those concerned with the field, including teachers. The significance of teaching controversial issues in this area has, however, recently been given renewed emphasis in England, both in the report on citizenship education by the Advisory Group on Citizenship – hereafter the 'Crick Report'[1] – (see the Crick Report, 1998, section 10), and in policy provisions and guidance for practice (Qualifications and Curriculum Authority, 2000, Appendix 2).

'Teaching controversial issues' in citizenship education is, as elsewhere, fraught with a range of well-recognized difficulties and complexities. This essay seeks to bring a number of these difficulties and complexities into clearer focus from a broadly philosophical perspective. Philosophical clarity alone is clearly insufficient for defensible and effective educational practice, and any claims about the necessity of philosophical clarity for such practice need to be made with caution. Certain kinds of philosophical clarity can be unhelpful to educational practice, and may even undermine it (McLaughlin, 2000a, especially pp. 450-53). Many of the questions surrounding the teaching of controversial issues in citizenship education can only be adequately dealt with by enquiring into matters of contextual detail, and in particular into what is actually happening in classrooms. While the primarily abstract preoccupations of philosophy constitute one of its limitations with respect to educational questions, it is in general true that the clarity afforded by a philosophical perspective can help teachers and educational policymakers to both identify and tackle significant difficulties and tensions relating to their work.

---

1   The Final Report of the Advisory Group on Citizenship, 22 September 1998, entitled *Education for Citizenship and the Teaching of Democracy in Schools*, is hereafter referred to as the 'Crick Report'. References to the Crick Report give paragraph numbers.

This essay has six sections. The first section brings into focus the concept of a 'controversial issue'. In the second section, some general points are made about teaching controversial issues. The third section discusses the rationale and principles for teaching controversial issues in citizenship education, and the fourth section explores some of the difficulties and complexities of this task. In the fifth section, attention is focused on a specific and neglected area of significance for teaching controversial issues in citizenship education: the interface of the public and non-public domains. The essay concludes with some reflections on the implications of the discussion for teachers and teaching, and in particular for teacher formation and training.

Controversial Issues

It is important at the outset to draw attention to how the term 'controversial issue' is being interpreted in this discussion. The Crick Report defines a controversial issue as one '... about which there is no one fixed or universally held point of view' (Crick Report, 1998, 10.2). Such issues, the Report continues, 'divide society' and invite conflicting explanations and solutions, including conflicting views about such matters as the origin of a given problem, and the principles that should be invoked in relation to its resolution.

In getting to grips with the notion of 'controversial issue', it is useful for the purposes of the present discussion to focus attention on the *grounding* of the controversy at stake. Some controversies involve little more than contingent social disagreement which is based on (say) ignorance, misunderstanding, prejudice or ill will. While all controversies involve the social fact of disagreement, they vary in the extent to which they are grounded in deeper and non-trivial disagreement about matters of (say) an epistemological or ethical kind. It is controversies grounded in deeper disagreements of these kinds, and not merely controversies *per se*, which are of particular educational significance. Dearden adopts an *epistemic* criterion of controversiality in his attempt to identify controversial issues apt for attention in the classroom. Dearden holds that '... a matter is controversial if contrary views can be held on it without those views being contrary to reason' (Dearden, 1984, p. 86). An emphasis on the grounds of disagreement is also a feature of Rawls' attempt to illuminate the nature of reasonable disagreement between reasonable persons via the notion of the 'burdens of judgement' (Rawls, 1993, pp. 54-8), involving '... the many hazards involved in the correct (and conscientious) exercise of our powers of reason and judgement ...' (Rawls, 1993, p. 56) and providing, for Rawls, an important basis for the democratic idea of toleration.

The kinds of disagreements of an epistemological or ethical nature which can underpin 'grounded' controversies can take many forms. A non-exhaustive indication of the character of a range of kinds of disagreement, drawn from a range of sources and arranged in order of ascending complexity, could include the following: (i) where insufficient evidence is as yet available to settle a matter, but where such evidence could in principle be forthcoming at some point; (ii) where evidence relevant to settling a matter is conflicting, complex and difficult to assess;

(iii) where the range of criteria relevant for judging a matter are agreed, but the relative weight to be given to different criteria in a given decision is disputed; (iv) where a range of cherished goods cannot simultaneously be realized, and where there is a lack of a clear answer about the grounds on which priorities can be set and adjustments made; (v) where the range of criteria relevant for judging a matter are broadly agreed, but there is dispute about the proper interpretation of a criterion or criteria, given the indeterminacy of many concepts; (vi) where there are differing kinds of normative consideration of different force on both sides of an issue, and it is hard to make an overall judgement; (vii) where there is disagreement about the criteria relevant for judgement; (viii) where the differing 'total experiences' of people in the course of their lives shapes their judgements in divergent ways; and (ix) where there is no agreement about whole frameworks of understanding relevant for judgement (Dearden, 1984, pp. 86-7; Bridges, 1986, pp. 21-2; Rawls, 1993, pp. 54-8).

An educationally significant feature of 'grounded' controversies of these kinds is that they afford scope for 'reasonable' differences of view to be held on the matters at stake. This consideration underlies Rawls' insistence that:

> It is unrealistic – or worse, it arouses mutual suspicion and hostility – to suppose that all our differences are rooted solely in ignorance and perversity, or else in the rivalries for power, status, or economic gain (Rawls, 1993, p. 58).

This is echoed in Bernard Crick's reminder that we are confronted by '... genuine differences ... not simply prejudices' (Crick, 2000, p. 45). A central element underpinning the notion of a 'grounded' controversy is captured in Rawls' claim that 'reasonable disagreement' arises from the fact that

> ... many of our most important judgements are made under conditions where it is not to be expected that conscientious persons with full powers of reason, even after free discussion, will all arrive at the same conclusion (Rawls, 1993; cf. Gutmann and Thompson, 1996, ch. 1).

Henceforward in this discussion, when I am referring to 'controversial issues', I am referring to 'controversial issues' in this 'grounded' sense, which involves the notion of reasonable disagreement. The notion of 'reasonable disagreement' is not, of course, wholly transparent or unproblematic, and we will return to it in due course.

This essay is concerned with the teaching of controversial issues, and does not examine the many other ways in which controversy impinges upon education. The respects in which many educational questions are themselves controversial scarcely require emphasis. A wide range of questions about the aims, values, processes, 'content', institutionalization, control and distribution of education are ones in relation to which reasonable people hold differing and sometimes conflicting views. Many educational issues, including those relating to citizenship education, are themselves controversial issues. (For a discussion of recent controversies concerning citizenship education, see McLaughlin, 2000b.)

Controversy about educational questions should not surprise us, because education is inextricably involved in fundamental questions about human good and value, such as 'What knowledge is of most worth?' and, ultimately, 'What sort of people should there be?' The focus of the present discussion, however, is on the specific question of the teaching of controversial issues to students.

Teaching Controversial Issues: Some General Points

A number of general points can usefully be made about the notion of 'teaching controversial issues'. Four are of particular significance for the present discussion.

First, 'controversial issues' do and should arise in many of the subjects (and, more broadly, areas of learning) which we invite students to engage in at school. (On the limitations of 'school subjects' as vehicles for appropriate learning, see Hirst, 1993.) Controversial issues are, in different ways, an integral part of many subjects and areas, and engagement with such issues is necessary if a proper understanding of the subjects and areas is to be achieved (Bridges, 1986, pp. 19-21). It is true that controversial issues of particular sensitivity arise in relation to the moral, religious, social and political domains (and therefore in citizenship education), but it is important to note that the teaching of controversial issues is an imperative and a concern which is – and should be – felt in many, if not all, areas of the school curriculum.

Second, 'teaching controversial issues' has not been neglected in recent educational practice and theory. Two of the most prominent expressions of interest and engagement in this matter are the Humanities Curriculum Project directed by Lawrence Stenhouse (Stenhouse, 1983; Pring, 1999) and the approach to moral education developed by Lawrence Kohberg, involving the exploration of moral dilemmas (Reed, 1997, chs 1-6).

Third, the notion of 'teaching controversial issues' requires some explanation. 'Teaching', here, should not be interpreted as necessarily involving – or being confined to – activities such as explanation or instruction. Properly understood, teaching is a polymorphous concept which can be embodied in many forms of activity, including discussion, debate and role-play. (On discussion as a form of teaching see Bridges, 1979.) Those who prefer notions such as 'handling controversial issues in the classroom' to 'teaching controversial issues' may have an impoverished idea of what teaching involves.

Fourth, the most fundamental aim of 'teaching a controversial issue' is typically articulated in terms of students achieving an understanding of the nature of the controversy in question, and having the ability and opportunity to develop and exercise independent critical judgement on the issues at stake. The grounds of the controversy in question are constant reference points, indicating what is to be understood and judged (see Dewhurst, 1992).

Teaching Controversial Issues: Rationale and Principles

The Crick Report articulates a case for including attention to controversial issues in citizenship education (Crick Report, 1998, 1.9; 5.4.1; section 10), expressing its 'strong belief', notwithstanding the difficulties, that '... offering pupils the experience of a genuinely free consideration of difficult issues forms a vital and worthwhile part of citizenship education' (Crick Report, 1998, 10.16). The Report argues that controversial issues are part of everyday life in various ways, and to neglect these issues educationally is to fail to prepare students for their lives (Crick Report, 1998, 10.4), as well as to omit an important part of their education more generally conceived (Crick Report, 1998, 10.5).

Bernard Crick articulates a case for including controversial issues in citizenship education for reasons which are more closely derived from the nature of politics itself. For Crick, politics is centrally concerned with '... the creative conciliation of differing interests, whether interests are seen as primarily material or moral' (Crick, 2000, p. 36) – since 'the recognition and tolerance of diversity' is thereby part of politics, it must also be part of any political or civic education. Crick insists: 'To stress deliberately "what we have in common" and to underplay differences is both a false account of politics and a cripplingly dull basis for a political education' (Crick, 2000, p. 37). Crick argues that, since constitutions and parliaments exist in order to conciliate, resolve and contain real and basic conflicts of interest and value, pupils seeking to understand politics must therefore be helped to understand '... what the basic conflicts in our society are' (Crick, 2000, p. 39). An engagement with controversial issues therefore seems part of the achievement of 'political literacy' as defined in the Crick Report: '... pupils learning about and how to make themselves effective in public life through knowledge, skills and values' (Crick Report, 1998, 2.11(c)).

The rationale for including attention to controversial issues in citizenship education is brought into focus by Crick's insistence that

> ... in politics and in morals there is no way of proving what is best. But there are ways of arguing reasonably, which at least exclude some possibilities. Everything that is possible is not therefore equally desirable. At the end of the day ... people will differ; but it is likely that they will differ less violently the more they know about the lives, motives and beliefs of those they differ from. Prejudice does not always vanish with greater knowledge, but it is usually diminished and made more containable ... (Crick, 2000, p. 45).

Crick's optimism in this matter is illuminated by Gutmann and Thompson's observation that 'deliberative' disagreements, or disagreements of a reasonable kind, do not run so deep that there is no point in argument. Such disagreements '... lie in the depths between simple misunderstanding and immutable irreconcilability' (Gutmann and Thompson, 1996, p. 16).

In terms of the principles which should govern the teaching of controversial issues in citizenship education, the Crick Report argues that teachers should help prepare pupils to deal with controversies 'knowledgeably, sensibly, tolerantly and morally', and teach them

> ... how to recognise bias, how to evaluate evidence put before them and how to look for alternative interpretations, viewpoints and sources of evidence; above all to give good reasons for everything they say and do, and to expect good reasons to be given by others (Crick Report, 1998, 10.1).

The qualities of mind specified as apt for enhancement by addressing controversial issues in citizenship education include:

> ... a willingness and empathy to perceive and understand the interests, beliefs and viewpoints of others; a willingness and ability to apply reasoning skills to problems and to value a respect for truth and evidence in forming or holding opinions; [and] a willingness and ability to participate in decision-making, to value freedom, to choose between alternatives, and to value fairness as a basis for making and judging decisions (Crick Report, 1998, 10.6).

The Report argues that teaching strategies should be adopted which ensure controversial issues are presented '... in a fair, acceptable and thoroughly professional manner ... [and] in a way that is most likely to stimulate the interest of pupils and achieve many of the basic aims of education for citizenship' (Crick Report, 1998, 10.11). It outlines a range of pedagogic vices which teachers should avoid in their handling of controversial issues, including biased selection and presentation of evidence, setting themselves up as the sole authority on matters of opinion, revealing their own preferences, inhibiting contributions from all pupils and the like (Crick Report, 1998, 10.9). Having outlined three general approaches to the teaching of controversial issues – the 'neutral chairman', 'balanced' and 'stated commitment' approaches respectively (Crick Report, 1998, 10.12) – the Report favours a mixture of methods judged as appropriate by individual teachers (Crick Report, 1998, 10.13; 10.14) in the light of a checklist of considerations relevant to ensuring that every aspect of a controversial issue is examined fairly and thoroughly (Crick Report, 1998, 10.15) – considerations which constitute publicly defensible criteria open to scrutiny (Crick Report, 1998, 10.16). (See also section 6, especially p. 42, Fig. 1.)

Teaching Controversial Issues: Difficulties and Complexities

Whilst the rationale and principles underpinning the teaching of controversial issues in citizenship education may seem persuasive and even compelling, a number of difficulties and complexities arise in relation to this activity which require attention. While a number of these difficulties and complexities are of a severely practical kind, attention will be paid here to a number of difficulties and complexities which have a more philosophical flavour to them. Two general difficulties and complexities will be identified and discussed briefly here, and in the next section an issue with particular significance for controversial issues in citizenship education will be explored in more detail.

The first general difficulty and complexity relates to the need to determine what is, and what is not, a controversial issue for the purposes of teaching in a given context. One does not need to be versed in the difficulties inherent in Rawls' notion of 'reasonable disagreement' to concur with Dearden that what is controversial is itself controversial (Dearden, 1984, pp. 92-3). Again, the difficulty of resolving this problem at the abstract level is magnified by transposing it to the level of the classroom, where the pupils' developmental stage and the context of the school may dictate which topics can appropriately be presented as controversial in a particular situation. It is one thing, for example, for students to call into question basic or fundamental democratic principles and values from the motive of genuine philosophical curiosity, and quite another to do so from (say) a racist perspective or a sheer desire to disrupt the lesson. Whether the school is a 'common' school or (say) a 'faith' school will determine what can be presented as controversial in that particular context. Further, in schools of all kinds the views and sensitivities of parents need to be borne in mind. Another difficulty with the general task of identifying the controversiality or otherwise of topics is that the precise ways in which a given topic might be said to be controversial enter into the equation. Controversy can arise at different *levels* (substantive first-order judgements about a particular matter, second-order considerations relating to identification and justification of the criteria which are relevant to the making of judgements, and so forth). A related aspect of complexity is the fact that controversies are rarely 'free-standing', but are often embedded in wide-ranging traditions of thought and practice.

The second general difficulty and complexity relates to the widely recognized need for ensuring a fair treatment of controversial issues, and avoiding forms of undue teacher influence. Criteria proposed for the judgements inherent in ensuring fairness in this matter – such as *balance* – are necessarily general and formal. (See, for example, criteria specified in statutory provisions for protection against bias in teaching – Crick Report, 1998, p. 56.) Such criteria therefore require interpretation and application in particular circumstances. In the case of 'balance', any interpretation of the notion involves evaluative judgements about the elements between which a balance is sought, and about the criteria for judging what constitutes a balance (Dearden, 1984, ch. 5). Unless these judgements are made explicit, the notion of 'balance' is little more than a vague statement of an ideal to be aimed at. What complicates matters is that judgements concerning balance need to be made not only in relation to abstract subject matter, but also in the dynamic and unpredictable context of the classroom. Variables which are relevant to achieving balance in this context include the composition of the individual group, the course of a particular discussion and the nature and timing of teacher action and reaction. Questions of balance are sensitive to teacher action and behaviour modes – Bernard Crick reminds us that the teacher can present even 'facts' with a sneer or with 'ecstatic benevolence' (Crick, 2000, p. 35). Teachers can reveal preferences in such tacit things as facial expressions, gestures and tones of voice (Crick Report, 1998, 10.9). There are also important temporal and holistic dimensions to the achievement of balance. Temporal considerations intrude because it is students' experience with a teacher over a period of time, and not merely in relation to particular topics, which is significant for the overall balance of the influence to which they are exposed. Holistic considerations are relevant because the student's experience in the citizenship education programme as a whole (including the ethos of the school, and community involvement and service) has an overall value 'impact'. For all these reasons, 'balance' is difficult not only to interpret and achieve, but also to monitor and inspect (see OFSTED, 2002).

We turn now to a more extended consideration of difficulties and complexities arising from a neglected aspect of citizenship and its educational requirements. In what follows, the Rawlsian language of 'public' and 'non-public' domains, values and forms of reasoning is adopted in ways which would require extended elaboration and defence in a fuller account.

Teaching Controversial Issues: Interface of Public and Non-public Domains

In his recent book, *Liberalism Beyond Justice*, John Tomasi argues that liberal democratic societies, and the theory in terms of which they are frequently articulated, have overemphasized a justice-based conception of citizenship and neglected its non-public dimensions (Tomasi, 2001, ch. 4). In Tomasi's view, more attention needs to be paid to the non-public virtues and personality traits which should characterize citizens in a liberal society, and to the ways in which citizens construct their lives as a whole in such societies.

Tomasi is concerned that liberal democratic societies end up by effectively, if not intentionally, imposing a single ethical doctrine on the whole of society via 'spillover effects' from liberal political forms. Public norms both underdetermine *and structure* the non-public lives of citizens (Tomasi, 2001, p. 43), thereby exerting a homogenizing effect. Tomasi's notion of 'alphabet people' provides an illuminating account of the series of differing relationships which liberal citizens may have with the complex evaluative structure of liberal democratic societies. According to his categorization, A-people give the values of autonomy and individuality a governing role in their lives as a whole, affirming ethical or comprehensive liberalism as a world view in both their public and non-public lives, and rejecting the validity of any ethical doctrine based on authority. B-people (whom Tomasi takes to be the vast majority of citizens) affirm liberal principles such as freedom and equality in their public lives, but do not affirm general or comprehensive doctrines in their non-public lives, which are characterized by a degree of muddle and variability. C-people affirm liberal principles in their public lives, but some general ethical doctrine based on religious authority in their non-public lives. D-citizens affirm comprehensive doctrines in both their public and non-public lives, and reject liberal principles and public reason, seeking (for example) to impose their distinctive beliefs on others politically (Tomasi, 2001, ch. 2).

Tomasi notes that liberal societies impose an unequal form of 'psychological taxation' on their citizens. A-people are likely to feel very much at home in such societies, since these societies do not conflict at any point with the values to which they subscribe.

D-citizens are likely to feel highly uncomfortable, but as they do not subscribe to basic features of liberal 'public reason', little can be done to remedy this in liberal democratic societies. C-citizens are a focus of Tomasi's concern, as they may be particularly aware of, and affected by, the homogenizing trends reported earlier. He holds that a liberal polity should be as welcoming as possible to '... the aims and self-understandings of all politically reasonable citizens' (Tomasi, 2001, p. 74).

For Tomasi, citizenship requires skilful exercise of non-public reason by diverse good souls (Tomasi, 2001, p. 71) as part of making a success of a life '... lived on the interface of public and personal identity components' (Tomasi, 2001, p. 75). He therefore sees ethical development in a liberal society as requiring individuals to find personal meaning in life across this interface (Tomasi, 2001, p. 84). This in turn requires citizens to deploy 'compass' concepts which are 'thick' and 'identity dependent', and provide a set of bearings in the background culture of a society, enabling citizens to discover what their political autonomy means to them in the light of their fuller conception of their own good, and guiding them in the way in which they should exercise their rights (Tomasi, 2001, ch. 3).

Tomasi therefore specifies a range of virtues in the liberal citizen which relate to the interface between the public and non-public domains, and affect such matters as the ability to achieve an appropriate equipoise between one's political standing and the fuller commitments characteristic of one's wider non-public life. What this requires of citizens of different kinds varies. Citizens who are religious believers, for example, require dispositions which enable them to resist the commercial and secular nature of modern society (Tomasi, 2001, p. 77).

His own proposals for civic education have extensive implications and require careful interpretation (McLaughlin, 2003a). He insists that civic education should be as concerned about the 'ethical situatedness' of students as with their political liberation (Tomasi, 2001, p. 95). Civic education must therefore '... address issues that lie deep in the moral worlds of individual citizens' (Tomasi, 2001, p. 88), in the interests of helping students explore the *fit* between the public and non-public views they affirm. For Tomasi, this process includes not merely discerning how the students' own non-public views support public views, but also how public norms support their non-public views (Tomasi, 2001, p. 86). However, one need not accept Tomasi's view of civic education as a whole to draw some important lessons from his general perspective on teaching controversial issues in education for citizenship.

He draws attention to an important point, noting that teaching children the detached, rights-based forms of thinking central to public reason can encourage those forms of thinking across all dimensions of the individual's life, transforming it '... beyond what the bare attainment of political autonomy requires' (Tomasi, 2001, p. 90). One of the important lessons Tomasi has to offer, regardless of the broader acceptability of his educational proposals, is that inattention to moral texture and complexity in citizenship education can obscure controversial issues and opportunities to teach children these issues explicitly and fairly, and also that such inattention can itself constitute a form of controversial educational influence.

As I have argued elsewhere (McLaughlin, 2003a, pp. 136-45), schools have a responsibility for ensuring that students grasp the moral texture and complexity inherent in both public and non-public values and forms of reasoning, and understand the interface between the two. The significance of this task for teaching controversial issues in citizenship education is that this moral texture and complexity must, in the interests of balance, be properly brought to bear on teaching controversial issues. In many cases these forms of texture and complexity partly constitute the nature and significance of the controversy at issue. Students must be invited to acknowledge critically the importance of public values and forms of reasoning for political purposes, but also to come to a clear understanding of their nature and scope. 'Respect', for example, should not be interpreted as requiring unequivocal acceptance as true or valuable of that which is respected. 'Civic' respect can be accorded to reasonable differences of view, but students should be made aware that what is worthy of 'civic' respect is not necessarily worthy of respect from every point of view. A C-citizen (in Tomasi's terminology), for example, may accept that a certain lifestyle may satisfy the criteria necessary for it to be legal and free from social censure, but still maintain that, seen in the perspective of their fuller view of life, the lifestyle in question is immoral. An invitation to extend mutual respect to all lifestyles within the 'civic' pale does not imply that every way of life is acceptable to all the others in any full sense of 'acceptable'. Similarly, 'tolerance' should not be interpreted as incompatible with (all forms of) disagreement. Continuing disagreement is in fact not only compatible with tolerance, but necessary for it. As Bernard Crick correctly insists, toleration is precisely based on '… respectful disapproval of other viewpoints' (Crick, 2000, p. 40). Nor should the notion of 'reasonable differences of view' about an issue be seen as necessarily implying in a relativistic way that the question of truth does not arise, or cannot arise, in this situation.

The relationship and fit between 'public' and 'non-public' values and forms of reasoning are important concepts which students must learn about in citizenship education. Neglect of the demands of moral texture and complexity in the kinds of ways illustrated can be distorting in a number of respects. It can distort not only the teaching of controversial issues in citizenship education, but also the student's grasp of the very nature of a democratic pluralist society, where we live among people we disagree with, on the basis of values and forms of reasoning which are (in part) intended precisely to protect difference, within unifying imperatives and forces. Attention must also be given to matters of moral texture and complexity in schools if those schools are to be maximally hospitable to important sub-groups in society, like the C-citizens identified earlier.

Teaching Controversial Issues: Demands on Teacher Formation and Training

The difficulties and complexities associated with teaching controversial issues in citizenship education confront teachers in an inescapable way. Given the intensely practical nature of the judgements involved, it is teachers who must (largely) determine what is or is not a controversial issue for the purposes of teaching in a given context. They must interpret and implement the demands of balance, and ensure that concepts of moral texture and complexity are adequately dealt with. Teachers are required to resolve these difficulties and complexities at classroom level, deploying a form of pedagogic *phronesis* or practical wisdom revealed in the kinds of questions they ask of students, the timing and prioritization of certain lines of argument, the extent to which neglected perspectives are reinforced at certain times, the extent to which certain individuals in the group are encouraged to participate, and other strategies. In order to fulfil central aspects of these requirements, the teacher must be *a certain sort of person*.

The Crick Report suggests teachers are '... professionally trained to seek for balance, fairness and objectivity' (Crick Report, 1998, 1.9). It is not clear that this is in fact the case to any significant extent, at least in relation to the kinds of difficulty and complexity which have been identified as intrinsic to teaching controversial issues in citizenship education. The Crick Report is conscious of the need for teacher training for citizenship education (Crick Report, 1998, 5.9). If the aim of citizenship education is to teach controversial issues in a serious and sustained way, the demands on teacher formation and training require urgent and sustained attention. Clearly, teachers must have a grasp of the kinds of philosophical point discussed in this essay, and they therefore should, to some extent, be 'philosophers' of their practice. However, they also need to situate this philosophical awareness and judgement in the context of a rich form of pedagogic phronesis, and become involved in the kinds of 'community of practice' in which this capacity can be developed and sustained. (On this question see, for example, McLaughlin, 2003b.) The exact form in which we can best develop and promote these capacities and opportunities for teachers is as yet unclear, although there are suggestive indicators from previous fruitful initiatives and experiments (Stenhouse, 1983). What is clear is that, in the indicated absence of sustained attention to the demands of teacher formation and training, the ambition of teaching controversial citizenship education issues effectively and justifiably, in the face of the kinds of difficulty and complexity we have noted, is likely to remain unrealized. Indeed, such inattention may lead to precisely the kind of distortive educational influence to which this ambition stands opposed.

References

Advisory Group on Citizenship ('Crick Report') (1998), *Education for Citizenship and the Teaching of Democracy in Schools*, Final Report of the Advisory Group on Citizenship, 22 September 1998, Qualifications and Curriculum Authority, London.

Bridges, D. (1979), *Education, Democracy and Discussion*, NFER, Windsor.

Bridges, D. (1986), 'Dealing with Controversy in the Curriculum: A Philosophical Perspective', in J.J. Wellington (ed.), *Controversial Issues in the Curriculum*, Blackwell, Oxford.

Crick, B. (2000), *Essays on Citizenship*, Continuum, London.

Dearden, R.F. (1984), *Theory and Practice in Education*, Routledge and Kegan Paul, London.

Dewhurst, D.W. (1992), 'The Teaching of Controversial Issues', *Journal of Philosophy of Education*, Vol. 26(2), pp. 153-63.

Gutmann, A. and Thompson, D. (1996), *Democracy and Disagreement*, Belknap Press of Harvard University Press, Cambridge, Mass.

Hirst, P.H. (1993), 'The Foundations of the National Curriculum: Why Subjects?', in P. O'Hear and J. White (eds), *Assessing the National Curriculum*, Paul Chapman Publishing, London.

McLaughlin, T.H. (2000a), 'Philosophy and Educational Policy: Possibilities, Tensions and Tasks', *Journal of Educational Policy*, Vol. 15(4), pp. 441-57.

McLaughlin, T.H. (2000b), 'Citizenship Education in England: The Crick Report and Beyond', *Journal of Philosophy of Education*, Vol. 34(4), pp. 541-70.

McLaughlin, T.H. (2003a), 'The Burdens and Dilemmas of Common Schooling', in K. McDonough and W. Feinberg (eds), *Citizenship and Education in Democratic Societies: Teaching for Cosmopolitan Values and Collective Identities*, Oxford University Press, Oxford.

McLaughlin, T.H. (2003b), 'Teaching as a Practice and a Community of Practice: The Limits of Commonality and the Demands of Diversity', *Journal of Philosophy of Education*, Vol. 37(2), pp. 339-52.

Office for Standards in Education (OFSTED) (2002), *Inspecting Citizenship 11-16 with Guidance on Self-Evaluation*, OFSTED, London.

Pring, R. (1999), 'Political Education: Relevance of the Humanities', *Oxford Review of Education*, Vol. 25(1&2), pp. 71-87.

Qualifications and Curriculum Authority (QCA) (2000), *Citizenship at Key Stages 3 and 4. Initial Guidance for Schools*, QCA, London.

Rawls, J. (1993), *Political Liberalism*, Columbia University Press, New York.

Reed, D.R.C. (1997), *Following Kohlberg. Liberalism and the Practice of Democratic Community*, University of Notre Dame Press, Notre Dame, IN.

Stenhouse, L. (1983), *Authority, Education and Emancipation*, Heinemann Educational Books, London.

Tomasi, J. (2001), *Liberalism Beyond Justice*, Princeton University Press, Princeton, N.J.

11

Developing Education for Citizenship

Ian Davies

Introduction

The introduction of citizenship education into secondary schools in England from August 2002 offers a number of challenges and opportunities. This essay reviews the recent history of attempts to introduce citizenship education (or variants of it) into schools and comments upon the failure thus far of widespread implementation. Drawing on a number of recently completed or current research projects, comments are made about the potential for success of the present initiative. Recommendations for action are made (in the form of examples, rather than a complete guide for implementation) which include the clearer identification of procedural or second-order concepts and, with reference to initial teacher education, that work should take place in international as well as other contexts. Although the scale of the challenge of implementing citizenship education is emphasized in this essay, I do believe that it is possible to succeed in that task and that, if we do, enormous benefits will be achieved.

Historical Context

Heater (1990, p. 336) has explained that:

> a citizen is a person furnished with *knowledge* of public affairs, instilled with *attitudes of civic virtue*, and equipped with *skills to participate* in the political arena [my emphasis].

There is increasing attention given, within the UK and elsewhere, to the promotion of citizenship education. However, although there are many exceptions, there has been very little done for citizenship education in England at any point up to and, perhaps, including the present (Davies, 1999). Heater (1977, p. 62) over thirty years ago, explained the reasons for the neglect: lack of a tradition of teaching and learning in this area; few teachers who are professionally committed to it; a belief that politics is solely an adult domain due to its complex and personal nature; and a fear of indoctrination. Generally, prior to the 1970s, if anything was done, it consisted of teaching information about institutions and constitutions to high-status academic students.

The first really significant mainstream development of interest in what would become known as citizenship education took place in the 1970s. This change occurred due to a number of factors. The age of majority was lowered to 18 in 1970, meaning that many would still be at school when voting for the first time. Research work relating to political socialization suggested both that young people were exposed to many political messages and that they were capable of being affected by this material (Greenstein, 1965; Connell, 1971), even if their level of actual knowledge showed appalling ignorance of basic societal features (Stradling, 1977). As a result of these factors, the Programme for Political Education evolved, with Crick as its leading figure. This Programme focused upon the promotion of 'political literacy', involving a wide definition of politics to allow for an issue-based (rather than a descriptive and constitutional) approach to which young people could relate. Political literacy also emphasized procedural – rather than substantive – values, such as respect for truth and reasoning and justice. There were additionally, beyond the boundaries of curriculum projects, a number of relevant whole-school initiatives which developed from a general concern with the democratization of education (Pring, 1999).

During the early 1980s a raft of 'new' or 'adjectival' educations (peace, anti-sexist, anti-racist, development) emerged. Although the fragmentation suggested by this range of initiatives makes it impossible to suggest a simple overarching framework, there was in some projects an emphasis on holistic approaches to global issues with an affective bias (e.g. Pike and Selby, 1988). From the late 1980s the officially sanctioned version of citizenship education was seen negatively by many. It was felt that it was being developed as a response to a perceived problem of youth crime, a shrinking welfare state in the face of an ageing population, and the reduction of the powers held by local government. The late 1980s version of citizenship seemed rather narrow, and unhelpfully associated with what one politician of the time referred to as the need for young people to recognize 'voluntary obligations' (Hurd, 1989). In other words, although young people could not be forced to take on the role hitherto played by the state, they were to be encouraged, very strongly, to accept that they had a responsibility to act for others.

The current citizenship agenda in England is perhaps an attempt to make the educational process rather more professional. Documentation produced by the relevant advisory group (Crick Report,[1] 1998) suggests that social and moral responsibility, community involvement and political literacy will be significant aspects of any characterization of citizenship. The National Curriculum orders for citizenship (DfEE/QCA, 1999) focus on three key areas: knowledge and understanding about becoming informed citizens; developing skills of enquiry and communication; and developing skills of participation and responsible action.

---

1   The Final Report of the Advisory Group on Citizenship, 22 September 1998, entitled *Education for Citizenship and the Teaching of Democracy in Schools*, is hereafter referred to as the 'Crick Report'. References to the Crick Report give paragraph numbers.

The nature of the activity during the last few decades suggests that there has been something of a confusing and confused situation. It seems that there has never been a point at which an initiative in this field has been, simultaneously, clearly articulated by academics and teachers, and legitimated by central and/or local government or professional bodies. The debates have been characterized largely by assertion and counter-assertion, as opposed to findings based on research into classroom practice or teachers' thinking. Above all, it is important to note the general lack of implementation of citizenship education (Whitty et al., 1994).

Developing Citizenship Education in the Late 20th and Early 21st Century: the Implementation of Educational Initiatives

Since the end of the 1990s three causal factors have seemed influential in the development of citizenship education. Firstly, Labour won the 1997 general election and the new government was determined to develop a strong communitarian approach to social policy. The 'Third Way' (Giddens, 1998) seemed to provide the key to the renewal of social democracy, involving forms of education which, although allowing for the development of basic skills, encouraged purposeful engagement with the goal of strengthening ties between individuals and groups.

Secondly, the notion of citizenship was seen as providing a way of establishing something both coherent and wide-ranging. Escaping from what some saw as the narrowness of, for example, political education or anti-racist education, citizenship would provide an overarching coherence, employing the three key strands of social and moral responsibility, community involvement and political literacy. Citizenship was seen as being both sufficiently flexible and robust to address matters of legal status (which has obvious salience at a time when prominence is given to asylum seekers) and, more widely, issues concerned with identity formation and one's ability to act effectively.

Thirdly, many other states had a form of education which addressed contemporary issues directly. Influences from within the European Union, as well as initiatives in many countries around the world, suggested that the education system in the UK was beginning to look unbalanced. The action that was taken within England and Wales was in a sense not free-standing.

The above factors, of course, imply the potential risk of the citizenship education agenda becoming dangerously overloaded. This danger can be explored with reference to debates that dominate the current agenda, only a limited number of which will be mentioned here.

Unless there is a reasonable degree of clarity about the nature of citizenship, there is little chance of effective implementation. Much contemporary thinking about citizenship is linked with the ideas of Marshall (1963). But this should not be taken to mean that there is a single and straightforward characterization (Gallie, 1964; Isin and Wood, 1999). Part of the difficulty of discussing citizenship is that it needs to be 'understood and studied as a mosaic of identities, duties and rights rather than a unitary concept' (Heater, 1999, p. 114).

This mosaic can be simplified by referring to two distinct traditions. Civic republicanism, generally, has insisted on the primacy of public life over private, with a perspective that individuals should search for ways to serve the community. Liberal citizenship, on the other hand, simply stated, emphasizes the importance of rights over duties. Part of Heater's answer to this dilemma of seemingly contradictory ideologies is to assert that 'by being a virtuous, community-conscious participant in civic affairs (a republican requirement), a citizen benefits by enhancing his or her own individual development (a liberal objective). Citizenship does not involve an either/or choice' (Heater, 1999, p. 117). This sort of thinking broadly supports that of others (e.g. Dagger, 1997, in his work on what he calls 'republican liberalism').

This accommodation between seemingly opposed traditions makes possible the development of some sort of coherent ideology for citizenship education. However, it does need to be recognized that this apparently attractive simple solution may be insufficiently rigorous. Wolfe (1999, p. 429), for example, has suggested that it has not yet been convincingly argued how 'putting the common good *ahead* of one's private interests is compatible with liberal values such as autonomy'. In other words, if we regard citizenship as being associated with two distinct traditions, it is felt by some that its key characteristics and underlying values are potentially in conflict. The possibility that teachers may give priority to one set of values over another, or present contradictory messages, needs to be considered.

It is necessary to ask whether the virtue of a broad-brush approach to citizenship education, which recognizes the essential nature of morality, communities, identity and so very many other issues, can be included without losing intellectual coherence. If the citizenship net is cast very wide, there is a possibility that the knowledge, skills and dispositions aimed at by citizenship education could be extended too far. Or – perhaps a slightly different way of saying the same thing – if the key terms are so ambiguous and contested their meaning is lost. Audigier (1998, p. 13) notes that:

> Since the citizen is an informed and responsible person, capable of taking part in public debate and making choices, nothing of what is human should be unfamiliar to him [*sic*], nothing of what is experienced in society should be foreign to democratic citizenship.

Unless we hold on to central features of citizenship (a few key substantive concepts principally related to power, explorations of identity, and investigations into the nature of practising citizenship by promoting action), it will be about everything and so it will be about nothing of any coherent worth. Perhaps even worse, it will be 'paradoxically reduced to the teaching of collective behaviours that conform to our cultural habits' (Audigier, 1998, p. 13). If we do not have a clear sense of what it is, and if we allow the continuation of a situation in which teachers and 'experts' seem to talk a different language in citizenship debates, there will simply be confusion.

This broad-brush approach to citizenship education carries with it dilemmas which can be more specifically characterized. The interaction at what could be described as a conceptual/geographical interface needs to be considered. It is possible to argue that characterizations of citizenship education have been developed which use geographical frameworks that are, in fact, a way of representing more substantial conceptual positions. Prior to the 1970s civic education, where it was delivered, was dominated by descriptions of some local, but more especially national, contexts. Although international considerations were not completely ignored (for example the League of Nations Union, the Council for Education in World Citizenship and the Parliamentary Group for World Government undertook valuable work), global understanding was not normally seen as a key issue until recent years. The structure of Whitehall (national government) provided the primary focus. Increasingly, since the 1980s, the influences of Europe and of global contexts have been noticeable although, of course, there have been recent analyses alleging that there is pressure for teachers to emphasize national identity as part of a strategy promoting cultural restorationism (Crawford, 1996; Phillips, 1998). The creation of the European Union has led to national governments responding to various initiatives (Davies and Sobisch, 1997; Convery et al., 1997), and debates about the meaning of globalization are ubiquitous.

These developments mean that there are a number of tensions (only two of which will be briefly mentioned here) that make the clear characterization of citizenship more complex. Is a debate on, for example, Europe, *really* about national issues, with the supposed centre of the discussion actually providing only an arena for conflict? And to what extent is a debate about citizenship dependent upon the existence of a polity? For example, those who argue in favour of global citizenship may be using a very different frame of reference from those who debate about the nature of a national citizenship, which carries with it certain more easily identifiable legal rights and obligations. Heater (1997) has shed some light on these issues by describing forms of citizenship that can be held in conjunction with state citizenship, referring to those which are *legally defined* and those which relate largely to *attitudes* that can be characterized vaguely or precisely. However, although this clarification is enormously helpful, it does have the effect of showing the huge difficulties associated with some of the rather simple and glib phrasing used by governments when exhorting teachers to implement citizenship education.

Implementation is also affected by the perception of crisis. There has always been greater interest in political learning at times of crisis (Stradling, 1987). Gollancz and Somervell (1914), Stewart (1938) and Cole (1942) all attracted mainstream attention at moments of crisis, but were perceived as voices in the wilderness at other points. During the 1970s there was a fear of the growth of extremist organizations. In the 1980s nuclear weapons and the unjust social exclusion of many, including women and black people, became particularly important. In the 1990s there was a perceived need to reduce the crime rate, shore up the welfare state by increasing the voluntary activity of young people, and cope with the problems presented by increasing fragmentation of identity. These were in many ways real crises, and some educational projects were spurred by them and perhaps even helped to alleviate them in minor ways. The cry for urgent action can still be heard. Marquand (1997, p. 33) talks of the choice we must make sooner or later 'between the free market and the free society', and Fukuyama (1997) claims that we are living through the 'great disruption'.

However, although there are some calls today for educational reform (and some of those calls are very relevant to the development of world citizenship, e.g. Nussbaum, 1997), the climate in Britain now, more than in recent years, is one of consensus in which the key targets are basic skills and increased examination success, which may help economic performance. However incomplete this consensus may be, I perceive it to be present. There may be evidence of continued low levels of civic engagement (Crewe et al., 1996) and there will always be those who refer to, and/or attempt to develop, moral panics, but as there is no strong positive evidence for a *generational* or *cohort* decline in political interest and activity (Jowell and Park, 1997), there are no very strong crisis cards to play. Whiteley (2002, p. 15) has argued that low voter turnout is a sign more of rationality than disaffection. Crises of international terrorism seem, at least in some cases, to lead to more rather than less civic activity (e.g. Apple, 2002; Giroux, 2002). While young people might be bored with politicians, this should not be confused with political apathy (White et al., 2000). Indeed, even some of those who do believe that generational shifts have occurred only argue that:

> Rising levels of education and economic security seem to be producing a gradual intergenerational shift toward placing less emphasis on respect for authority (Inglehart, 1996, p. 661).

In the current climate it is likely that data used by political sociologists, such as Inglehart, will be interpreted to suggest that the critical awareness targeted by those who worked for political education in the past has already been achieved. This may, according to Prime Minister Blair, already have gone too far. 'Duty,' he says, 'is an essential Labour concept' (Blair, 1995), and there are increasing numbers of academics who wish to agree with him (e.g. Bottery, 1999).

Some Tensions and Issues in Schools

Within schools there are particular tensions that are relevant to the implementation of citizenship education, three of which will be mentioned here. The findings reported below are from one research project conducted with teachers and school students for the purpose of identifying challenges and opportunities for citizenship education (Davies and Evans, 2002).

Firstly, citizenship education is perceived as having a low status within schools, and yet is regarded as the central purpose of education. Teachers have traditionally been drafted into the timetable to cover citizenship-type issues when their own specialist subject has left some slight availability. Little or no assessment takes place, and qualifications are not normally awarded or highly regarded. A number of respondents suggested to us that citizenship education should not become 'too demanding of time'. One of the young people from a community-based project remembered her time in PSE lessons: 'it's half an hour a week, sit, talk with your friends, collapse, that's it'. One teacher in a post 16 context talked of the 'woeful lack of knowledge' about political matters. In two institutions we were told that the title 'citizenship' is 'a turn-off' and will not be used. 'The biggest issue,' according to one teacher, 'is how to make it interesting for the 98 per cent who aren't particularly interested, and that's the key issue'. And yet many teachers have entered the profession with high ideals of making the world a better place. Citizenship, as one teacher commented, is 'the watchword for everything'.

Secondly, there seems to be a tension between the way in which politicians urge schools to help in the creation of a better society and the debates that take place between teachers about the best way to proceed. It is to be expected (and to be welcomed) that policy recommendations include the proposal to aim 'at no less than a change in the political culture of this country the UK both nationally and locally' (Crick Report, 1998, 1.5). However, there is as yet no widespread agreement about the way to teach citizenship. Of course, it would be unrealistic and unhelpful to expect complete uniformity of perspective. However, there is a need for some greater clarity if we are not to pretend that political rhetoric is a substitute for educational action. The wide-ranging characterizations of citizenship used by respondents may not always be regarded positively. We would suggest that some of the possibilities suggested to us by some young people (e.g. cleaning graffiti from walls) or by some teachers (e.g. 'mowing lawns') are not necessarily by themselves satisfactory ways forward.

Thirdly, it is very difficult indeed to specify the acceptable boundaries that could be used when discussing matters to do with a pluralistic society. There has been some very useful elaboration of some of the difficulties in promoting consensus within pluralism (e.g. Dahl, 1982; Kymlicka, 1995), but there are few theoretical answers and very limited guidance about what can be done. This point also relates to the nature of the citizenship education which is promoted. One teacher referred to the danger of a citizenship education programme that just 'chugged along', insofar as there would be 'volunteering only and not learning citizenship'. This may be a particular challenge if conceptions of citizenship are limited. School councils are at times perceived as not working effectively. The 2002 Green Paper on 14-19 education promoted a model of citizenship which seemed to owe little to reflective critical engagement, and more to community volunteering. Other recent research suggests that teachers often perceive citizenship as something to do with enacting responsibilities in a local context (Davies et al., 1999).

Ways Forward?

The above discussion may seem to present almost intractable difficulties, but ultimately the value of educational research and scholarship depends on the ability of professionals to do something. Brief outlines of two current projects with which I have been working, with a range of others, are given below to illustrate approaches which, while not necessarily models of good practice, may provide a means of stimulating thinking and action.

The Department for Education and Skills sponsored a project during 2001-2002 which focused on procedural concepts. The project team intended to help teachers to go beyond asking students to memorize details of specific cases, and also to go further than having students consider the nature of the contexts and substantive concepts which may relate to a number of cases. The ambitious position would be to assert that by identifying procedural concepts it would be possible to invite students not just to think *about* citizenship, but to think *as* citizens. Teachers and others would be encouraged to move away from citizenship as 'merely' a goal, and allow for the possibility of a clearer identification of what students need to do and how they should think in order to demonstrate effective learning. Practical classroom materials for use in history, English and Personal and Social Education classrooms have been produced.

The central ideas behind the project are not new. Similar work has already taken place in other subjects. Our understanding of educational goals for students of history, for example, has been vastly improved by the clearer identification of what is needed for them to think as historians. We were, for example, attracted by the following statement from Lee and Ashby:

> Teaching that systematically builds on prior understandings and assessment that rewards their development are both central to achieving progression. Of course, algorithmic approaches are possible in many forms of teaching and experience in the United Kingdom unsurprisingly suggests that they are likely to be widespread where teachers do not themselves have a good grasp of the ideas they are attempting to teach. This may be the case even when entry standards are high (a first or upper second class in a degree) (Lee and Ashby, 2000, p. 215).

Although the specific content and context of what is to be studied must always be emphasized, we are struck by the fact that it has now been possible in history to produce more valuable educational work by identifying the procedural concepts which characterize the field. This means that students know what they have to learn, and also allows them to focus on the levels of understanding that can and should be reached in relation to each concept. School students of history can now focus their attention not just on learning information (e.g. names and dates), studying contexts (e.g. the nineteenth century) or learning about substantive concepts which are often tied to particular events (e.g. revolution). Rather, history teachers can concentrate on improving students' understanding through a clearer appreciation of such procedural concepts as evidence, cause and change. These procedural concepts can be seen as the essential part of 'doing' the subject. A shift is made in that area from learning history to being an historian.

The concepts can then be developed to show levels of performance which allow for more effective and precisely targeted teaching approaches. We now know for example that, when we look at children's conceptions of rational understanding in history, their thinking tends to conform to a pattern. Once something is known about these patterns, then it may be easier to understand what pupils are thinking and to assist their development by more precisely formulated approaches to teaching.

This combination of knowledge of the procedural concepts and knowledge of pupils' thinking may be a potent force for improvement. The levels of thinking about the past have been characterized in the following way. At the lowest level, pupils see only a baffling series of unrelated events. At a slightly better level, the people of the past are viewed as being simply unintelligent. Thereafter, three forms of empathy (everyday, restricted and contextual) characterize the ways in which pupils show the first real signs of appreciating the nature of the past (Lee et al., 1995). This approach thus seeks to develop a way of knowing, rather than presenting pupils with things to know. It is an approach which is seen as being 'suited to the education of citizens in a liberal democracy', as it helps students 'to develop the ability and the disposition to arrive at reasonable informed opinions' (Seixas, 2000). It is about understanding the processes of citizenship and being citizens, as opposed to learning things about citizenship.

Given that the preference is for active engagement, our procedural concepts are expressed in the form of active verbs. The three areas are explaining, tolerating and participating. Expressed slightly more fully, these areas would involve developing understanding dispositions and abilities associated with:

1. rationality grounded in a critical appreciation of social and political realities;
2. toleration within the context of a pluralistic democracy; and
3. participation arising from an acceptance of one's social and political responsibilities and appreciation of one's own rights and entitlements.

These concepts have been selected following a careful consideration of the nature of the citizenship Order, a review of the literature and discussion with experts (academics and teachers). It is, however, a very provisional list and it is hoped that it will be modified and expanded in the future. It is, of course, necessary to relate the concepts to substantive concepts of citizenship, otherwise it would be possible for school students to explain, tolerate and participate in any lesson or activity in the school or community.

Having asserted that there is something essential for citizenship education wrapped up in these procedural concepts, we need to be able to explain how they relate generally to an overarching sense of citizenship, and how they themselves can be seen as being made up of necessary features. This being so, our materials are based around a key concept such as inequality or justice or identity. The materials and activities will be designed to encourage students:

1. to explain their views, their understandings and their arguments;
2. to tolerate, accommodate and reflect upon opinions and views that may be different from their own; and
3. to participate in the consideration and debate of these ideas in the classroom and (ideally) use this experience and understanding in their life outside school.

Citizenship Learning by International Exchange

A second example of recent work which attempts to assist in the implementation of citizenship education is concerned with initial teacher education. There are a number of positive initiatives developing currently, including a project sponsored by the Teacher Training Agency (see *www.ittcitized.info*), but I will elaborate here only on a project that has an international focus.

A number of partners in Europe and Canada are working to promote the very necessary development of international experience which encourages better understanding of global citizenship and citizenship skills applied beyond the narrow boundaries of the nation state. The choice of Canadian and European collaboration was, of course, partly driven by the desire to build upon existing personal and professional links, as well as a desire to respond to funding opportunities. However, the collaboration is in many ways ideal for providing us with insights into the issues outlined above in this essay. Both Europe and Canada are good examples of the tensions (creative and otherwise) which arise from debates about citizenship. Three issues – political unification, uniformity or plurality of culture, and the relative weight to be given to economics – seem particularly relevant to our work.

Firstly, there is uncertainty about the distribution of powers, given the emphasis, on one hand, on a Europe of the regions or a Brussels-led Union and, on the other, to the relative power of the federal and provincial Canadian legislatures. Second, the purposes of citizenship are thrown into stark relief in both Canada and Europe, with arguments in both areas about cultural identity (linguistic in the arguments over the use of English and 'Englishness' but also, more fundamentally, in relation to powers to be held by aboriginal peoples). In Canada the struggle for recognition by the francophone minority is significant, as well as the more general issue of the essential distinctiveness of Canadians and Americans. In Canada there are increasing pressures to respond to the multicultural nature of the society. Toronto schools, for example, are the most multicultural and multilingual in the world, with approximately 53 per cent of secondary students having English as their first language and more than 47,000 (24 per cent of) elementary students born outside Canada. Thirdly, there are debates on both sides of the Atlantic about the extent to which economic matters should be considered as an essential component of citizenship, with some in Europe and Canada claiming that this is the principal (or sole) reason for continued collaboration.

The essence of the project is an exchange of student teachers between Canada and Europe. Universities in three European countries (the UK, Sweden and Germany) and three Canadian provinces (Ontario, New Brunswick and Prince Edward Island) are co-operating to allow student teachers to spend six weeks on the other side of the Atlantic. Our grand aim is that the exchange will allow for a greater understanding among young people of the changing nature of citizenship, their rights and responsibilities as citizens, and the complexities of membership of different and sometimes conflicting contexts (from local to global), so that they can make informed decisions as future voters, workers, parents and community participants. It is hoped that, through the exchanges and workshops envisaged in this project, student teachers will be challenged to question and reflect upon the fundamentals of citizenship, such as loyalty, patriotism, identity formation and forms of civic participation. They will encounter multiple perspectives on key national and global issues and trends; and they will be introduced to a variety of successful practices in education for citizenship, as developed by the partner institutions.

The principal focus of the exchange is a placement in a school where it will be possible to learn about citizenship and also to teach it. However, there are extra activities planned that will heighten their awareness of citizenship issues in both Canada and Europe. In addition, students from the participating universities who do not themselves take part in the exchanges will become involved in the project by meeting and working alongside the mobile students (i.e. those who take part in the exchange) on a variety of projects and tasks. That work includes workshops with practising teachers; visits to places of interest in the spheres of national politics and government; and opportunities to develop resources and activities which can be tried out in the classroom.

Home institutions are organizing preparatory activities for the mobile students. These will include an introduction to the culture of the host institution's country, training in basic language skills (where necessary), and discussion of some key concepts and perspectives relating to citizenship. An international practice teaching handbook, containing advice on cross-cultural exchange as well as introductions to the education systems of partner countries, will be produced and distributed to all mobile students. In addition, mobile students will be prepared to make presentations, either individually or in teams, within their host school and community about their home country, including its cultural, educational and political systems. Students' portfolios will be sent to the host institution prior to the exchange, enabling the most appropriate school placements to be found.

During their exchange period, mobile students will be asked to undertake small-scale research projects in which they will investigate questions such as: What are the knowledge, skills of participation and dispositions toward citizenship of students and teachers you have met? What is the orientation toward citizenship represented in the official curriculum? How does citizenship education look on the ground – particularly when compared with the intended curriculum? The research projects will serve as a vehicle to promote reflection on, and to make coherent, the multiple experiences each mobile student will encounter. The completed projects will also be accepted by the home institution as fulfilling a requirement for teacher certification.

Throughout the project we are attempting to evaluate the extent to which a recognizable impact has been made. This involves assessing the effectiveness of the exchange experience in terms of meeting the relevant goals of each institution's teacher education programme; the personal and professional development of mobile student teachers; the development of awareness and skills in the area of education for citizenship; and the development of intercultural understanding.

The above brief outline does not do full justice to the nature of the project or to the hopes attached to it. It should perhaps be read merely as an indication of our determination to encourage teachers to reflect on the complexities of citizenship, to look beyond narrow national considerations and to become effective actors and participants in bringing the benefits of citizenship education to others.

Conclusion

Citizenship education presents a great many challenges. However, the descriptions of the projects given above may provide some stimulus for others to develop ways around seemingly intractable difficulties. By drawing attention to these projects, I wish to argue that the nature of citizenship can be seen coherently if we decide to explore specific areas. We need to consider a coherent conceptual meaning of citizenship education in a way that breaks down the barriers between knowledge, skills and understanding, and allows students to focus on the process of being a citizen. We need to employ an appropriate and targeted set of pedagogical strategies which encourage young people to enjoy the conceptual engagement that relates to key processes. We should ensure that students may participate in a range of contexts, including those that go beyond the local, regional and national. International experience (real as well as virtual) is an achievable option and should be seized. Such work clearly has the power to motivate. Further, this sort of work could help students to develop the skills to operate effectively in a range of contexts and also explore whether global citizenship is itself a category which can carry meaning.

The growth of school subjects is a slow and complex business, and perhaps citizenship education presents challenges which have not previously been experienced. We will need a good deal of flexibility from government agencies involved in the inspection of our work and, importantly, support from others not associated directly with government, if initiatives are not to be stifled. If, however, we can set – meaningfully, coherently but flexibly – the parameters for citizenship education and deepen our understanding of what counts as good work, then there will be opportunities for some of the loftier ambitions of Crick and others to be fulfilled.

References

Advisory Group on Citizenship ('Crick Report') (1998), *Education for Citizenship and the Teaching of Democracy in Schools*, Final Report of the Advisory Group on Citizenship, 22 September 1998, Qualifications and Curriculum Authority, London.

Apple, M. (2002), Patriotism, Pedagogy and Freedom: On the Educational Meanings of September 11, *http://www.tcrecord.org* (26 June).

Audigier, F. (1998), *Basic Concepts and Core Competences of Education for Democratic Citizenship: An Initial Consolidated Report*, Council of Europe, Strasbourg.

Blair, T. (1995), 'End the Take and Give Away Society', *The Guardian*, 23 March 1995.

Bottery, M. (1999), 'Getting the Balance Right: Duty as a Core Ethic in the Life of the School', *Oxford Review of Education*, Vol. 25(3), pp. 369-86.

Cole, M. (1942), *Education for Democracy*, Allen and Unwin, London.

Connell, R.W. (1971), *The Child's Construction of Politics*, Melbourne University Press, London.

Convery, A., Evans, M., Green, S., Macaro, E. and Mellor, J. (1997), *Pupils' Perceptions of Europe*, Cassell, London.

Crawford, K. (1996), 'Neo-Conservative Perspectives on Culture and Nationhood and Their Impact upon the School Curriculum in England and Wales', *Children's Social and Economics Education*, Vol. 1(3), pp. 208-22.

Crewe, I., Searing, D. and Connover, P. (1996), 'Citizenship: The Revival of an Idea', in Citizenship Foundation, *Citizenship and Civic Education*, The Citizenship Foundation, London.

Dagger, R. (1997), *Civic Virtues: Rights, Citizenship and Republican Liberalism*, Oxford University Press, Oxford.

Dahl, R. (1982), *Dilemmas of Pluralist Democracy*, Yale University Press, New Haven, Conn.

Davies, I. (1999), 'What Has Happened to the Teaching of Politics in Schools in England in the Last Three Decades and Why?', *Oxford Review of Education*, Vol. 25(1&2), pp. 125-40.

Davies, I. and Evans, M. (2002), 'Encouraging Active Citizenship', *Educational Review*, Vol. 54(1), pp. 69-78.

Davies, I. and Sobisch, A. (1997), *Developing European Citizens*, Sheffield Hallam University Press, Sheffield.

Davies, I., Gregory, I. and Riley, S.C. (1999), *Good Citizenship and Educational Provision*, Falmer Press, London.

Department for Education and Employment (DfEE)/Qualifications and Curriculum Authority (QCA) (1999), *Citizenship: The National Curriculum for England*, Her Majesty's Stationery Office, London.

Fukuyama, F. (1997), *The End of Order*, Social Market Foundation, London.

Gallie, W.B. (1964), *Philosophy and Historical Understanding*, Chatto and Windus, London.

Giddens, A. (1998), *The Third Way: The Renewal of Social Democracy*, Polity Press, London.

Giroux, H. (2002), 'Democracy, Freedom and Justice after September 11th: Rethinking the Role of Educators and the Politics of Schooling', *http://www/tcrecord.org* (26 June).

Gollancz, V. and Somervell, D. (1914), *Political Education at a Public School*, Collins, London.

Greenstein, F. (1965), *Children and Politics*, Yale University Press London.

Heater, D. (1977), 'A Burgeoning of Interest: Political Education in Britain', in B. Crick and D. Heater, *Essays on Political Education*, Falmer Press, Lewes.

Heater, D. (1997), 'The Reality of Multiple Citizenship', in I. Davies and A. Sobisch (eds), *Developing European Citizens*, Sheffield Hallam University Press, Sheffield.

Heater, D. (1999), *What is Citizenship?*, Polity Press, Cambridge.

Hurd, D. (1989), 'Freedom Will Flourish Where Citizens Accept Responsibility', *The Independent*, 13 February 1989.

Inglehart, R. (1996), 'Generational Shifts in Citizenship Behaviours: The Role of Education and Economic Security in the Declining Respect for Authority in Industrial Society', *Prospects*, Vol. 26(4), pp. 653-62.

Isin, E.F. and Wood, P.K. (1999), *Citizenship and Identity*, Sage, London.

Jowell, R. and Park, A. (1997), *Young People, Politics and Citizenship – a Disengaged Generation?*, Paper delivered at the Citizenship Foundation Annual Colloquium, The Citizenship Foundation, London.

Kymlicka, W. (1995), *Multicultural Citizenship*, Clarendon, Oxford.

Lee, P. and Ashby, R. (2000), 'Children's Understanding of History', in P.N. Stearns, P. Seixas and S. Wineburg (eds), *Knowing, Teaching and Learning History*, New York University, London.

Lee, P., Dickinson, A. and Ashby, R. (1995), 'Progression in Children's Ideas about History', in M. Hughes (ed.), *Progression in Learning*, BERA Dialogues 11, Multilingual Matters, Clevedon.

Marquand, D. (1997), *The New Reckoning: Capitalism, States and Citizens*, Polity Press, Cambridge.

Marshall, T.H. (1963), 'Citizenship and Social Class', in T.H. Marshall, *Sociology at the Crossroads*, Heinemann, London.

Nussbaum, M. (1997), *Cultivating Humanity: A Classic Defense of Reform in Liberal Education*, Harvard University Press, Cambridge, Mass.

Phillips, R. (1998), 'Contesting the Past, Constructing the Future: History, Identity and Politics in Schools', *British Journal of Educational Studies*, Vol. 46(1), pp. 40-53.

Pike, G. and Selby, D. (1988), *Global Teacher, Global Learner*, Hodder and Stoughton, London.

Pring, R. (1999), 'Political Education: Relevance of the Humanities', *Oxford Review of Education*, Vol. 25(1&2), pp. 71-88.

Seixas, P. (2000), 'Schweigen! Die Kinder! Or, Does Postmodern History Have a Place in the Schools?', in P.N. Stearns, P. Seixas and S. Wineburg (eds), *Knowing, Teaching and Learning History*, New York University, London.

Stewart, M. (1938), *Bias and Education for Democracy*, Oxford University Press, Oxford.

Stradling, R. (1977), *The Political Awareness of the School Leaver*, Hansard Society, London.

Stradling, R. (1987), *Political Education and Politicization in Britain: A Ten Year Retrospective*. Paper delivered at the International Round Table Conference of the Research Committee on Political Education of the International Political Science Association, Ostkolleg der Bundeszentrale für Politische Bildung, Köln, March 9-13 1987.

White, C., Bruce, S. and Ritchie, J. (2000), *Young People's Politics: Political Interest and Engagement amongst 14- to 24-Year-Olds*, Joseph Rowntree Foundation, York.

Whiteley, P. (2002), 'Stay-at-Home Citizens', *The Guardian*, 1 May 2002.

Whitty, G., Rowe, G. and Appleton, P. (1994), 'Subjects and Themes in the Secondary School Curriculum', *Research Papers in Education*, Vol. 9(2), pp. 159-81.

Wolfe, D. (1999), 'Visions of Citizenship Education', *Oxford Review of Education*, Vol. 25(3), pp. 425-30.

Index